REGNUM STUDIES IN MISSION

Christology in Dialogue with Muslims

A Critical Analysis of Christian Presentations of Christ for Muslims from the Ninth and Twentieth Centuries

REGNUM STUDIES IN MISSION

Series Preface

Regnum Studies in Mission are born from the lived experience of Christians and Christian communities in mission, especially, but not solely, in the fast growing churches among the poor of the world. These churches have more to tell than stories of growth. They are making significant impacts on their cultures in the cause of Christ. They are producing 'cultural products' which express the reality of Christian faith, hope and love in their societies.

Titles in the Regnum Studies in Mission series are the fruit of rigorous research to the highest international standards and always of authentic Christian engagement in the transformation of people and societies. These books have been created for the world. The formation of Christian theology, missiology and practice, in the twenty-first century, will depend to a great extent on the active participation of growing churches contributing biblical and culturally appropriate expressions of Christian practice to inform World Christianity.

Series Editors

REGNUM STUDIES IN MISSION

Christology in Dialogue with Muslims

A Critical Analysis of Christian Presentations of Christ for Muslims from the Ninth and Twentieth Centuries

I. Mark Beaumont

Foreword by David Thomas

First published 2005 by Paternoster Press.
Reprinted 2011 by Regnum Books International

Regnum is an imprint of the Oxford Centre for Mission Studies
St. Philip and St. James Church
Woodstock Road
Oxford, OX2 6HR, UK
www.ocms.ac.uk/regnum

09 08 07 06 05 04 03 8 7 6 5 4 3 2 1

British Library Cataloguing in Publication Data
A catalogue record for this book is available from the British Library

ISBN 978-1-506475-28-8

Typeset by Kyoko Beaumont

Distributed by 1517 Media in the US and Canada

To all the family past and present

Contents

FOREWORD

The task of explaining the belief that Christ was both human and divine is even more challenging in dialogue between Christians and Muslims than it is in Christian self-understanding. This is because Muslims already possess in their scripture a detailed biography of Jesus the Messiah, son of Mary, a human messenger who both proclaims the radical oneness of God and explicitly denies that he himself is divine or God's son. For this reason a recurrent theme in Muslim writings on Christianity from the earliest times is the scrutiny of claims that in Christ the eternal, unlimited Deity became one with a temporal, circumscribed human. And on grounds both logical and scriptural – derived not only from the Qur'ān but also from informed readings of the Bible – Muslims have questioned and ultimately rejected it.

The apologetic challenge to say exactly who Jesus was and why he has been acclaimed as human and divine, example for all and saviour of all, has been taken up by many theologians and missionaries. In recent times distinguished minds have sought to explain his significance in full recognition that new faith contexts demand new expressions of doctrine. In this book Mark Beaumont looks at four representative attempts, Hans Küng and Kenneth Cragg whose restatements show continuity with the past, John Hick who dramatically reduces Christ's figure to human dimensions, and an anonymous Arabic biography which casts the story of Jesus in Qur'ānic form and language. With unerring adroitness he pinpoints the main features of the Christologies they propose, and evaluates their loyalty to normative belief as they try to show a Christ whom Muslims might be persuaded to find attractive or at least to understand.

But this is only a part of his achievement. Drawing upon his expertise in Arabic language, Beaumont sets alongside these modern re-modellings of the person of Christ another series that survives in the earliest extant records of encounters between Christians and Muslims. From an examination of texts that derive from the ninth century he presents the Christologies of Arab Christian theologians who both lived in Muslim society and shared the thought world of Muslim contemporaries. Here they endeavoured to preserve the doctrines which their respective denominations had striven to identify, and at the same time to employ new forms of explanation and illustration in order to show to their Muslim counterparts that God really was in Christ, and that unless he was, he could not be perceived in all his sublime goodness.

This fascinating section brings to a wider audience ideas and a portion of history that have been known to only a few for far too long. In the last part of the book Beaumont compares the Christologies of the early Arab Christians featured in it with those of the contemporary scholars he examines, and is able to demonstrate the continuing problems and possibilities that attach to presenting Christ to the Muslim world.

Of course, this task continues. Here Beaumont has given it fresh impetus by showing what has been done, and by suggesting what can be done and should be done.

Dr David Thomas
Centre for the Study of Islam and Christian-Muslim Relations
The University of Birmingham

PREFACE

This book is substantially the same as the PhD awarded by the Open University in 2003, through the Oxford Centre for Mission Studies. I have now taken the opportunity to refer to writing published after the presentation of my thesis in preparation for publication.

I am grateful for the financial sponsorship of Birmingham Christian College and the Spalding Trust. Dr Richard Massey, Principal of Birmingham Christian College, first encouraged me to engage in research on Christian dialogue with Muslims and has been constant in his enthusiastic support.

Dr David Thomas, my main supervisor, introduced me to ninth century Christian apologetics for Muslims and never flagged in his belief that I could complete the task of interpreting largely unknown theologians for our times. Dr Hugh Goddard and Rev Colin Chapman helped me particularly with the modern period. To all of them my thanks.

Arabic texts are translated by the author unless otherwise acknowledged. Arabic long vowels are marked by overlining and the following consonants are underlined; ح = h̲; ص = s̲; ض = d̲; ط = t̲; ظ = z̲.

INTRODUCTION

This book analyses Christian presentations of Christ for Muslims in the most creative periods of Christian-Muslim dialogue, the first half of the ninth and the second half of the twentieth century. In these two historical moments, Christians made a serious effort to present their faith in Christ in terms that fully take into account Muslim perceptions of him, with a view to bridging the gap between Muslim and Christian convictions. While these Christian writers gave reasons for their own Christological beliefs, they also attempted to argue for their Christology on the basis of Islamic concepts. Rather than merely expound a received Christology composed from within a totally Christian environment, they entered into a Muslim framework of thought to show the validity of a Christian view of Christ in terms that Muslims might understand as credible.

Since Christians and Muslims have such different perceptions of Christ, it may appear to be futile for Christians to try to enter into dialogue with Muslims about him. However, there can be no escape from the fact that Christians understand their identity from the person of Christ, his teaching, his actions, his spiritual dynamic, and that the continuing life of the mainstream church has been bound up with the worship of Christ as the eternal Son become human. Given that Muslims think of Christ as a prophet who brought essentially the same message as Muhammad, that God is one and is to be worshipped alone, they have never understood their identity as being bound up with Christ. In Islam, Christ's words, work and spiritual dynamic were not unique among the messengers of God, but can be seen in other prophets too.

The difficulty of establishing a dialogue is compounded by two denials of Christian faith in Christ: the rejection of the idea of divine sonship, and the denial of the death of Christ by crucifixion. Muslims have not accepted the title "Son of God" for Christ, and they have held that Christ was taken up to heaven without going through death. These denials cut right to the heart of the developed faith of the church, where Christ is the Incarnate Son of God who gave his life to redeem others from sin. Christians have reacted to these Muslim ideas about Christ in three different ways. Firstly, they have regarded Islam as a completely false ideology and therefore have adopted an aggressive policy of propagating Christian truth without taking Islamic perceptions into account. Secondly, they have distanced themselves from Muslims so that no real communication arises on these contentious issues. Thirdly, they have attempted to take Muslims seriously as people of good faith whose views of Christ need to be understood and related to in a genuine attempt to make sense of Christian faith for them. This third approach is studied here, because it is imperative for Christians to learn to live with Muslims in the global community without falling into the errors of aggression or withdrawal. The approach of peaceful dialogue is a better way than defiant proclamation or complete indifference.

The subject of Christian presentations of Christ for Muslims has not been studied in great detail. While the topic is referred to in recent treatments of Christian-Muslim dialogue, such as in Kate Zebiri's *Muslims and Christians Face to Face*, Montgomery Watt's *Muslim-Christian Encounters. Perceptions and Misperceptions*, Chawkat Moucarry's *Faith to Faith: Christianity and Islam in dialogue*, and Mahmut Aydin's *Modern Western Christian Understandings of Muslims Since the Second Vatican Council,* no book length study has appeared to date. Some of the book length studies of Muslim attitudes to Christ have looked at Christian presentations of Christology for Muslims. Neal Robinson's *Christ in Islam and Christianity: The Representation of Jesus in the Qur'ān and the Classical Muslim Commentaries*, refers to Christian interpretations of the Qur'ān but does not offer a detailed analysis of these Christian contributions. Oddbjorn Leirvik's *Images of Jesus Christ in Islam: Introduction, Survey of Research, Issues of Dialogue*, briefly outlines several Christian presentations of Jesus in dialogue with Muslims, but as the title suggests, the chief concern of the survey is with Muslim contributions. This book aims to fill the gap by examining the most creative Christian writing on Christ for Muslims from the long history of Christian-Muslim encounter.

The outstanding Christian presentations of Christ for Muslims came from the ninth and twentieth centuries. By the ninth century, Middle Eastern Christians were engaged in oral and written dialogue with Muslims about their faith in exceedingly detailed terms. The fact of continuing Islamic rule of the largely Christian Middle East led Christian theologians to treat Muslim intellectuals as dialogue partners whom they needed to convince of the rationality of the Christian faith. By this time, the credibility of the Christian faith was at stake, with nominal Christians converting to Islam in increasing numbers. Thus the apologetic writing of the ninth century has both Muslim and Christian audiences in mind. It shows on the one hand that Christology was not completely alien to Islamic belief, and on the other, that it was acceptable for Christians to hold such views even in a society ruled by Muslims.

Part One expounds and analyses the writing of three apologists from the early ninth century, Theodore Abū Qurra, Ḫabīb ibn Khidma Abū Rā'iṯa, and `Ammār al-Baṣrī. These writers are the only ones known to have written on Christology for Muslims in the early ninth century, and helpfully they represent the three major Christian communities of the Middle East in that period which were divided by different views of the Incarnation. No other comparable writings are extant from the formative period of Islamic rule in the Middle East. Later apologists such as Yaḫyā ibn `Adī from the tenth century and Paul of Antioch from the twelfth, have little to add to the innovative work of Abū Qurra, Abū Rā'iṯa and `Ammār al-Baṣrī. It is regrettable that the Christological apologetics of these theologians remains virtually unknown. Seppo Rissanen's comparative analysis of the writing of Abū Qurra and Abū Rā'iṯa in his *Theological Encounter of Oriental Christians with Islam during Early Abbasid Rule* is exceptional. The absence of the three theologians from Kenneth Cragg's chapter on early Arab Christian apologists in *The Arab Christian* is an indication of the need for these writers to be better known.

Part Two studies the twentieth century Christian theologians, Kenneth Cragg, Hans Küng and John Hick, who engaged in oral and written dialogue with Muslims about Christ. Their desire to relate Christian thinking about Christ to Islamic presuppositions is a product of recent efforts to treat Muslims as genuine dialogue partners. While some Christians have thought that dialogue with Muslims should avoid discussion of Christology, these three have felt that tackling the differences between Christians and Muslims over Christ is essential to dialogue. Cragg, Küng and Hick are the notable representatives of creative Christological dialogue in recent times. There are a number of writers who have dialogued with Muslims from a fairly traditional Christological perspective like Cragg. The best examples are David Shenk's dialogue with B.D. Kateregga in *Islam and Christianity*, Robert Caspar's answers to questions posed by Tunisian Muslims *Trying to Answer Questions*, and Thomas Michel's *Pour Comprendre le Christianisme: Un Chrétien présente sa foi aux Musulmans*. However, they do not match Cragg's innovative approach to Muslims. Küng and Hick have no competition for inclusion, since they are the only twentieth century apologists to present Christ on the basis of modern gospel scholarship rather than the teaching of the Apostles or the Creeds of the church.

There has not been much analysis of modern Christian dialogue about Christ with Muslims. Cragg's Christology in dialogue has been reviewed by Christopher Lamb in *The Call to Retrieval: Kenneth Cragg's Christian Vocation to Islam*. Hossein Nasr, who dialogued with Hans Küng in the 1980's, named only Hick and Küng as Christian theologians who have carried out serious dialogue with Muslims in an article in the 1998 volume of *The Muslim World*, "Islamic–Christian Dialogue – Problems and

Obstacles to be Pondered and Overcome". Yet the central Christological concerns of Hick and Küng still await a critical exposition. Therefore an analysis of the presentations of Christ for Muslims by Cragg, Hick and Küng is offered here, showing how these three theologians have contextualised Christology in an Islamic context. Since humanity lives in a global village at the beginning of the twenty-first century, it is time to take stock of attempts to do theology in the Muslim sector of the village.

The method employed in this book is to set the Christological apologetics of the six writers from the ninth and twentieth centuries in the context of writing on Christ for Muslims that preceded them. The ninth century Arab apologists were preceded by important contributions in Greek and Syriac, designed mainly to help Christians cope with life under Islamic rule. The new reality of the ninth century writing in Arabic is the effort made to reach a Muslim audience as well as a Christian one. The fact that Abū Qurra and Abū Rā'ita engaged in debate with each other over Christological differences enables a contrast to be drawn between inter-Christian dialogue and Christian-Muslim dialogue in the ninth century. By comparing their writing for a specifically Christian audience with that designed for Muslims, it is possible to understand their apologetic method. The apologetic method of each writer is then compared, in order to draw conclusions about the way in which Islamic concepts influenced their work and the Christology they advocated.

The twentieth century theologians are studied in the light of the most important Christological writing for Muslims from the post-enlightenment era that preceded them. Knowledge of Islam that came in the wake of the enlightenment enabled dialogue to re-emerge after centuries of indifference or diatribe. By the nineteenth century, some Christians were beginning to make use of this knowledge to engage in debate about Christ with Muslims. The difference between the ninth century and the post-enlightenment nineteenth and twentieth centuries, is the situation of the two groups of writers. The ninth century apologists were living under Islamic rule with the constraints of censorship that this implied. However, their twentieth century counterparts are Western European theologians, only one of whom has lived in the Islamic world. The fact that Cragg and Küng openly criticised Islamic beliefs is a mark of their freedom from constraint. Such criticism is absent from the ninth century writers. A need emerges from the analysis of the modern Western apologists for a more dynamic approach to dialogue that would enable Christians living in Islamic societies to relate their faith to Muslims. An attempt to do this has come from a dramatic version of the life of Christ, which combines material from the four gospels with language taken from the Qur'ān, to create a portrait of Christ that relates to Islamic thought patterns. This approach to Christology may point a way forward for Christians in the global context in which they find themselves.

The book is structured into two clusters of chapters, concerned in Part One with three ninth century theologians, and in Part Two with three twentieth century theologians. Part One is preceded by a study of Muslim beliefs about Christ, which create the context for dialogue, and Part Two is followed by a study of the future prospects for dialogue on Christ. Chapter One outlines the teaching of the Qur'ān about Christ and the various ways in which Muslims have interpreted that teaching down to recent times, and establishes the main difficulties in the way of dialogue that arise from the Qur'ānic denials of Christ's sonship and crucifixion. Chapter Two sets the scene for the study of the three ninth century apologists by examining the references to dialogue about Christ in the writing of John of Damascus from the first half of the eighth century. The earliest apology for Christianity in Arabic from the second half of the century provides evidence of the way the Islamic context was provoking a Christian response. The debate between Timothy I and the Caliph al-Mahdī in 781-2 points out the issues that Muslims raised in dialogue with Christ.

Chapter Three is devoted to the Christological writing in Arabic of Theodore Abū Qurra. Short treatises written for catechetical purposes are compared with others addressed to Muslims, to show how he dealt with Christology in dialogue with Muslims. His aim was to defend a Christian account of Christ by showing that it is not inconsistent with Islamic convictions. Chapter Four expounds the more detailed Christological writing of Abū Rā'iṯa. As a Jacobite miaphysite theologian, he debated with Melkite diophysites such as Abū Qurra, as well as with Muslims. A comparison is made between the two types of writing to discern how his Christology differs from one audience to another. Like Abū Qurra, he seeks to uphold the rationality of Christology for his Muslim audience. His direct appeal to the Qur'ān in support of the Incarnation is an outstanding feature. Chapter Five studies the only two known pieces of writing by `Ammār al-Basrī. These are both apologetic works in which the Incarnation is defended in the face of Islamic doubt. `Ammār's aim is to show the internal coherence of the idea of the Incarnation as the best form of revelation. Chapter Six draws together the common themes of these ninth century apologists as well as their distinctive contributions to dialogue on Christology, and studies Muslim reactions to Christology in the ninth and early tenth centuries. This chapter acts as a summary of Part One, evaluating the importance of the early ninth century for Christological dialogue.

Chapter Seven opens Part Two with a summary of the subsequent history of dialogue up to the nineteenth century. Two innovative apologists are considered as suitable background to the writers of the second half of the twentieth century. The German missionary, Karl Pfander and the Egyptian Coptic Christian Ibrāhīm Lūqā both attempted to present Christ from a Muslim point of view, arguing that a Christian perspective can be seen to grow out of a Muslim one. Their common approach differs in detail, but sets the tone for the creative apologetic of a later period. Chapter Eight gathers together the significant writings of Kenneth Cragg on Christology for Muslims. His innovative Christian readings of the Qur'ān are analysed along with his insistence on the need for Muslims to rethink their concept of God's relationship with the world. Chapter Nine examines the dialogical activity of Hans Küng and John Hick, who entered into dialogue with Muslims after establishing a reputation as philosophical theologians. Their concern to write theology at a global rather than Western level is tested in dialogue, as is their capacity to represent their fellow Christians. Chapter Ten outlines the Christology behind an anonymous Life of Christ in Arabic, which seeks in an unusual and innovative way to combine material from the four gospels and the Qur'ān. This is a significant event in contextualising Christology for Muslims, since the thought of the Qur'ān is so thoroughly interwoven into the Christian story, and may point to a future method of Christian-Muslim dialogue. Chapter Eleven summarises Part Two by analysing the Christologies of the twentieth century writers in the context of dialogue in the light of Muslim response.

Chapter Twelve concludes the study by evaluating the ways in which different aspects of Christology have been dealt with in dialogue from both the early and recent periods. The significance of the apologetic method of those living in the Muslim world is noted in comparison with the approach of those living in the Western world. The chapter closes with a glance at future prospects for dialogue between Christians and Muslims on Christ.

Abbreviations

BCIIS	*The Bulletin of Christian Institutes of Islamic Studies*
BHMIIS	*The Bulletin of the Henry Martyn Institute of Islamic Studies*
BDEC	*The Blackwell Dictionary of Eastern Christianity*
CSCO	*Corpus Scriptorum Christianorum Orientalium*
EI	*The Encyclopaedia of Islam*
IBMR	*International Bulletin of Missionary Research*
IRM	*The International Review of Mission*
ICMR	*Islam and Christian-Muslim Relations*
JA	*Journal Asiatique*
JSS	*Journal of Semitic Studies*
LAB	*The Living Arabic Bible*
MSJ	*Mélanges de L'université Saint Joseph*
MW	*The Muslim World*
NTS	*New Testament Studies*
OC	*Oriens Christianus*
PO	*Parole de L'Orient*
P.I.S.A.I.	Pontificio Istituto di Studi arabi e Islamici
POC	*Proche-Orient Chrétien*
RSO	*Revista degli Studi Orientali*
TAV	*Today's Arabic Version*
WCC	World Council of Churches

Chapter One

The Islamic Context for Dialogue on Christology

Christian dialogue with Muslims about Christ has always been affected by the portrait of him found in the Qur'ān, which both affirms and denies convictions held about Christ by Christians. The Qur'ān affirms that Christ was born of the virgin Mary,[1] that he had a special measure of God's Spirit,[2] that he healed the sick and raised the dead,[3] and that he brought God's message to his people Israel which confirmed the *Torah* previously given through Moses.[4] In addition, the Qur'ān makes claims about Christ that the Christian gospels do not, that he made a bird from clay,[5] that he predicted Muhammad's coming,[6] and that he was taken up to heaven instead of being put to death.[7] The Qur'ān denies that Christ sought for faith in himself,[8] that he should be called God's Son,[9] and that he died by crucifixion.[10]

Qur'ānic Affirmations of and Additions to Christian Convictions about Christ

Born of the Virgin Mary

Sūra 3:45-49 contains a speech by a group of angels to Jesus' mother, Mary, announcing details about the baby she is to conceive by God's power. He is to be 'a word' from God, and is to be called 'the Messiah'. He will be esteemed by men and by God as among those closest to God. He will speak to people while still a child before his adult work begins. He will be especially pure in character. In *sūra* 19:19-21 a solitary angel appears to Mary in human form and announces that God is giving Mary a 'pure boy'.

---

[1] *Sūra* 19:19-21.
[2] *Sūra* 2:87, 253; and 5:110.
[3] *Sūra* 5:110.
[4] *Sūras* 3:49-51; 5:46; and 61:6.
[5] *Sūras* 3:49; and 5:110.
[6] *Sūra* 61:6.
[7] *Sūra* 4:158.
[8] *Sūras* 5:116f; and 43:57-64.
[9] *Sūras* 2:116; 4:171; 6:101; 9:30; 10:68; 17:111; 18:4; 19:35, 88-92; 21:26; 23:91; 25:2; 37:152; 39:4; 43:81f; 72:3; and 112:3.
[10] *Sūra* 4:157.

To Mary's retort that no man has touched her, the angel replies that it will happen because it is easy for God to do what he has decreed.

Only Jesus has a beginning like this among the other messengers of God he is identified with in the Qur'ān. Others had human fathers but he did not. Subsequent Muslim interpretation of the birth of Jesus has usually insisted on virginal conception. Qur'ān commentator Fakhr al-Dīn al-Rāzī (d. 1210) suggested that either God breathed into Mary so that she conceived or the angel Gabriel did, but there was no question of a human father being involved.[11] Yūsuf `Alī confirms this view in recent times. "Mary the mother of Jesus was unique, in that she gave birth to a son by a special miracle, without the intervention of the customary physical means."[12] A dissenting voice can be heard in the Aḫmadi commentator, Muḫammad `Alī, who held that Jesus was conceived in the same way as all women conceive.[13]

While it appears that Christ's conception is unique among the prophets, *sūra* 3:59 makes a comparison between the conception of Jesus and the beginning of the human race. The conception of Jesus is like the creation of the first man Adam, since God created Adam from dust and said to him 'be', and Adam came into existence. The context of this comparison is a dispute about the significance of Jesus' virginal conception. Muḫammad is instructed to argue with those who doubt the comparison. The historian Ibn Isḫāq (d. 767) reported that Muḫammad debated with Christians from Najran and Ethiopia about the divinity of Jesus. The Christians argued that Jesus had a unique status among humans as a result of his conception without a human father. Muḫammad replied that God created Adam without a male or female parent. Therefore the creation of Jesus was no more unique than that of Adam.[14] This use of the comparison as an argument against a Christian view of the virginal conception has reappeared throughout the history of Islam. The ninth century Muslim apologist `Alī ibn Rabbān al-Ṯabarī appealed to Adam's lack of human parents as a refutation of the Christian idea of the Incarnation.[15] The twentieth century Muslim apologist, Abdul Hamid, argued that the Christian conviction of the uniqueness of Jesus as a result of his virginal conception is flawed, since

[11] Fakhr al-Dīn al-Rāzī, *Al-Tafsīr al-Kabīr,* on *sūra* 19:16-22. See the discussion by N. Robinson, 'al-Rāzī and the Virginal Conception', *Islamochristiana* 14 (1988), 1-16, 14f.

[12] Y. `Alī, *The Meaning of the Holy Qur'ān* (Lahore: 1934), on *sūra* 3:42.

[13] M. `Alī, *The Holy Qur'ān* (Woking: 1917), on *sūra* 19:22.

[14] A. Guillaume, *The Life of Muḫammad: a Translation of (ibn) Isḫāq's "Sīrat Rasūl Allāh"* (London: 1955), 657.

[15] `Alī ibn Rabbān al-Ṯabarī, 'Al-Radd `alā al-naṣārā', in D. Thomas, 'The Miracles of Jesus in Early Islamic Polemic', *JSS* 39 (1994), 221-243, 221f.

"God can create a man without a father, or even without father and mother."[16]

Therefore, the Qur'ānic account of the birth of Jesus seems to be coloured by a dispute between Muhammad and his Christian contemporaries over the interpretation of Jesus' conception. Jesus is conceived in an unusual way but this does not make him absolutely unique. This is because the first man, Adam, was also conceived in an abnormal fashion. The conception of Jesus demonstrates the continual ability of God to create without being tied to normal methods. When he chooses he needs only to say, 'be', and it will take place. In the use of Adam as a parallel to Jesus, Christians are asked to accept that the conception of Jesus cannot be interpreted as the entrance of the divine nature into the human realm. The appeal to Adam serves to reduce the impact of Jesus' uniqueness. Jesus was uniquely conceived without a human father, but Adam was created in a unique way too with neither a father nor mother. Christians would be hardly likely to argue that Adam was divine as well as human. Thus, in the Muslim perception of Jesus, the virginal conception is understood as confirming, not the entrance of the divine into the human, but the magnificence of the creative energy of the Lord of all worlds.

Endowed with God's Power

The unusual circumstances of his conception are actually a sign of God's power in Christ's life. As a newborn child he knows about his future work for God. In *sūra* 19:30 he defends his mother's integrity in the face of family disgrace by testifying to God's call on his life. "I am God's servant. He has given me the book and made me a prophet." In other words, Mary's family must not think that his birth is disgraceful, but on the contrary, should honour her for bearing him. Jesus is a precocious personality in the Qur'ān; not only is his conception spectacular, but his maturity of thought is beyond compare for such a young child. According to *sūra* 3:49, he knows that his future work will involve the performance of miracles of healing and raising the dead. These remarkable predictions by the newborn Jesus are not actually followed up by a set of stories describing these miracles, but they remain anticipated promises of what is to come. Nevertheless they are confirmed as having actually taken place in *sūra* 5:110, where God addresses Jesus after the completion of his prophetic ministry; "You healed the blind and the lepers by my permission and you gave life to the dead by my permission." The infant Jesus went on to perform exactly what God commanded him.

In *sūra* 3:49 the infant who prophesies his future work says he will make a bird model from clay, breathe on it, and it will become a real bird. The

[16] A. Hamid, *Islam and Christianity* (New York: 1967), 65.

prediction is confirmed by the divine review of his life's work in *sūra* 5:110; "you created a clay model of a bird by my permission. You breathed on it and it became a (real) bird by my permission." While references to Jesus healing lepers, giving sight to the blind, and raising the dead in the same texts confirm the testimony of the gospels, this transformation of a clay model into a living bird is a different type of story from the miracle stories found there.[17] Therefore the Qur'ān both confirms aspects of Jesus' work in the gospels and gives supplementary information that alters the perception of his activity. Giving life to clay is not part of Jesus' ministry in the canonical gospels, but giving life to people is central to his mission.

Some early Muslim interpreters of the infant Jesus' predictions noted that the Christian accounts of Jesus' life differed. The historian al-Ya`qūbī (d. 891/2) noted that the New Testament gospels omitted any account of Jesus speaking in infancy. However, he took the view that the four gospel writers tended to disagree with each other on important aspects of the life of Jesus.[18] In his *Reply to the Christians*, the Muslim philosopher al-Jāhiz (d. 868/9) reported that Christians denied the accuracy of the Qur'ānic account of Jesus speaking as an infant because "it is not found in the gospels, or stories of the life of Jesus, or in the prophecies of his coming."[19] Al-Jāhiz went on to affirm the veracity of the Qur'ānic story.

Muslim interpretation of the miracles of Jesus has focused particularly on whether Jesus had creative power in himself given by God, or whether he was merely a channel for God's creative work. Ibn al-`Arabī (d. 1240) held the first view. Jesus possessed the spirit of God in an unusual manner because God had endowed Jesus with a spiritual nature that enabled him to do work that would normally be done by God alone. "Jesus came forth raising the dead because he was a divine spirit. In this the quickening was of God, while the blowing itself came from Jesus ... Jesus' raising of the dead was an actual bringing to life."[20] According to this interpretation, the miracle is attributed to both God and Jesus. Fakhr al-Dīn al-Rāzī, held the second view. He notes that only in this context does the verb *khalaqa* have a subject other than God. Therefore, Jesus had in himself no creative power, since the expression 'by God's permission', rules out such a possibility.

---

[17] The story is found in the non-canonical Infancy Gospel of Thomas, and the Arabic Infancy Gospel, both of which may derive from fifth century Syriac sources. See J.K. Elliott, *The Apocryphal New Testament* (Oxford: 1993), 75 & 103.

[18] Al-Ya`qūbī, *Historiae,* vol.1,77, in A. Ferré, 'L'historien al-Ya`qūbī et les Évangiles', *Islamochristiana* 3 (1977), 65-83, 68.

[19] Abū `Uthmān al-Jāhiz, 'Reply to the Christians', in I.S. Allouche, 'Un Traite de Polemique Chrétienne-Musulmane au IX'e Siècle', *Hesperis* 26 (1939), 131.

[20] Ibn`Arabī, *The Bezels of Wisdom,* trans. R.W.J. Austin, (London: 1980), 176. See also A. D'Souza, 'Jesus in ibn `Arabī's Fuṣūṣ al-Hikam', *Islamochristiana* 8 (1982), 185-200, 194.

The permission of God must mean 'by God's causing and determining', so the breath of life does not belong to Jesus as an inherent power, but works through him at the point of the miracle.[21] These two ways of understanding Jesus' miraculous ability illustrate tensions within Islamic tradition over the relationship between God and Jesus. On the one hand, Jesus seems to have creative power in himself by virtue of a special possession of God's spirit. This appears to mark Jesus out from other prophets. The ability to breathe life into the inanimate or the dead is not the typical work of prophets. On the other hand, to isolate Jesus' role from other prophets is to open the door to a false estimation of Jesus. His activity was fundamentally the same as all the other prophets, to be God's instrument in whatever way he was summoned to be. If God causes all human action then it follows that all prophetic activity is actually God's work. Jesus cannot be given credit for the power of God at work through him.

A minority view of the miracles of Jesus can be found in the writings of the tenth century mystical Brethren of Purity who read a spiritual message from them. When Jesus gave sight to the blind he applied "spiritual substances to the eyes". He told his disciples that he had come to heal them "from the sickness of disobedience, false thinking, bad character traits, and bad actions."[22] A similar spiritualising of the miracles is found in M. `Alī's twentieth century commentary on the Qur'ān. For instance he understands the table of food sent down from heaven at Jesus' request in *sūra* 5:114f as heavenly food for the heart that gives spiritual knowledge.[23]

Although the miracles of Jesus are outstanding, the Qur'ān also records other prophetic miraculous activity. Moses produced water from a rock,[24] threw a rod on the ground, which became a snake,[25] which then swallowed up other rods that had turned to snakes.[26] If Moses performed miracles by God's permission, then it cannot be true that Jesus had creative power in himself. The ninth century Muslim apologist Abū `Īsā al-Warrāq (d. 861) argued that if Jesus' miracles proved the presence of the divine nature in him as Christians claimed, then the miracles of Moses must prove that he had the same divine nature in him. Christians cannot single out Jesus from other miracle workers for divine status.[27]

---

[21] Fakhr al-Dīn al-Rāzī, *Al-Tafsīr al-Kabīr,* on *sūra* 3:48. See N. Robinson, 'Creating Birds from Clay: a Miracle of Jesus in the Qur'ān and in Classical Muslim Exegesis', *MW* 79 (1989), 1-13, 11.

[22] The Brethren of Purity, *Epistles 3 and 4*, in Y. Marquet, 'Les Ihwān al-Safā et Le Christianisme', *Islamochristiana* 8 (1982), 129-158, 144 and 150.

[23] M. `Alī, *The Holy Qur'ān*, on *sūra* 5:114f.

[24] *Sūra* 2:60.

[25] *Sūra* 7:107.

[26] *Sūra* 7:117.

[27] Abū `Īsā al-Warrāq, 'Against the Trinity', in D. Thomas, *Anti-Christian Polemic in Early Islam* (Cambridge: 1992), 92.

Confirming the Torah Given to Israel through Moses

In *sūra* 3:49 angels announce that Jesus will have a specific message for the people of Israel, and this is confirmed in *sūra* 43:59, "We made Jesus an example for the children of Israel." Jesus himself twice speaks to the children of Israel. In *sūra* 5:72 he challenges them to serve God; "Children of Israel, worship God, my Lord and yours", and in *sūra* 61:6, he claims that God has sent him to them with a message about the past; "Children of Israel, I am God's messenger to you, to confirm the *Torah* which you already possess." Confirmation of the *Torah* seems to mean clearing up disagreements that have arisen among the Jews concerning the correct interpretation of the *Torah*, according to *sūra* 3:48f. He will tell them what they are allowed to eat, making lawful what had been forbidden by faulty understanding. He claims a God-given authority to interpret the *Torah* correctly. Nevertheless, there are no actual examples of Jesus' interpretation of food laws.

Sūra 5:46 indicates that Jesus was given a book that contained God's message; "We gave Jesus the gospel in which is guidance and light." The contents of the gospel are not specified as such, though in *sūra* 43:63 Jesus understands the book to contain wisdom for the children of Israel: "I have come to you with wisdom to clarify what you disagree about. Fear God and do what I say." Yet the nature of these disagreements is not made clear. The following verse provides a possible context for disagreement; "God is my Lord and yours; so worship him. That is the straight path." The straight path is total loyalty to God, and deviation from absolute commitment to him leads to disagreement. The way to avoid divergence of opinion is to wholeheartedly focus on God himself. This appears to be the heart of the message contained in the gospel given to Jesus.

Jesus not only confirmed the messages of the past, he also predicted the coming of Muhammad in the future. In *sūra* 61:6 Jesus proclaimed to Israel that he was God's messenger whose task was to confirm the law already given and also to announce the coming of a prophet "whose name is Ahmad." The eighth century biographer of Muhammad, Ibn Ishāq (d. 767), connected this prophecy of Ahmad with Jesus' promise of a 'comforter' in the gospel of John 14:16. He claimed that the Syriac word for 'comforter' had the same meaning as the name 'Muhammad', and therefore Jesus was looking forward to the arrival of the Prophet of Islam.[28] This connection of the Qur'ān and the fourth gospel has become an accepted feature of Muslim apologetic addressed to Christians. Yusuf `Alī argues that Ahmad 'the praised one' is a close parallel to the Greek word Periklytos. In John 14:16,

[28] A. Guillaume, *The Life of Muhammad: A Translation of (ibn) Ishāq's "Sīrat Rasūl Allāh"*, 103f.

the Greek word Parakletos is a corrupt reading for Periklytos. "In the original saying of Jesus there was a prophecy of our Holy Prophet."[29]

Qur'ānic Denials of Christian Convictions about Christ

Christ did not Seek for Faith in Himself

In *sūra* 5:116f God interrogates Jesus about his teaching; "Jesus, Mary's son, did you say to people - take me and my mother as gods alongside God?" After rigorous denials Jesus professes, "I only told them what you commanded me; worship God, my Lord and yours." Under cross-examination, Jesus testifies to the central message of the gospel that the children of Israel are to worship God to the exclusion of any other object of devotion. Jesus protests that the allegation is groundless, since he never put himself forward as a focus of devotion, nor did he present any other human being for the people of God to worship. Perhaps this is an example of the kind of disagreement mentioned in *sūra* 43:63. Jesus' impact on the people of Israel was such that some were offering him the kind of worship that ought to have been reserved for God alone. But it was not Jesus' intention to attract faith in himself. Possibly the authority with which he spoke led some to worship him, or maybe his powerful deeds led others to treat him as having divine power in his person and so to offer him worship as a divine being. Could the special status of Mary as bearer of Jesus have led some to think of her as worthy of worship?

Muslim commentators have understood this dialogue between God and Jesus as a denial of Christian belief in the Trinity. Al-Rāzī's discussion is the most thorough of the major Qur'ān commentators. He believes that Christians invented the story that Jesus called on his disciples to regard himself and his mother as divine. This idea grew out of the miracles they performed in the name of Jesus and Mary. Christians attributed the miraculous power to Jesus and his mother rather than to God.[30] In his comments on *sūra* 4:171, al-Rāzī thinks that Christians developed a belief that God's attributes indwelt Jesus and Mary. This lies behind the command not to speak of 'three' when God is 'one'. He sees a development in Christian thought based on devotion to Jesus and Mary in the first instance, because the concept of the threefold nature of God grew from that initial aberration. Christians believe "that it is possible for the attributes (*sifāt*) to indwell Jesus and Mary, and that is tantamount to blasphemy."[31] What is attributed to God cannot be attributed to humans, but Christians failed to

---

[29] Y. `Alī, *The Meaning of the Holy Qur'ān*, on *sūra* 61:6.
[30] Al-Rāzī, *Al-Tafsīr al-Kabīr,* on *sūra* 5:116.
[31] *Ibid.*, on *sūra* 4:171.

preserve adequate distinctions between the human and the divine. Therefore, the Qur'ān corrects the false worship of Christ in the Christian tradition. This line of interpretation has become standard. Yūsuf `Alī's comment on *sūra* 5:116 is typical; "Jesus disclaims here any knowledge of the sort of things that are attributed to him by those who take his name."[32]

Christ is not God's Son

This failure to hold to the unity of God is seen especially in the way Christians call Jesus God's Son. *Sūra* 4:171 connects false ideas about the trinity with the notion that Jesus is Son of God; "People of the book … Do not go beyond what is right in your religion. Confess God's truth; the Messiah, Mary's son, is only a messenger … Do not speak about a trinity … since God is one. Far be it for him to have a son." Somehow Christians have erred from the truth given to them by Christ and have invoked the wrath of God. *Sūra* 9:30 shows the limits of divine tolerance; "The Christians say the Messiah is God's son ... May God destroy them." But the truth is that God does not have the sort of relationship with a man that the idea suggests, because God does not restrict himself to the world he has made by being connected with Jesus as if they were in the same family. "It is not for God to have a son. May he be glorified! When he decides anything he only has to say concerning it, 'be', and it comes into existence."[33]

For the Qur'ān commentator al-Ṯabarī (d. 923) the naming of Jesus as God's son undermines the unity of God. By introducing concepts of fatherhood and sonship, Christians take away from God's true nature, since the Christian idea introduces a necessary connection between God and Jesus that reduces God's freedom and power. But the truth is that "God created the heavens and the earth from nothing, and he created the Messiah without a father by his power and authority."[34] Al-Rāzī takes this insight further by arguing that a son would take some of the greatness from God because he would have to carry the seed of his father. It would be far better to call Jesus God's 'servant' rather than God's son.[35]

The truth cannot contain any hint of a biological connection between Jesus and God. Christians ought to give up naming Jesus as son in order to remove any suspicion of such a thing. Muẖammad himself testifies in *sūra* 43:81 that the sonship of Jesus was an idea that he had encountered but had rejected as false prophecy; "if the Compassionate had a son I would be the first to worship [him]." While Muẖammad respected Christians he had met,

---

[32] Y. `Alī, *The Meaning of the Holy Qur'ān*, on *sūra* 5:116.

[33] *Sūra* 19:35.

[34] Abū Ja`far al-Ṯabarī, *Jāmi` al-Bayān fī Tafsīr al-Qur'ān*, on *sūra* 2:116.

[35] Al-Rāzī, *Al-Tafsīr al-Kabīr*, on *sūra* 2:116.

he failed to understand how they could offer worship to a supposed divine son. Part of his mission was to try to bring sense to the Christians of his day.

Recently M.M. Ayoub has questioned the longstanding tradition of interpreting sonship in a biological sense. He points out that the Qur'ān does not use the term *walad* to refer to Jesus; "the Qur'ān nowhere accuses Christians of calling Jesus the *walad* offspring of God."[36] The Qur'ān uses the verb *ittakhadha* meaning 'took to himself', which does not suggest physical generation but rather a relationship of adoption.[37] It remains to be seen whether this novel reading of the Qur'ān will be adopted by other Muslims, but it does suggest a fertile approach to finding common ground with Christians over a title that is central to the portrait of Christ in the gospels.

Christ did not Die on the Cross

Sūra 4:157f clearly denies that Christ died on the cross; "The people of the book said, we killed the Messiah, Jesus, Mary's son, God's messenger. But they did not kill him. They did not crucify him. Rather it seemed so to them ... No, God raised Jesus to himself." In the context, the people of the book were Jews in Jesus' day who sought for his death but who were denied the result they hoped for. Interpreters of this text have often followed al-Ṯabarī in his view that the disciple who betrayed Jesus "took on the likeness of Jesus" and was mistaken for his master. "God raised Jesus and they only crucified the one that looked like him."[38] For example, the twentieth century apologist Z.H. Assfy holds that after Jesus was taken from prison to heaven, Judas, who betrayed Jesus, was "miraculously transformed to resemble Jesus in all his physical features", and was crucified.[39] However, al-Rāzī thinks that such an idea would lead to doubt in the transmission of reports, and doubt might follow concerning any sacred law. A better interpretation would be that the Jews took a man whom they killed and claimed that he was Jesus. Al-Rāzī is aware of the strength of the Christian conviction that it was Jesus who died rather than another. "The only way Muslims can argue against this is to ask whether the disciples of Jesus at the time of the crucifixion were mistaken."[40]

---

[36] M.M. Ayoub, 'Jesus the Son of God: A Study of the Terms *Ibn* and *walad* in the Qur'ān and Tafsīr Tradition', in Y.Y. Haddad and W.Z. Haddad (eds.), *Christian-Muslim Encounters,* (Gainesville: 1995), 65-81, 65.

[37] *Ibid.*

[38] Abū Ja`far al-Ṯabarī, *Annals* vol.2:735f, in M. Hayek, *Le Christ de L'Islam* (Paris: 1959), 224.

[39] Z.H. Assfy, *Islam and Christianity* (York: 1977), 56f.

[40] Al-Rāzī, *Al-Tafsīr al-Kabīr,* on *sūra* 4:157f.

A minority view has been to accept the fact of his death but to deny that the spiritual reality of Christ was affected by the event. The tenth century Brethren of Purity thought that Jesus was actually killed by crucifixion, but that his soul was not harmed even though his body perished.[41] M.M. Ayoub has put forward a similar view. The Qur'ān denies "the power of men to vanquish and destroy the divine Word, which is forever victorious." He makes room for the crucifixion of Jesus as a historical fact. The Qur'ān teaches that men cannot destroy the word of God even though they can kill the body of the messenger.[42] Nevertheless, the denial of the death of Jesus as a historical reality remains dominant in contemporary Muslim thought. For example S.H. Nasr believes that "the non-crucifixion of Jesus is the one irreducible fact separating Christianity and Islam."[43]

A consequence of the denial of the death of Christ on the cross has been the assumption of the majority that Christ was raised up without going through the process of death. This is seen in al-Ṯabarī's interpretation quoted above, that God raised Jesus before the one who looked like him was seized and crucified. Several of the sayings attributed to Muḫammad assume that Christ was raised alive and will return again to bring God's message.[44]

Conclusion

The Qur'ān affirms, adds to and denies aspects of the life of Christ found in the gospels. The virginal conception is accepted as true but a Christian understanding of the Incarnation is ruled out. The miraculous work of Jesus is affirmed, but not a Christian veneration of Jesus' miraculous power as proof of his divinity. His teaching does challenge Jewish convictions, but is essentially the same as that of Moses, since Jesus' authority is no greater than that of previous messengers. In his prophetic teaching he looks forward explicitly to the coming of Muḫammad, whose authority he endorses. Christians are wrong to worship Christ since he called on his followers to worship God alone, they are wrong to use language of Jesus that implies a biological link with God, because God cannot be limited to a human level. They are also wrong to claim that Jesus died by crucifixion, because his exaltation bypassed the plans of his enemies.

---

41 The Brethren of Purity, *Epistle 44*, in Y. Marquet, 'Les Ihwān al-Ṣafā et Le Christianisme', *Islamochristiana* 8 (1982), 129-158, 146.

42 M.M. Ayoub, 'The Death of Jesus; Reality or Delusion', *MW* 70 (1980), 96-117, 103.

43 S.H. Nasr, *Islamic Life and Thought* (London: 1981), 210.

44 See for example *Saḫīh Muslim*, vol.1:287, "Jesus son of Mary will come down to you and will break the cross, kill the pig, abolish the tax on non-Muslims, and provide an abundance of money so that nobody will need to accept charity."

The implications for Christians of the three denials of the Qur'ān are serious. If Christ did not seek for faith in himself then a major focus of New Testament and subsequent Christian faith is misplaced, and needs to be radically altered in favour of pure monotheism. If God did not have a son then many New Testament texts must be rewritten to avoid making the claim that God is the father of his son Christ. If Christ did not die on the cross then the ending of his life in the four gospels must be adjusted accordingly, and the teaching of the Apostles about the saving effects of his death on the cross must be abandoned.

The following study of Christian dialogue with Muslims about Christ shows how Christian apologists have dealt with these challenges while maintaining a belief in the divinity and humanity of Christ. Since there will be an increasing need for Christians to take the Islamic context into proper account in articulating their faith in a plural world, consideration of the most creative responses to these challenges should enable them to "give a reason for (their) hope in a gracious and respectful way".[45]

[45] *The First Letter of Peter*, 3:15f.

Chapter Two

The Beginning of Dialogue on Christology in the Eighth Century

The arrival of Muslim rule in the traditionally Christian sectors of the Middle East, in the fourth decade of the seventh century, brought a direct challenge to the churches to give an account of Christ in the light of the Islamic understanding of him. If the Qur'ān offered a correct account of Christ then Christians would sooner or later have to defend their conviction that Jesus Christ was the eternal Son of God who had become human to rescue humanity from the results of sin through his death on the cross. Incarnation and atonement were at the heart of Christian faith but these central doctrines were under attack from the new religion that had taken control over this section of the Christian world. The denials of the Incarnation and the atonement by the new rulers forced Christians to account for these doctrines, not only to those who regarded them as false, but also to nominal Christians who were adopting the new religion. This task was made more complicated by the fact that Middle Eastern Christians were divided into three communities characterised by particular Christologies. Muslim intellectuals could easily charge Christians with incoherent interpretations of Christ that stood in need of a simpler and more rational treatment.

The challenge of defending Christology from the charge of incoherence was essential to the ongoing vitality of the three communities, both to stem the flow of members to Islam and to stake a claim to intellectual respectability within the Islamic Empire. Christology now had to be thought out in the light of Islamic claims concerning Christ. By the late eight and early ninth centuries Christian theologians from each of the three communities were producing Christological writing of great sophistication. This was mainly due to a climate of intellectual exchange between thinking Muslims and Christians that would not be paralleled until modern times. During this period Muslim intellectuals were studying the Greek heritage passed on to them by Christians who were engaged in translating Greek texts into Arabic. The openess of Muslims to the cultural values of Christians provided a basis for two-way communication between rulers and ruled. By the end of the ninth century Muslim attitudes to Christians had narrowed to such an extent that creative dialogue had become circumscribed and Christians found themselves marginalised from public intellectual discourse.

This chapter examines two major and two minor contributions to dialogue about Christ in the eighth century. While there are indications of dialogue about Christ between Muslims and Christians from the seventh century,[1] the earliest known written defence of Christian belief about Christ comes from John of Damascus (d. c. 750), after his retirement from service in the Muslim government in the second decade of the eighth century. John was a member of the Greek speaking churches that followed the Christological affirmations of the councils of Ephesus and Chalcedon, and was later to be regarded as one of the doctors of the Eastern Orthodox churches for his systematic account of the faith. John referred to Islam as one of many heresies of his era, which may reflect a widespread view of the new movement among Christians.[2]

An anonymous defence of the Christian doctrines of the Trinity and the Incarnation in Arabic came from the Greek speaking Chalcedonian churches in Palestine possibly before 750, showing that Christians were beginning to adopt the language of Islam at least to engage in debate with Muslims. It most probably was the work of the monastic communities of South Palestine, which John had joined after his retirement, and shows a familiarity with the Qur'ān that demonstrates a willingness to approach Muslims on their terms in order to uphold Christian truth.[3]

From the eighth decade of the century comes the written report of a dialogue between the Caliph al-Mahdī and the Patriarch of the Nestorian churches in Baghdad, which seems to have taken place just after Timothy was consecrated Patriarch in 780.[4] Timothy was invited by al-Mahdī to give an account of a range of Christian beliefs that differed from Islamic

---

[1] There is a report in Syriac of a dialogue between John Sedra, the Jacobite Patriarch of Antioch (631-48) and a Muslim leader, in which the Patriarch is asked to justify his belief that Christ is God. John appeals to the prophecies of the Messiah in the Old Testament, but does not engage with specifically Muslim convictions about Christ. See F. Nau, 'Un colloque du patriarche Jean avec L'émir des Agaréens et faits divers des années 712 à 716,' *JA* 5 (1915), 225-79.

[2] See D.J. Sahas, *John of Damascus on Islam* (Leiden: 1972), 42-44; and S.H. Griffith, 'Melkites, Jacobites, and the Christological Controversies in Arabic in Third/Ninth-Century Syria', in *Syrian Christians Under Islam,* (Leiden: 2001), 19-22. For a convenient introduction to the apologetic methods of John of Damascus, as well as Timothy I, Abū Qurra and `Ammār al-Basrī see J-M. Gaudeul, *Encounters and Clashes,* vol. 1 (Rome: 1984), 28-38.

[3] See S.K. Samir, 'The Earliest Arab Apology for Christianity (c. 750)', in S.K. Samir and J.S. Nielsen (eds.), *Christian Arabic Apologetics during the Abbasid Period (750-1258),* (Leiden: 1994), 57-60; and S.H. Griffith, 'The Monks of Palestine and the Growth of Christian Literature in Arabic', *MW* 78 (1988), 1-28, 21f.

[4] Timothy describes his debate with the Caliph in a letter to the priest Sargis in 782/3. See Epistle 59 in *Les Lettres du Patriarche Nestorien Timothée I,* (ed.) R.J. Bidawid, (Rome: 1956), 42f.

teaching. Timothy's grasp of Muslim thought is evidence of a climate of dialogue cultivated by the early `Abbasid Caliphs in which Muslim and Christian theologians developed extensive knowledge of each other's beliefs. The dialogue has been preserved in Syriac and in Arabic, and for the most part shows Timothy offering answers to al-Mahdī's questions, with occasional counter-questions raised by Timothy. Al-Mahdī's questions concentrate on the Trinity, the Incarnation, the Scriptures and the status of the prophet Muḫammad, since these were the most significant areas of disagreement between Muslims and Christians.[5]

The Nestorian community had a substantial presence in the region of Baghdad, which had become the seat of the `Abbasid Caliphs, and this accounts for the way that al-Mahdī treated Timothy as the leader of the Christians. Nestorians had been forced to live beyond the borders of the Roman Empire during the fifth century and had settled mainly in Mesopotamia, from which they established churches further east. Their language was Syriac, but the fact that an Arabic version of the dialogue became available in the last decade of the century shows that the language of Islam was becoming important not just for communication with Muslims, but also for Christian instruction.[6]

John of Damascus: Dialogue with Muslims about Christ

During his retirement from public office, John wrote three treatises, which he put together under the title *Pege Gnosis* 'The Fount of Knowledge'. The first treatise, *Dialectica*, is a study of philosophy, the second, *De Haeresibus*, describes one hundred heresies, and the third, *De Fide Orthodoxa*, expounds orthodox belief. The hundredth heresy in *De Haeresibus* is 'the Heresy of the Ishmaelites', and includes answers to questions posed by Muslims on the Trinity, the Incarnation and Scripture.[7]

Dialogue on Christ in The Heresy of the Ishmaelites

John's treatment of Christology in this chapter on Islam refers to an accusation made by Muslims that Christians associate Christ with God in an unacceptable way "by saying that Christ is the Son of God and God."[8] John suggests two ways of replying to this challenge. Firstly, it could be mentioned that the prophets that preceded his coming foretold the divinity

[5] See H. Putnam, *L'Église sous Timothée I: 780-832* (Beirut: 1975).
[6] See A.S. Atiya, *A History of Eastern Christianity* (London: 1968), 95.
[7] Greek text with English translation in D.J. Sahas, *John of Damascus.*
[8] John of Damascus, *The Heresy of the Ishmaelites,* in Sahas, 137.

of Christ, since Muslims accept them as genuine prophets of God. However, he realises that Muslims might deny the validity of such prophecy on the grounds that the prophetic writings have been tampered with to such an extent that they can no longer be trusted to contain original prophetic utterance. This is early testimony for the Islamic conviction that the Jews tampered with their scriptures.[9]

John thinks a second type of response may be more fruitful. Christians could quote the Muslim belief that "Christ is Word and Spirit of God."[10] and say "if the Word is in God it is obvious that he is God as well." Denial of this argument by Muslims would result in an inadequate understanding of the nature of God, so that the Christian can say; "if, on the other hand, this is outside of God, then God, according to you is without word and without spirit." In John's logic, since Muslims wish to deny that Christ is God they have to accept that the word and spirit are split off from God as a result of the appearing of Christ. Christians can drive the point home; "thus trying to avoid making associates to God, you have mutilated him."[11]

John has chosen to avoid dealing with the sonship of Christ raised in the original allegation that Christians associate Christ with God in the wrong way by calling him Son of God. He has focussed instead on the Qur'ānic affirmation that Christ is word and spirit from God in order to put Muslims on the defensive over their understanding of God's attributes of word and spirit. However, a Muslim may have replied that Christ carried the word of God, which he declared to the Jews, and was empowered by the spirit of God in a similar way to other prophets. As a result no association of Christ with God need be made.

---

[9] The Qur'ān speaks of corruption of the Scriptures in the possession of the Jews. *Sūra* 3:78, "There is a group (within the People of the book) who distort the book with their tongues … They say this is from God, but it is not from him" along with *sūra* 7:162, "Evildoers (among the People of the book) changed the word that was spoken to them", have been widely understood by Muslims to demonstrate the unreliability of the Jewish Scriptures. It is clear from John's argument that appeal to Messianic prophecy, which was characteristic of New Testament and Patristic Christology, could not be used with ease in an Islamic context.

[10] See *sūras* 3:45 and 5:110.

[11] John of Damascus, *The Heresy of the Ishmaelites*. In Sahas, 137.

Dialogue between a Muslim and a Christian Attributed to John[12]

Though attributed to John, this dialogue is found among the writings of Abū Qurra (d. c. 829) who may have edited the work. Since the content of this dialogue corresponds more closely to *De Haeresibus* than the writing of Abū Qurra, it is likely that it comes from the eighth century even if not from John himself. This dialogue concerns Christology and the source of good and evil.[13] Since the Muslim is addressed in the third person as 'he' and the Christian in the second person as 'you', it is clear that this is a piece of advice for Christians in their encounter with Muslims rather than an apology written directly for Muslims. Once again it is suggested that the Christian refer to Christ as Word and Spirit of God, but now the argument turns on whether Word and Spirit are created or not. If the Muslim says that the Word and Spirit are created, the Christian should ask; "before God created the Word and the Spirit, did he have neither Spirit nor Word?" In reply, the Muslim asks the Christian whether the words of God are created or uncreated. The Christian is warned to be careful in making a response. If he says that God's words are uncreated, the Muslim might argue that this does not make the words of God, "gods to be worshipped". Likewise, Christ is not a god to be worshipped, even if he is an uncreated word of God. In the light of this, the Christian is advised to make a clear distinction between the words of God and the Word of God. The words of God are gathered in the Scriptures, but the Word of God is Christ who is the true uncreated Word of God.[14]

Here the use of the Qur'ānic title "a word from him" throws up problems for the Christian. Discussion of the eternity of the Qur'ān among Muslims seemed to provide a useful parallel for talk about the eternal Word becoming human. However, though Muslims might believe in the eternity of the Qur'ān, they did not think of the word of God as existing in time in the way that Christians believed that Christ was the eternal Word in time. The appeal to this Qur'ānic title for Christ is not repeated in ninth century apologetics probably because the lesson taught here had been learnt. The dialogue also advises Christians how to speak about the divine and human natures of Christ. If a Muslim wonders how God can eat, drink and sleep, Christians should reply that the human nature performed those actions but that the divine nature did not. If the Muslim asks whether the divine nature

---

[12] Sahas (p. 102) believes that although the text in its present form does not come from John's hand, the content is a product of his thought. However, S.H. Griffith (*Melkites*, p. 22) doubts whether the attribution can be supported. R.G. Hoyland thinks that it may have been constructed from John's teachings, but not written by John himself. See his *Seeing Islam as others saw it* (Princeton: 1997), 489.

[13] Sahas gives the Greek text with an English translation by J.W. Voorhis from 'The Discussion of a Christian and a Saracen', *MW* 25 (1935), 266-273.

[14] *Dialogue Between a Christian and A Muslim*, in Sahas, 151.

died on the cross then the Christian must say that only Christ's human nature died.[15]

Evaluation

John's approach to dialogue on Christology is firstly to recognise the way Muslims see Christ. Rather than repeat the affirmations of Orthodox Christology he builds his case on foundations acceptable to Muslims. While they refuse to speak of him as God's son, they call Christ God's word and spirit, therefore John begins his answer to the question about sonship with this Muslim affirmation about Christ. If Christ is word and spirit from God then surely he shares attributes of God in such a way that makes him divine as well as human.

Secondly, John avoids areas of outright denial, thus he does not discuss why Christians call Jesus God's Son. He also declines to appeal to Christian Scripture since he is aware of Muslim hesitation about the authenticity of the text. The issue of *taḫrīf* had become important in Muslim attitudes to the Jewish and Christian scriptures. Rather than appeal to the authority of the sacred text, John counsels Christians to develop arguments that depend on ideas acceptable to Muslims themselves with a view to reaching Christian conclusions. This type of apologetic argument that seeks to make a reasonable case for Christology on grounds acceptable to Muslims comes to full flourish in the early ninth century writing studied in chapters three to six.

An Anonymous Apology for Christianity[16]

From the same Palestinian region in which John wrote comes an apology not in Greek, but in Arabic, which attempts to explain Christian faith to Muslims. The date of the apology is not certain, but it may have been written in the 740's.[17] The apology differs in style from John's dialogue

[15] *Ibid.*, 153.

[16] The Arabic text (Sinai 145) is edited with an English translation by M.D. Dunlop as *A Treatise on the Triune Nature of God* (London: 1899).

[17] Gibson's version of the treatise omitted "a few pages from the end" (introduction vi). S.K. Samir discovered on one of those pages the following statement; "If this religion was not truly from God, it would not have stood firm nor stood erect for seven hundred and forty-six years." See S.K. Samir, 'The Earliest Arab Apology for Christianity (c. 750)' in S.K. Samir and J.S. Nielsen (eds.), *Christian Arabic Apologetics during the Abbasid Period (750-1258)*, (Leiden: 1994), 57-116, 61. Samir's belief that this statement probably reflects a date just before 750 is accepted by S.H. Griffith in 'The Monks of Palestine and the Growth of Christian Literature in Arabic', *MW* 78 (1988), 1-28, 21. This presupposes counting 746 years from the birth

framework, since here Muslims are not addressed in the third person as in John's writing, but in the second person as 'you', with Christians in the first person as 'we'. This apology is more of a long discourse addressed to Muslims rather than a debate with questions and answers. The context of the work is Muslim criticism of Christian belief just as it was in John's work, but the writer quotes from the Qur'ān in order to defend Christian faith to a much greater extent than John's single Qur'ānic reference to Christ as word and spirit from God. If this apology is the product of the generation following John then Christians were beginning to use Arabic to formulate theology by the mid eighth century.

The treatise opens with an explanation of Christian belief in the Trinity in terms governed by the Muslim concern for the worship of one God; "we do not worship another God alongside God in his Word and Spirit."[18] The writer responds to the allegation made against Christians that they do this with Christ. The proof that only one God is worshipped is found in "the book God sent down on his prophet Moses" where God created the world by his word and his spirit.[19]

The Sending of the Word

When the writer comes to the relationship between God and his Word he deals with the Qur'ānic denial of the sonship of Christ. "We do not say that God brought forth (*walada*) his Word, as humans give birth to offspring."[20] Christians think of the Father bringing forth the Word as the sun produces rays, or the human mind words, or fire heat. Just as there cannot be heat without fire or rays without sun, or words without a mind, so there cannot be the Word of God without God. The writer quotes from the Qur'ān to support this view. "Believe in God and his word; and also in his spirit, who is sent down from your Lord as mercy and guidance."[21]

The sending of the Word is set in the context of the Biblical account of the creation and fall of humanity and the history of Israel. Figures common to the Bible and the Qur'ān, Noah, Abraham, Lot, Moses and David, are all referred to, and no incidents in Old Testament history are mentioned that do not occur in the Qur'ān. The weakness of Israel lies in the power of the

---

of Christ, but if the beginning of the church is in mind then a date in the 780's is more likely, according to M. Swanson, *Folly to the Hunafā`*, PhD thesis presented to P.I.S.A.I. (Rome: 1992). He specifies 788 in 'Some Considerations for the Dating of *fī tatlīt allāh al-wāhid* (Sinai Ar. 154) and *al-gāmi` wugūh al-īmān* (London, British Library op. 4950)' in *PO* 18 (1993), 118-141, 140.

[18] *A Treatise on the Triune Nature of God,* (ed.) M.D. Gibson, 75.

[19] For the Qur'ānic phraseology see *sūras* 3:4 and 5:44.

[20] *Ibid.*, 77.

[21] *Ibid.* The quotation is an amalgam of *sūras* 4:171 and 16:102.

Devil who continually succeeds in drawing the people away from God, so the Word is sent to deal with Satanic power once and for all, "by putting on weak human nature taken from pure Mary."[22] The purity of Mary is emphasised in the succeeding section, enabling the writer to show that the Word took on a human nature that was undefiled by any weakness. "Christ was born of the pure Mary by the Holy Spirit without her being touched by a man. God from God, light from light, Word and Spirit; a perfect human, with mind and body, yet without sin."[23] Expressions from the Nicene creed "God from God, light from light" and also from the Chalcedonian definition "a perfect human, with mind and body, yet without sin" are built into the presentation.[24] Here is a weaving together of Islamic and Christian ideas to produce the elements of a Christology that might appeal to Muslim readers, or at least not seem totally removed from Islamic principles.

Qur'ānic support for the divinity of Christ is found in Jesus' creative power. "Christ created whereas only God creates. You will find in the Qur'ān that Christ spoke and created from clay what looked like a bird, then blew on it and it became a [real] bird by God's permission."[25] Further proof for the divinity of Christ comes from his forgiving sin, feeding the hungry, casting out evil spirits, giving the Holy Spirit to his disciples, ascending to heaven, judging humanity and granting eternal life to the righteous. None of these could be performed by a human being, but only by God who "veiled himself in a sinless human being".[26] The author attaches data from the New Testament to the miracle story from the Qur'ān to create a composite account of Christ's divine power in a bid to anchor the idea of divinity in the creative actions permitted him by God.

There is no treatment of the death and resurrection of Christ. The notion of a sacrificial death for sin is not prominent elsewhere in the treatise. This may be accounted for by the facts that the edited document is incomplete, and that the subjects of the extant treatise are the Trinity and Incarnation. The salvation of humanity from the power of Satan seems to come through the Incarnation of the Word without reference to the cross; "God defeated Satan by clothing himself with human nature".[27] The cross releases

---

[22] *Ibid.*, 83.

[23] *Ibid.*

[24] The Nicene Creed composed in 325 stated that Christ was "the Word of God, God from God, Light from Light." See the text in J. Stevenson, *A New Eusebius* (rev. ed.) (London: 1987), 344. The Chalcedonian definition written in 451 confirmed the Nicene Creed and added statements about the human and divine natures of Christ; "perfect in Godhead, perfect in manhood, truly God and truly man, consisting of a reasonable soul and a body … like us in all things apart from sin." See the text in J. Stevenson, *Creeds, Councils and Controversies* (London: 1966), 337.

[25] Gibson, 84; referring to *sūras* 3:49 and 5:110.

[26] *Ibid.*, 85.

[27] *Ibid.*, 83.

humans from the consequences of sin rather than the power of the Devil; "He crucified sin by his crucifixion and put an end to death, which was inherited from Adam's disobedience, by his own death".[28] The author mentions the cross only this once, but often refers to salvation from Satan. At one point the coming from heaven and the returning to heaven takes place without reference to Christ's death and resurrection. "He came down from Heaven to save Adam's descendants from Satan and his evil, and then he ascended to Heaven where he had come from".[29] Perhaps there is a deliberate attempt to play down the significance of the cross in order to avoid losing the Muslim reader.

Evaluation

This early apology in Arabic firstly seeks to defend Christian beliefs by addressing Muslim criticisms found in the Qur'ān. Christians do not associate Christ with God as another god, they do not speak of three divine beings, and they do not think of God bringing forth offspring as humans do. Secondly, there is an attempt to find positive support for Christian beliefs in the Qur'ān. Muslims are to believe in God, his Word and his Spirit, therefore the Qur'ān teaches the unity of God in his Word and his Spirit, which is what Christians hold. Christ had the power to create according to the Qur'ān, so this is a proof of his divinity. The Qur'ān teaches that Christ is raised to a position of greatness in God's presence, which supports the Christian belief that he sits at God's right hand to rule the world.

Thirdly, Christology is presented positively from three sources; prophesy from before the coming of Christ, the gospel accounts of him, and the tradition of the church about Christ. About half of the extant document expounds prophesy of Christ and its implications for Christology; Christ is "God with us", he will rule the nations, he will guide them into all truth, and all nations will come to serve him. He also takes away the sin of the world. Much of the rest of the treatise appeals to the gospels to show Christ's divine power and authority; his authority to forgive sin, his power to feed the hungry, his authority over evil spirits and illnesses, are all proof of his divine nature. The creeds sum up the Biblical evidence by declaring that Christ is "God from God", but also a perfect human who never sinned. The author does not elaborate on the sinless human character of Christ but his concern is to demonstrate Christ's divinity. The relationship between the divine and human natures of Christ is only briefly touched on. Christ

[28] *Ibid.*, 84.
[29] *Ibid.*, 86.

honoured all humanity by clothing himself with human nature, which in Christ's case had already been purified before "he put it on".[30]

The treatise is addressed to Muslims, but is not a dialogue as such. It is a discourse that attempts to give an explanation of Christian faith for a Muslim readership by incorporating Muslim conceptions of Christ that are not impossible to reconcile with Christian ones. However, Muslim counter-argument is not really included in the presentation, so it is not easy to determine what kind of response might have been made to the treatise. Nevertheless, this merger of Qur'ānic data with Christian faith is noteworthy, setting an example for future generations of a respectful discourse between Christians and Muslims about Christ. While the course of ninth century apologetics was to follow a debate format, the discourse approach re-emerged in the modern era. Chapter seven shows that the discourse method of the Anonymous Apology was favoured alike by a European missionary in the nineteenth century and an Egyptian Copt in the twentieth, and chapter ten examines a late twentieth century life of Christ that blends Qur'ānic and gospel texts together in the manner of this apology.

Dialogue between the Caliph Al-Mahdī and the Nestorian Patriarch Timothy I

This dialogue, which took place shortly after Timothy became Patriarch of the Nestorian church in Mesopotamia in 780, exists in Syriac and Arabic. Timothy no doubt produced the longer Syriac version for fellow members of the Nestorian community, whereas he probably had a shorter Arabic text made for Muslims as well as for Christians who were more familiar with Arabic than Syriac. It is possible that Timothy wrote the Arabic version himself, but it is more likely that he supervised the translation, since the rest of his extant writing is in Syriac. While these written versions may not be transcriptions of the oral debate, it is hardly likely that the questions posed by the Caliph were put on his lips unless he actually asked them. The reality

[30] *Ibid.*, 94. The image of the Word of God clothing himself with human nature goes back at least to Tertullian's *Against Praxeas*, 27, written around 213. "The Word was in flesh; but we must ask how the Word was made flesh; whether by transformation into flesh or by being clothed therewith. The latter surely." Text in H. Bettenson, *The Early Christian Fathers* (London: 1969), 123. See also Athanasius (c. 296-373) *Against Arius*, 1:42, "The Word was not degraded by receiving a body … Rather he deified what he put on", and 2:7, "just as Aaron put on his robe, so the Word took earthly flesh." Text in Bettenson, 279 and 281.

of Muslim rule set limits to the use of the Caliph as a literary device to show the pre-eminence of the Christian case.[31]

The Caliph asks virtually all of the questions, allowing Timothy the occasional counter-question. The fact of Islamic rule meant that although Christians were numerically strong they could not assume a position of intellectual dominance. While Nestorian scholars translated Greek texts into Arabic for the Caliph it did not follow that they could mount a challenge to Islamic convictions with ease.[32] The Caliph had the true revelation and Timothy was under pressure to give an account for Christian beliefs that seemed not to concur with that revealed truth. The Caliph scrutinises Timothy's understanding of the Trinity, the Incarnation, and the Bible. The section on Christology is mainly concerned with Christ's relationship with God.

The Relationship between the Divine and Human in Christ

Al-Mahdī thinks that Christians believe in a biological connection between God and Jesus via Mary. "How can someone like you, knowledgeable and wise, say that the most high God took a wife and had a son?"[33] Evidently al-Mahdī reads the Qur'ān in this way, since no Christian would ever have claimed that Mary was married to God.[34] Timothy simply denies the allegation and avoids using sonship terminology altogether, in favour of "the Word of God", who "appeared in the flesh for the salvation of the world."[35]

---

[31] The Syriac text is edited and translated into English by A. Mingana as 'The Apology of Timothy the Patriarch before the Caliph Mahdi', *Woodbrooke Studies* II, (1928), 1-162. Mingana believes that the dialogue took place in 781/2, and that the Syriac text followed soon after. The Arabic text is edited by L. Cheikho in *Al-Machriq* 19 (1921), 359-374, and 408-418. This version is reproduced with a French translation by H Putnam in *L'Église sous Timothée I* (Beirut: 1975). Putnam thinks that the Arabic version is a later summary of the Syriac one from around 794/5. See Hoyland, *Seeing Islam as others saw it,* for a discussion of authorship. He thinks both versions are literary creations that do not transcribe the actual debate, but do reflect discussions taking place between Christians and Muslims.

[32] For the translation work of Nestorian scholars see A.S. Atiya, *A History of Eastern Christianity,* 252f.

[33] *Dialogue between the Caliph Al-Mahdī and the Nestorian Patriarch Timothy I.* In Putnam, appendix, 7.

[34] The Qur'ān does not make this allegation, but al-Mahdī probably understood *sūra* 4:171 to imply that Jesus, the son of Mary, had been transformed by Christians into Jesus, the son of God, via Mary, in strictly physical terms.

[35] Putnam, appendix, 7.

Al-Mahdī insists on discussing Christ's sonship, knowing that Christians believe in it. Timothy makes a distinction between Christ's eternal sonship and his temporal one.

> "We believe that the Messiah was born of the Father as his Word and that he was born of the Virgin Mary as a man; and that his birth from the Father is eternal before time, and that his birth from Mary took place in time without a human father."[36]

However, al-Mahdī spots a difficulty with the two births. If the Messiah has two points of origin, does not this mean two separate Christs? "So there are two Messiahs, one temporal and the other eternal; the eternal is a god coming from God and the temporal is a man from Mary."[37] Timothy concedes two separate points of origin for the divine and human natures of Christ, but argues that after the Incarnation there is complete unity between the divine and human in him. "There are not two Messiahs or two Sons but one Messiah and one Son who has two natures, divine and human, because he is the Word of God who took a human body and became a man." (*sāra insānan*)[38] This sounds as though the Word found a ready-made body from Mary, but the use of the verb *sāra* introduces another dimension to the discussion. The Word once was not human, but by uniting in time with the human nature taken from Mary, the Word became human.

Al-Mahdī does not accept that two types of nature can be united without losing their distinctiveness. Timothy appeals to the way a human being is a combination of mind and body; Christ is a combination of the divine and human, but no less a unity than any human with a mind and body.[39] Here is the same argument found in *The Anonymous Apology*, but Timothy goes beyond the earlier work in his vocabulary. A new technical term for

---

[36] *Ibid.*

[37] *Ibid.*, 9.

[38] *Ibid.*, 10. Timothy argues in the tradition of Antiochene Christology that stressed the union of two natures in Christ. Theodore of Mopsuestia (c. 350-428) gave a similar answer to those who thought that two natures in Christ meant two sons. "The fact that we speak of two natures does not mean that we are forced to speak of two Lords or two sons." *Sermons on the Catechism,* 8:14. Text in H. Bettenson, *The Later Christian Fathers* (London: 1970), 167.

[39] Putnam, appendix, 10. The use of the duality of the human person as body and mind as a support for two natures united in Christ was a feature of Antiochene Christology. Theodoret of Cyrus (c.393-466), who had attempted to defend Nestorius before agreeing to his anathematization in 451 at the Council of Chalcedon, provides an example of this argument. "In the case of one man we divide the natures, speaking of a mortal body and an immortal soul, but the two, we say, are one man. It is even more reasonable to acknowledge the distinction of the natures of God, who assumed, and man who was assumed." *Refutation of the Twelve Chapters or Anathemas of Cyril*, 3. Text in Bettenson, *The Later Christian Fathers.* 271.

Incarnation appears, which becomes standard in subsequent Christian writing in Arabic. "The Word of God had, as a result of his Incarnation (*bi tajassudi-hi*), two distinct natures, one divine and the other human."[40] *Tajassud* is the verbal noun of *tajassada*, "to become embodied". In the Qur'ān, the noun *jasad* is found, meaning "body", but the idea of becoming embodied is absent. Whether *tajassud* was first used in this dialogue is not certain, but it is the first surviving record of its use in Christian writing in Arabic. Christians were being forced to develop theological terms in the language of their Muslim rulers, which meant coining new expressions in Arabic not found in the stock of Islamic discourse.

The Death of Christ

This dialogue contains the first recorded debate on the crucifixion between Muslims and Christians. John of Damascus and the writer of *The Anonymous Apology* did not enter into discussion of the Qur'ānic denial of the death of Jesus by crucifixion. Here al-Mahdī raises the issue of the death of the divine nature if the Christian story is true. If Christ really did die on the cross, then it must follow logically that the divine nature died there also. But if Christians believe God is eternal how can they hold that the eternal Word was put to death? Al-Mahdī asks; "Is it possible that God died, supposing that he [Christ] is God?" Timothy replies; "In so far as he was God, Christ did not die; but in so far as he was human, in his human nature he died."[41] Timothy gives the same answer that John of Damascus recommended; the divine nature cannot die otherwise the eternal One would cease to exist. Though both Timothy the Nestorian and John the Chalcedonian were united on this point, it raised a profound problem for both types of Christology. The union of divine and human in Christ seemed to operate up to the death of Christ and no further. When Christ died there must have been a separation of the divine and human natures. The divine was spared death, but the human had to submit to it. Therefore the supposed union of two natures lacks cogency for Muslims.

Al-Mahdī does not press this inconsistency but simply quotes *sūra* 4:157; "They did not crucify him."[42] The Qur'ān denies the crucifixion of Christ so no further discussion is necessary. Now Timothy quotes from *sūra* 19:33, where Jesus says; "Peace be on me, the day I was born, the day I die, and the day I am raised alive", and interprets this to mean "that Jesus died and was brought to life."[43] Al-Mahdī does not accept the chronology

---

[40] Putnam, appendix, 10.

[41] *Ibid.*, 44.

[42] *Ibid.*, 45.

[43] *Ibid.* This use of *sūra* 19:33 reappears in subsequent Christian apologetic for the historicity of the death of Christ up to modern times. For example, Bill Campbell

placed on the text by Timothy; "Jesus is not yet dead but he is going to die." This is early testimony to the stories contained in the *Hadīth*, that Jesus will return at the end of the age to preach Islam and then die for the first time.[44]

Timothy continues to answer al-Mahdī by refusing to accept that Jesus can ascend to heaven without dying. "If Jesus is not dead he would not have ascended to heaven. But it is affirmed by you that the ascension of Jesus to heaven and his resurrection took place a long time ago, as your book testifies."[45] Timothy sees a basic contradiction between the plain meaning of *sūra* 19:33 and al-Mahdī's interpretation of it. How can the future dying of Jesus be possibly reconciled with Jesus' own statement of his death preceding his ascension? As far as Timothy is concerned, Al-Mahdī has reversed the order of the dying and raising of Jesus in such a way as to render meaningless the text of the Qur'ān. Timothy does not argue that the Qur'ān contradicts itself, but rather that al-Mahdī's reading of the Qur'ān is faulty.[46]

Al-Mahdī produces another argument to deny the death of Christ on the cross. "Jesus was honoured by God who did not deliver him into the hands of the Jews so that they could kill him."[47] This is an early example of the standard Muslim assertion that God would not allow a prophet to suffer such an ignominious death. Timothy's reply quotes the gospel of John 10:17f; "The Father loves me because I lay down my life of my own free will" and makes the comment that the Jews crucified Jesus not because he was weak, but because he decided to die of his own will.[48] Presumably this rescues God from blame for allowing the Messiah to die, but Timothy does not make the point. The debate on the crucifixion therefore ends on different conceptions of what God allowed to happen to Christ. For al-Mahdī, God does not allow his prophets to be defeated, but for Timothy, God allows Christ to die by his own choice.[49]

---

asked a Tunisian taxi driver who had denied that Christ died; "What about the verse where God is speaking and says – Oh Jesus, I will cause you to die and raise you to myself – doesn't that say that Jesus died before he rose again?" The taxi driver replied that the two statements don't have to be in chronological order. See W. Campbell, *The Qur'ān and the Bible in the Light of History and Science* (Marseille: 1986), 161.

44 See *Sahīh Muslim,* vol.1:72, 287-293.

45 Putnam, appendix, 46.

46 This approach to dialogue has been revived in the modern era. See especially Kenneth Cragg's Christian readings of the Qur'ān in chapter eight.

47 Putnam, 48.

48 *Ibid.*

49 B.D. Kateregga uses the argument in, *Islam and Christianity* (Grand Rapids: 1981), 140. "According to the true belief of Islam, it would seem most inappropriate for the

Evaluation

This dialogue graphically displays the concerns Muslims have with Christian faith in Christ. Firstly, Muslims suspect that there is a biological link between Jesus and God in the thinking of Christians, which undermines the character of God. Secondly, the idea that Christ has two natures seems to the Muslim mind to be a logical impossibility since it would result in two separate beings rather than one. Thirdly, the Christian claim that Christ died on the cross proves the logical absurdity of the two natures concept, because it ought rationally to follow that both natures died there and not just the human. Finally, the supposed death of Christ by crucifixion must undermine both the dignity of Christ's status as a prophet and the power of God to protect him.

Timothy's method is to avoid giving offence at all costs in the way that he answers the Caliph's questions. Thus he never criticises the Qur'ān as such but only the Caliph's interpretation of particular Qur'ānic texts. Indeed his purpose in referring to these texts is to find a credible Islamic basis for the fact of the crucifixion. His general approach to answering questions about Christian doctrine is to make a reasoned case based on the coherence of the beliefs themselves. The four objections raised by the Caliph are dealt with in this fashion.

Timothy answers the first objection by denying that Christians hold to a physical connection between Christ and God. The other three objections are dealt with by accepting the apparent problem while offering a different perspective on it. The second objection is met by explaining that the two natures in Christ have two points of origin but an ultimate unity. The divine is from eternity, the human is from within time, but after the union of the eternal and the temporal there is a unity of being. As far as the third objection is concerned, Timothy's concession that only the human nature died on the cross seems to confirm al-Mahdī's point that the unity of the two natures is actually broken by the death of Christ. The fourth objection is countered by an appeal to the Qur'ānic text that seems to say that Christ's death comes before his being raised. However, he does not offer a defence of the appropriateness of the crucifixion of a prophet.

Towards Ninth Century Dialogue on Christology

From John's cryptic advice to Christians in their conversation with Muslims to the detailed debate between Timothy and al-Mahdī is a journey short in time but long in theological development. John wrote in Greek for

---

Messiah to die through a shameful crucifixion. God, who is just, would not permit the righteous Messiah to suffer in that manner."

Christians. *The Anonymous Apology* was an Arabic document for Christians with a Muslim readership in mind. Timothy's dialogue would have been conducted in Arabic, and the Arabic text would have been produced for Muslims as well as for Christians.

The Anonymous Apology presents a Christology based on the Bible with some Christological language taken from the Nicene creed and the Chalcedonian definition. However, the treatise does not give a Muslim response to the Christology put forward. Timothy, on the contrary, was required to answer questions about Christological ideas that were unacceptable to Muslims, so he was forced by the circumstances of the interview to mount a defence of Christology as best he could. Timothy's style of argument was to show the intelligibility of the two natures Christology when understood properly. If his Muslim questioner could be helped to see the inner consistency of the language used then the dialogue would be worthwhile.

Timothy's apologetic method of giving reasoned answers to difficult questions was further developed by the three ninth century apologists, Abū Qurra, Abū Rā'iṯa and `Ammār al-Baṣrī, whose work will be examined in chapters three to six. Whether any of them were familiar with Timothy's dialogue with al-Mahdī is uncertain, but they all followed the same method of finding principles on which to base their arguments for the validity of their Christology with which Muslims might agree. However, these early ninth century writers show a depth of engagement in dialogue between Christians and Muslims that went much further than the three examples from the eighth century that have been reviewed here.

Chapter Three

The Christology of Theodore Abū Qurra in Dialogue with Muslims

Theodore Abū Qurra

Abū Qurra (c.755-c.829) was the leading Middle Eastern Chalcedonian theologian in the generation after John of Damascus, but little is known about his life, apart from a few details given in two Syriac Chronicles, *The Chronicle of Michael The Syrian*, and *The Anonymous Chronicle of 1234*. The former mentions that Theodore was Bishop of Harrān in Syria before being deposed by the Patriarch Theodoret of Antioch, and that he travelled to Egypt and Armenia around 813-4 to promote Chalcedonian orthodoxy.[1] Patriarch Theodoret was in office between 785 and 799 and therefore Theodore probably was Bishop of Harrān sometime during those years.[2] The latter chronicle says that Abū Qurra was involved in a debate with the Caliph al-Ma'mūn (813-833) in the year 829.[3] Sidney Griffith adds together these biographical items to give a career spanning forty years, assuming he was thirty years of age in 785.[4]

Among his writings are a number of apologetic treatises for Jews, Muslims and Christians concerning Christology. For Christians, he defended the Chalcedonian definition against those who did not accept it.[5] For Jews, he attempted to show that Jesus was superior to Moses in his ability to perform miracles in his own name so proving that he was divine.[6]

---

[1] See J-B. Chabot, *Michel le Syrien* vol. 3 (Paris), 32-34.

[2] See I. Dick, 'Un continuateur arabe de saint Jean Damascène: Theodore Abuqurra, évêque melkite de Harran', *POC* 12 (1962), 209-23 and 319-32; 13, (1963), 114-29, and S.H. Griffith, 'Reflections on the Biography of Theodore Abū Qurrah', *PO* 18 (1993), 143-170. See also the accessible summary of his biography in *BDEC*, (Oxford: 1999).

[3] See J-B. Chabot, *Anonymi Auctoris Chronicum ad A.C. 1234 Pertinens, CSCO* 109 (1937), 22f.

[4] See S.H. Griffith's 'Reflections', 149.

[5] See his "Confession of the Orthodox Faith" (ed.) I. Dick in 'Deux Écrits Inédits de Théodore Abuqurra', *Le Muséon* 72 (1959), 53-67.

[6] See his 'Treatise on the Holy Law of Moses and the Prophets who predicted the Messiah', (ed.) C. Bacha in *Un Traite des Oeuvres Arabes de Théodore Abou-Kurra* (Paris: 1905).

For Muslims, Abū Qurra produced at least three treatises on Christology. These are concerned with the problem of attributing Incarnation to God,[7] the nature of the Sonship of Christ,[8] and the necessity of the suffering of Christ for the forgiveness of sin.[9] The existence of treatises in Arabic addressed to such a variety of audiences shows how the language of Islam had, by the turn of the ninth century, become the common means of discourse in the Middle East. His treatise comparing Moses and Jesus assumes that Jewish readers understand Arabic. His Confession of the Orthodox Faith is essentially a catechetical piece to educate fellow Melkite Christians in the errors of alternative Christologies and the rightness of the definition of Chalcedon. This is written in complex theological language designed for serious students of theology, perhaps indicating that the traditional Church languages of Greek and Syriac were giving way to Arabic.

Abū Qurra emphasizes aspects of Christology relevant to the audience. For example, in his writing for Jews he explicitly engages with Jewish convictions about Moses who he compares with Christ. In the Treatise on the Holy Law of Moses he addresses Jews directly in the fashion "you say Jew", and goes on to argue that what Jews revere about Moses can hardly be compared with the reality of the Messiah and his accomplishments. Moses was able to perform miracles by God's power but not by his own ability, whereas the Messiah was able to perform miracles in his own name and to "empower others to do similar work in his name."[10] The treatise engages with exposition of the Old Testament, arguing that Moses and other prophets looked forward to the coming of the Christ of the New Testament.[11] His Confession of the Orthodox Faith is quite different in content. Here there is no discussion of Scripture but a detailed defence of Chalcedonian Christology over against alternative views. This treatise is addressed to fellow Chalcedonians to help them have confidence in the rightness of their faith in Christ. Neither Jews nor Muslims are in his sights in this presentation. When he writes for Muslims there is no discussion of alternative Christologies but only a defence of his own. Two of his treatises for Muslims relate to the impossibility for Muslims of the divine nature

[7] 'A reply to the one who refuses to attribute the Incarnation to God', (ed.) C. Bacha, in *Les Oeuvres Arabes de Théodore Aboucora Évêque d'Harran* (Beyrouth: 1904), 180-186.

[8] 'God has a Son who is his equal in Nature and exists forever with him', in Bacha, (1904), 91-104.

[9] 'There is no forgiveness of sin without the suffering of the Messiah on behalf of humanity', in Bacha, (1904), 83-91.

[10] 'Maymar fī taḫqīq nāmūs mūsā al-muqaddas wa-l-anbīyā' aladhīna tanabā`u `alā al-masīḫ', in Bacha, (1905), 9.

[11] Abū Qurra writes in the tradition of Justin Martyr (d.c.165), whose *Dialogue with Trypho the Jew* likewise argues for the superiority of Christ over Moses.

uniting with the human nature in Christ, and are written as answers to questions Muslims ask in a "we say to you" format. The treatise on the suffering of Christ is an exposition of why Christians believe in the death of Christ for sin, but even here Muslims are addressed as "you".

Abū Qurra then wrote for widely different audiences, tailoring his argument for the group in mind. His presentation for Jews is a very detailed study of the Old Testament, not of immediate interest to Muslims. His debate with alternative Christian presentations of Christology was only of interest to Christians. Answering questions Muslims ask Christians was firstly an aid to fellow Christians in their encounter with Muslims, and secondly a means of making Christian faith more understandable to Muslims. Abū Qurra seems to have been successful in reaching a Muslim audience, given that among others `Īsā ibn Sabīh al-Murdār (d. 840) wrote a refutation of his writing entitled *Kitāb `alā Abī Qurra al-naṣrānī* (Against Abū Qurra the Christian), which is unfortunately no longer extant.[12]

Abū Qurra's treatise on the Incarnation is one of the first known Christian attempts to deal with the possibility of Incarnation on Islamic terms of reference. His appeal to the image of God seated on his throne as a way of showing, as he sees it, that the immanence of God is a shared premise between Christians and Muslims, marks a new departure for Christian presentation of Christ for Muslims. His treatise on the sonship of Christ is also innovative in its appeal to the anthropomorphic language of the Qur'ān as a way of showing that the language of God as Father and Christ as Son can be understood in an analogous fashion. If God hears without physical ears then he can be Christ's Father without any physical connection. The third treatise on the atonement seeks to ground forgiveness in the concept of justice, which he argues must not be overruled by God's mercy. The death of Christ provides the balance between mercy and justice by joining the two together in a way that would not otherwise be possible. While not discussing the Qur'ānic denial of Christ's death on the cross, he does put forward a new argument for the purpose of the cross that relates to Muslim concepts of forgiveness.

In order to discover to what extent Abū Qurra developed his Christology as a result of dialogue with Muslims, his Confession of the Orthodox Faith written for a Christian audience may be compared with the three apologetic pieces for Muslims. The comparison shows that while not developing new Christological concepts in dialogue, Abū Qurra did provide arguments for Christological beliefs that were based on principles derived from Islamic teaching.

---

[12] See *The Fihrist of al-Nadīm,* vol. 1, (ed. and tr.) B. Dodge, (New York: 1970), 394.

Confession of the Orthodox Faith

This confession is written as a statement of faith with the formula "I believe" along with refutations of several unorthodox views, suiting a catechetical purpose. There are no references to Jewish or Muslim views, and debate is only with Christians. The purpose of the treatise seems to be a comprehensive summary of Orthodox belief for fellow Chalcedonian Christians, probably designed for the theological training of clergy. The opening section deals briefly with the Trinity before the much longer Christological main body of the text, which offers a critique of five faulty Christologies, those of Nestorius, Eutyches, Dioscorus, Severus, and the Maronites, which all fail to depict adequately the union of divine and human natures in Christ. The Christological section of the confession opens with a statement of Orthodox Christology. The eternal Son, begotten (*al-mawlūd*) from the Father before time, who is God from God, came down from heaven in the last days for our salvation. He became Incarnate (*tajassada*) through the Holy Spirit and the Virgin Mary. He became human (*ta'annasa*) in such a way that he formed for his hypostasis a living body with a rational and intelligent mind. He became a perfect man (*sāra insānan kāmilan*) like one of us, except without sin. He remained perfect God (*illāhan tamman*) as he is eternally, since his becoming human (*ta'annus*) did not entail any change. For he still is the eternal Son after becoming human (*ta'annus*). He has two natures (*ṯabi`atain*) and one hypostasis; the divine nature which the Father and the Spirit have, and the human nature that became his at his Incarnation (tajassud), which each one of us has.[13]

Abū Qurra here expounds the definition of the council of Chalcedon that Christ had two natures and one hypostasis. He then goes on to defend this description of Christ against the alternative views of Nestorius, Eutyches, Dioscorus, Severus, and the Maronites. a) Nestorius was guilty of saying that the one born of Mary had a different hypostasis from the one eternally begotten of the Father, so that he could not confess that Mary is the mother of God. b) Eutyches, Dioscorus and Severus were wrong to state that Christ had only a divine nature but not a human one. This would be to introduce change, suffering and death into the divine nature. c) The Maronites claimed that the human nature of Christ did not have a human will or human action. But this strips the human nature of Christ of its real character.[14] Abū Qurra closes the debate with a description of the union of the two natures.

---

13 Abū Qurra, 'Imāna al-urthūduksīya', (ed.) I. Dick, in 'Deux Écrits Inédits de Théodore Abuqurra', 56f.

14 *Ibid.*, 57f.

> "The divinity abides in the Incarnate Word (*fī tajassudi al-kalimati*), not subject to any limitation, suffering or death, which belong to the human nature … Both divine and human natures belong to the divine Word, so the Word of God Incarnate (*al-kalimatu-llāhi al-muta'annasi*) is limited by the human nature."[15]

Therefore, a Chalcedonian view of the union of divine and human natures means that the limitations of the human nature affect Christ without undermining the integrity of the divine within him.

Abū Qurra uses the terms *tajassud* and *ta`annus* for the Incarnation interchangeably, even though *tajassud* implies becoming embodied, while *ta`annus* means becoming human. *Tajassud* was used in the Arabic translation of Timothy's debate in the last decade of the eighth century, when Abū Qurra was in Harrān. Despite disagreement between the Chalcedonians and Nestorians, they share a common vocabulary in Arabic, which shows how much interchange there was between the rival Christian communities in Mesopotamia. However, the fact that Abū Qurra's confession is composed in Arabic rather than the Syriac traditional to the churches of Harrān may mean that Chalcedonians were ahead of Nestorians in the use of Arabic for preaching and teaching. The early search for new expressions in Arabic for Christian ideas came perhaps from them rather than Nestorians.[16] This suggestion may be supported by the second term for the Incarnation *ta'annus*, which is not found in the Qur'ān, though the related term *insān* (human being) is common. The verb *ta'annasa* (he became human), the state of being *ta'annus* (his having become human), and the descriptive *muta'annas*, appear in the confession. Abū Qurra uses these terms more frequently than *tajassud*. This may be because becoming human is more suggestive of the union of the divine with a fully independent human nature than the mere embodiment of the divine. There was no dispute between Nestorians and Chalcedonians on the full humanity of Christ. Both held to a union of two distinct natures, so there is no surprise that both Timothy and Abū Qurra use the phrase *sāra insānan* (he became a man). Christ was a particular human being, not simply a body in which the divine nature dwelt. Here Nestorians and Chalcedonians could line up against the one nature miaphysites who held that the eternal Word took flesh and always acted as the thinking and willing centre of Christ.[17]

---

[15] *Ibid.*, 59.

[16] This is despite the fact that Nestorians were given greater access to the `Abbasid Caliphs in Baghdad than Chalcedonian Christians. See J. Joseph, *The Nestorians and their Muslim Neighbors* (Princeton: 1961), 27. Nestorians spoke Arabic but wrote in Syriac before the `Abbasids set up their capital in Baghdad. See P.K. Hitti, *History of the Arabs* (London: 1970), 84.

[17] See chapter four for an exposition of one nature Christology

The confession could have been written even if Islam had not come to Harrān in northern Mesopotamia. Even though it is an Arabic tract, it does not address Muslims, nor does it allude to Islamic concerns with Christology. In the three treatises for Muslims on Christ, however, the content shifts from confession of faith to apologetic, from argument with other Christians to argument with Muslims, from defence of the Chalcedonian definition to defence of the possibility that the divine became human. But in shifting the focus in these ways, Abū Qurra is dealing with issues that simply were not part of traditional Christological discourse among theologians in the Middle East. The Islamic understanding of Christ was now forcing theologians to mount a much more elaborate defence of Christology than had been attempted before. The first of these treatises is a response to the Muslim view that if God is transcendent then the embodiment of the divine is impossible, and if Christ suffered then he cannot be divine.

A Reply to the One who Refuses to Attribute the Incarnation to God

This apology attempts to answer a question raised by Muslims about the Incarnation. "You ask us how the divine Son could take a body and experience suffering. We answer that God is not effaced or cancelled out by appearing to his creation."[18] Abū Qurra proceeds to develop his answer by quoting several Old Testament texts to the effect that God can be simultaneously seated on his throne and in touch with the whole world. Thus God can be in one location and in all places at the same time. He then applies this duality to the embodiment of the divine nature in Christ. "The eternal Son is in every place … He is not at all limited or restricted, apart from being in the body in which he experienced pain and suffering."[19]

The body of the eternal Son is akin to God's throne as a location of divinity such that it does not in any way reduce the capacity of God to be God when united with the human body. The choice of the throne analogy from the Bible may have been inspired by Muslim discussion of texts in the Qur'ān that referred to God sitting on a throne.[20] Although he makes no appeal to the Qur'ān in his exposition of four Biblical texts containing the image of God's throne, he appears to be inviting his Muslim reader to

[18] Abū Qurra, 'Maymar fī-l-radd `alā man yankaru li-llāh al-tajassud', in C. Bacha, *Les Oeuvres Arabes de Théodore Aboucarra Évêque d'Harran,* 180-186, 180.

[19] *Ibid.,* 182.

[20] There are eighteen references to God's throne in the Qur'ān. See *sūras* 7:52, 9:130, 10:3, 13:2, 17:44, 20:4, 21:22, 23:88 and 117, 25:60, 27:26, 32:3, 39:75, 40:15, 43:82, 57:4, 81:20, 85:15.

notice that both the Bible and the Qur'ān speak of God limiting himself to one particular place while at the same time being everywhere. If the Muslim grants that the unlimited God can limit himself to a throne then the Christian claim that the eternal Son lost nothing of his divine status by taking a human body may not seem so contradictory after all. Seppo Rissanen suggests that the throne texts of the Qur'ān were a major point of debate among Muslims in the late eighth and early ninth centuries.[21] To be sure, there was discussion about the anthropomorphisms of the Qur'ān between the Mu`tazila, who denied that God had attributes, and the Traditionists who held that he did. Al-Ash`arī (d. 935-6) reported that "all the Mu`tazila agree that God is one with nothing resembling him. He is the hearing and seeing one without being matter, spirit, body, shape, flesh and blood, person, substance or accident … He is not limited by space or affected by time."[22] The fact that the contemporary miaphysite Abū Rā'iṯa discusses the session of God on his throne by directly quoting from the Qur'ān provides support for a debate between Muslims in which Christians were engaged.[23]

Abū Qurra has a Muslim respond to the use of the throne texts to allow God to limit himself to a human body while still ruling the universe by denying the validity of the comparison. "It is undeniable that God sits on the throne but he does not take up residence in the body … The throne is pure but the human body is not suitable for God."[24] Abū Qurra suggests that far from being unsuitable, the human body is the crown of God's creative work and perfectly free from corruption. "God does not abhor residence in the finest aspect of his creation … God does indeed abhor impurity in humanity, but the body taken from Mary was not touched by sin."[25] He quotes The Letter to the Hebrews 4:15 to support the purity of the human nature of Christ, and backs this up by several quotations from Isaiah on the righteous character of the Messiah. The upshot of these Biblical references is that "the body was not taken from the virgin Mary before the Holy Spirit cleansed it from all trace of sin. The eternal Son took from Mary a body which was pure, clean, immaculate, and beautiful in order that the divine could reside there."[26] Abū Qurra is able to avoid the idea that human nature is unsuitable for union with the divine. If the power of God could fashion a pure human nature from Mary then the Muslim

---

[21] See S. Rissanen, *Theological Encounters of Oriental Christians with Islam during Early Abbasid Rule* (Åbo, 1993), 120-123.

[22] Abū-l-Ḫasan `Alī al-Ash`arī, *Kitāb Maqālāt al-Islāmīyīn wa Ikhtilāf al-Musallīn,* (ed.) H. Ritter (Wiesbaden: 1963), 155.

[23] For Abū Rā'iṯa's contribution see chapter four.

[24] Abū Qurra, 'Maymar fī-l-radd', 183.

[25] *Ibid.*

[26] *Ibid.*, 184.

objection to the divine entering the human is groundless. In fact the divine nature enabled Christ to remain unpolluted throughout his life.

> "After taking up residence, the divine nature became the source for the human nature of all of the glory of divinity, righteousness, wisdom and power. However the eternal Son restricted the glory of his divinity and did not reveal it in his body when he lived among people. He let human activity appear in his divinity; eating, drinking, sleeping, and the like."[27]

As a result Abū Qurra feels confident that he can lean on his Muslim questioner to acknowledge the suitability of this human body as a residence for the divine nature. "It would be astonishing for anyone to deny the residence of God (*hulūl allāh*) in the human body which we have shown is the most perfectly suited aspect of his creation."[28] If the Muslim still wants to protest that the divine cannot associate with his creation then how can he accept that God was present in a thorn-bush from which he spoke to Moses or in the pillar of cloud that guided Israel? Then again Moses consulted God in the tabernacle. Just as God sat between the cherubs on the Ark of the Covenant so he was sustaining the world at the same time. "Therefore the eternal Son was in heaven and on earth and in every place necessary to communicate with people in this human body which he took from the immaculate Mary."[29]

Evaluation

This is one of the first known attempts to argue for the possibility of the Incarnation with Muslims who denied it. The eighth century writing already surveyed tended to expound what Christians believed about the Incarnation without using Islamic categories of thought to defend it. In this apology Abū Qurra tries to clear the ground for the concept of Incarnation by arguing that human nature is not unsuitable for God to dwell in if it is properly prepared by him. To back this up he refers to God's session on a throne as a helpful parallel to the Incarnation. Abū Qurra may have known of contemporary Muslim discussion on the anthropomorphisms of the Qur'ān, and here makes his own contribution to the discussion. Assuming that the throne cannot sully God's character, or limit him to time and space, a position shared by all Muslims, he argues that the union of divine and human natures in Christ similarly does not sully God's character or limit him to time and space. This is the kind of argument that would have been taken seriously by Muslim intellectuals of his day, though a thoroughgoing belief in the transcendence of God on their part would have provoked the

---

[27] *Ibid.*, 185.
[28] *Ibid.*
[29] *Ibid.*, 186.

reply that 'indwelling' is beyond the bounds of acceptable interaction between God and creation.

He may also be alluding to the purity of Christ mentioned in *sūra* 19:19 at the announcement of the gift of a pure child to Mary. If this is so, Abū Qurra is appealing to Qur'ānic texts that support Christian ideas, in order to demonstrate that the Incarnation can be supported by Muslims on the basis of Islamic premises. By appealing to two notions familiar to Muslims, God's session on a throne, and the perfection of Christ's character, he argues that Muslims can believe in the Incarnation on terms acceptable to them. This is an apologetics of persuasion, which appeals to concepts held by the dialogue partner. Ultimately the apology seeks to head off the anathema of 'associating' human nature with God by showing that God may in fact associate with his world in a fashion that does not undermine his dignity. Nevertheless, Muslims would have argued that pure transcendence acts as a brake on such a speculative notion as Incarnation, even if the human material taken by God is specially prepared and purified. What Abū Qurra succeeds in doing here is to present Incarnation in a way that takes seriously Muslim reservations, so that the idea of Incarnation may not simply be dismissed as fantastic nonsense.

God has a Son who is his Equal in Nature and who Exists Forever with Him

In this apology Abū Qurra deals with the alleged problem of God giving birth to a son, an accusation implied by several Qur'ānic texts though none is explicitly quoted in the apology. The Muslim challenge comes in the following form; "How can God give birth in the light of the fact that a man only has offspring after intercourse with a woman? Surely it is not right to speak this way about God?"[30] Abū Qurra calls this a futile question. The Muslim might as well ask how God exists in the light of the fact that humans only exist by eating and drinking. Surely it cannot be right to speak of God in that way? The same goes for God seeing or hearing. Does such language imply that God has eyes and ears like people do?[31] He has a question for the Muslim; "If you accept that God can be called the one who hears and the wise, and these titles do not demean him, why can't you accept that he can be called the Father in the same way?[32] After an exhaustive study of Old and New Testament texts Abū Qurra declares that the Son is not part of the created order at all, nor has he a beginning in time.

[30] Abū Qurra, 'Maymar yaḥqiqu an li-llāh ibnan huwa `adilu-hu fī-l-jawhar wa lam yazill ma`a-hu', in Bacha, *Les Oeuvres Arabes*, 91-104, 94.

[31] *Ibid.*, 95.

[32] *Ibid.*, 96f.

God cannot be accused of "taking a son to himself", since the Son lives forever with the Father and is equal in nature to him.[33] Muslim discussion of the anthropomorphisms in the Qur'ān reappears in this treatise. The Mu`tazila denied that God had attributes of seeing or hearing even though he is called the all seeing and all hearing repeatedly in the Qur'ān. The Traditionists held that he did see and hear although humans cannot know how he did so.[34] Abū Qurra joins the debate by ignoring the division among Muslims over the seeing and hearing of God, and by emphasising that both camps accept that the language of hearing and seeing is applicable to God without compromising his character. This is a similar approach to the discussion of the throne of God in the earlier treatise.

The treatise goes on to explore whether attributes such as wisdom are separate from God's nature. Just as the book of Proverbs personifies 'wisdom' which yet remains fully an attribute of God, so the New Testament speaks of the Son of God in personally distinct terms yet he remains fully divine.[35] This section of the treatise is focused on the nature of the Trinity, especially Old Testament support for the activity of God's Word and Wisdom. At the outset of the lengthy exposition of Scripture Abū Qurra gives a brief statement of his Christology; "The Holy Church testifies that the Messiah is perfect God and perfect man. He has two natures, one divine and the other human."[36] This is a much simpler statement than that given in his Confession of the Orthodox Faith, and illustrates the two different contexts of his writing. The Confession is a detailed defence of Chalcedonian Christology over against rival views within the Christian world of the Middle East. This apology on the nature of Christ's sonship is concerned to defend the possibility of sonship for God as an eternal rather than temporal reality. Only Muslims and Jews would have needed to hear such an argument. Here Muslims are the audience. Conversely, Muslims did not need to hear detailed discussion of rival Christological positions among Christians. For them the issue was the suitability of the terminology of sonship, rather than the mechanics of the union between divine and human natures.

---

33 *Ibid.*, 97f.

34 See al-Ash`arī, *Maqālāt.*

35 Abū Qurra, 'Maymar yahqiqu an li-llāh ibnan', 98. This use of wisdom is first found in the apologetics of the Patristic era. See Irenaeus, *Against Heresies,* 4:22:1, where the Word is the Son and Wisdom is the Spirit of God. "God always has, at his side his Word and Wisdom, the Son and the Spirit. Through them and in them he created all things of his own free will." See also Tertullian, *Against Praxeas,* 6. "Wisdom speaks – the Lord created me as the beginning of his ways, for his works (Prov 8:22) that is, he created and begat his own consciousness." Texts in H. Bettenson, *The Early Christian Fathers* (London: 1969), 76f. and 119.

36 Abū Qurra, 'Maymar yahqiqu an li-llāh ibnan', 99.

Evaluation

Abū Qurra appeals to anthropomorphic language of God hearing and seeing. As with the discussion of God's session on a throne, he appeals to debate among Muslims themselves over the way to interpret human concepts applied to God. If there are Muslims who understand such language in a metaphorical sense, then they ought to be able to interpret Christian talk of God in a similar fashion. The upshot is that Fatherhood can then be interpreted in a metaphorical sense. This is an important position for Abū Qurra to adopt since it allows Muslims to think about Fatherhood and Sonship along the same lines as hearing and seeing. However, the Muslim denial of fatherhood for God prevents any proper discussion of the sonship of Christ, and Abū Qurra realises that the prior question of the nature of God himself needs to be answered before any purely Christological discussion can proceed with Muslims.[37]

Discussion of God's wisdom extends the range of debate about the attributes of God. John of Damascus appealed to the attribute of God's word to argue that while God's speech cannot be distinct from him yet it subsists independently.[38] Abū Qurra makes the same point about God's wisdom. In the Bible, God's wisdom seems to have personal, almost human characteristics, yet is an aspect of God's nature. On this basis God's son has individual human characteristics but still is fully identified with God's nature. Faced with a Muslim audience that questioned the possibility of divine attributes having a distinct existence, Abū Qurra attempts to show that such a possibility is not inconsistent with God's character. As far as Christ is concerned, the double attribution of natures, divine and human, is only a logical extension of the idea of wisdom acting 'alongside' God, yet being essentially God at work. If Muslims can accept the personification of God's wisdom, then it should not be too difficult for them to appreciate the union of divine nature with human nature in Christ. The weakness in this argument lies in the assumption that Muslims will accept the personification of wisdom. While the appeal to the hearing and seeing of God is based on Qur'ānic concepts, here the appeal to wisdom is not. Whether Muslims would have been impressed with exposition of the Bible is doubtful without a Qur'ānic base to the discussion. In this desire to communicate Scripture to Muslims, Abū Qurra shares in the approach of *The Anonymous Apology* from his own Chalcedonian community.[39]

---

[37] This is the burden of Kenneth Cragg's apologetic in the twentieth century. See chapter eight.

[38] See John's argument in chapter two:16.

[39] See the emphasis placed on exposition of Scripture in *The Anonymous Apology on Christianity* in chapter two:18f.. In the nineteenth century, Karl Pfander relied on Biblical support for Christ's purity of character mentioned in *sūra* 19:19. But, unlike

There is no Forgiveness for Sin without the Suffering of the Messiah on behalf of Humanity

In this treatise Abū Qurra questions the Islamic belief that God's forgiveness can be obtained directly without the help of an intermediary.[40] He argues that it is a mistake to think that God's mercy is greater than his justice. God's law must not be rendered futile by its requirements being overruled by kindness on his part. Therefore, in order to balance justice with mercy God sent his eternal Son to fulfil the just requirements of his law on behalf of those who had failed to keep them.[41] Underlying this argument is the Qur'ānic denial that one human being can atone for the sin of another.[42] Abū Qurra's method is to expound the Biblical idea that the Messiah would die for the sins of others, without directly engaging with the way the Qur'ān deals with human sin. The treatise is basically a presentation of the Biblical notion of the need for perfect purity before God, which only Christ fulfils, by the purity of his human nature at his conception.[43] Thus Christ achieves salvation for others on the strength of his suffering the punishment due to them for their sin. In this way the justice of God is co-ordinated with his mercy.

Quite soon into the treatise comes a detailed description of the coming of the Son into the world in language reminiscent of Abū Qurra's Confession of the Orthodox faith.

> "The eternal Son, begotten of God before time, of the nature of God and equal to him, came down from heaven out of his compassion for the descendants of Adam, and indwelt (*halla*) the womb of Mary the immaculate virgin by the Holy Spirit. He took (*ittakhadha*) a body (*jasadan*), making it like himself with a mind and being (*nafs*). He became human (*ta'annasa*) by the Holy Spirit and the virgin Mary."[44]

Abū Qurra introduces a phrase not found in his Confession of the Orthodox Faith; "He took a body" (*ittakhadha jasadan*). The verb *ittakhadha* is found in the Qur'ān in several texts denying that God took to

---

Abū Qurra, he began his exposition with Islamic concepts. See chapter seven:116-119.

[40] Abū Qurra, 'Maymar fī anna-hu la yaghfiru li-ahad khatīyati-hi illā bi-awjā` al-Masīh allatī hallat bi-hi fī sha'n al-nās', in C. Bacha, *Les Oeuvres Arabes*, 83-91.

[41] *Ibid.*, 83f.

[42] See *Sūra* 6:70, "Each person comes to death with that which he has earned. He has no patron or intercessor alongside God. Even if a complete ransom were offered it would be unacceptable." Intercession for sin is also denied in *sūras* 7:53, 30:13, 32:4, 39:43f, 40:18, and 74:48.

[43] Abū Qurra, 'Maymar f»-anna-hu', 86-91.

[44] *Ibid.*, 85f.

himself a son.[45] Perhaps Abū Qurra is aware of the difficult connotations of this verb, and seeks to set the idea in a better context. If it is the eternal Son who takes a human body, then it should be clear to his Muslim reader that Christians do not claim that God took a son. Rather, the already existing Son took human nature. The expression "he took a body" could be taken to imply that the eternal Son found a ready-formed human body to enter. That Abū Qurra does not intend this sense is clear from the explicatory phrase which follows; "making the body like himself". The eternal Son therefore fashions the human body until it becomes fit for his indwelling. The union with the body taken from Mary only occurs at the end of this creative process.

The apology continues by explaining that according to the Old and New Testaments forgiveness can only come through the death of the Messiah. His suffering for sin had been predicted "by all the prophets."[46] A substantial exposition of Scripture ends with this challenge to Muslim readers; "You have heard from the books of God that there is no forgiveness without the cross of the Messiah. There is no fulfilment of the requirement of the law except through the shedding of his blood on behalf of the living and the dead."[47]

Abū Qurra does not attempt to address the apparent denial of the cross in the Qur'ān. He simply assumes that Christ was crucified as described in the New Testament. Any other means for receiving the forgiveness of God apart from the cross of Christ is illusory. "We in the Christian community receive forgiveness when we accept the sufferings of the Son for our sins. But non-Christians who do not accept the sufferings of the Messiah for their sins will die in their sins."[48]

Evaluation

Abū Qurra's approach to the atonement of Christ differs from that of the Patriarch Timothy, who sought to argue for the death of Christ on the basis of the teaching of the Qur'ān.[49] Abū Qurra nowhere appeals explicitly to the Qur'ān in this treatise. Rather he bases his appeal on the Biblical insistence on sacrifice for sin as the means of forgiveness, with the self-giving of Christ as the pinnacle of this process. His final words strike a

---

[45] See *Sūra* 2:116, "They say God took a son" (wa qālū ittakhadha allāhu waladan). Four other texts are similar; *sūras* 10:68, 18:4, 19:88, and 21:26. *Sūra* 72:3 links the taking of a son with the taking of a wife, offering a biological understanding of *ittakhadha*.

[46] Abū Qurra, 'Maymar fī anna-hu', 87.

[47] *Ibid.*, 89.

[48] *Ibid.*, 90.

[49] See Timothy's argument that Christ predicted his death according to *sūra* 19:33 in chapter two:24f.

strident note. Christians understand forgiveness correctly, and more to the point, actually embrace God's forgiveness. However, this is not the case with others, who can have no assurance of God's forgiveness if they fail to believe in the death of Christ. Such a dismissive attitude to Muslim notions of forgiveness would no doubt alienate his supposed audience, which shows Abū Qurra to be a polemicist here rather than an apologist.

He seems unconcerned with any Muslim accusation that the Bible is corrupt, which is at variance with al-Mahdī's questioning of Timothy on this point, and John of Damascus' awareness of the problem.[50] Perhaps he believed that some Muslims might be persuaded by an interpretation of the Bible that could be aligned with Islamic thought. Abū Qurra's aim is to show the necessity of the sacrificial death of Christ by spelling out the conditions laid down in the Bible. So the truth of Christ's sacrificial death for sin is based on the premise that God must judge sin rather than overlook it. Thus all are judged guilty and none can be forgiven without some kind of external means. In this way Christ provides the way for God to forgive without forsaking justice. Whether Muslims would be impressed with such an argument is doubtful given the denials of the crucifixion of Christ and human ransom for sin in the Qur'ān. His unwillingness to tackle these Qur'ānic beliefs, even in an indirect manner, means that his argument for the death of Christ as an atonement for sin would most probably fail to convince a Muslim.

Conclusion

Abū Qurra's Christology in dialogue with Muslims is largely a defence of the Nicene-Chalcedonian tradition. His summary creed at the conclusion to his treatise on sonship speaks of Christ as "perfect God and perfect man."[51] The language of the detailed description of the Incarnation in the treatise on the forgiveness of sins reflects the Creed of Contantinople; "The eternal Son begotten of God before time … came down from heaven and became human by the Holy Spirit and the Virgin Mary."[52] He translates the

[50] John cautioned his fellow Christians about appealing to prophetic predictions of Christ in dialogue with Muslims since they did not accept the prophecies as genuine. See chapter two:14f. Al-Mahdī questioned Timothy at length about inconsistencies in the Biblical text. See H. Putnam, *L'Église sous Timothée I*, appendix.

[51] As in the definition of the Council of Chalcedon, "perfect in Godhead … perfect in manhood", in J. Stevenson, *Creeds, Councils and Controversies*, 337.

[52] Compare with the Creed of Constantinople; "The only-begotten Son of God, begotten from the Father before all ages … came down from heaven and became incarnate from the Holy Ghost and the Virgin Mary", in *Creeds, Councils and Controversies*, 335.

orthodox creeds into Arabic, finding terminology to suit the purpose. Thus, for example, the descent of the Son is *ḥulūl*; a term found in the Qur'ān in other contexts, but now pressed into service for the indwelling of God in human nature. The terms for the Incarnation *tajassud* and *ta'annus* appear to be neologisms. The roots are Qur'ānic but the verbal forms are not. Abū Qurra may not have developed these new Arabic expressions himself, but he was one of the first Christians to use them. He upholds the faith of Chalcedon in a way that would interpret the truth of that Christology for Muslims. One example of a new interpretive departure is his use of the phrase "took a body", which is hardly a translation of credal vocabulary into Arabic. Abū Qurra uses the verb *ittakhadha* (took), a term found in the Qur'ān in the context of Islamic Christology. The Qur'ān denies that God took a son, but Abū Qurra affirms that the Son took a body. As a result the Muslim reader would be more able to understand the kind of 'taking' Christians believed in.

Abū Qurra weaves expositions of Scripture and tradition into answers to questions Muslims ask Christians on Christology. His treatment of the atonement of Christ is less a set of answers to questions and more a careful presentation of the Biblical notion of sacrifice for sin. There is an Islamic conviction underlying the whole treatise, that the Merciful and Compassionate forgives wrongdoers. Abū Qurra seeks to argue that God must be just as well as merciful, and that the balance between justice and mercy lies in the self-offering of the perfect eternal Son. The death of the Son is therefore a better solution to the problem of wrongdoing than the simple exercise of mercy.

The two treatises on Incarnation and sonship are constructed on a dialogical framework of "you ask, and we reply". He shows inventiveness in his answers in four different ways. Firstly, he uses the idea of God's session on a throne to raise the issue of God's relationship to his creation in a way that Muslims could relate to from their own interpretation of this Qur'ānic conception. Did God literally sit on a throne? Even if the answer is affirmative, the conclusion ought to be that God's apparent limitedness does not cancel out his ubiquity. If Muslims are prepared to grant this truth, then God can be Incarnate in Christ while still ruling the universe. Secondly, the appeal to the purity of Christ enables another idea familiar to Muslims to be put to use in defence of the Incarnation. God's character is not undermined by relationship with a pure form of human nature. Only union with sinful human nature would demean the creator.

Thirdly, the reference to God's seeing and hearing helps Abū Qurra to suggest to his Muslim reader the possibility of metaphorical language in the Qur'ān. If Muslims can think of the anthropomorphisms of the Qur'ān in that sense then the metaphorical use of Fatherhood for God should not be ruled out of court by Muslims. Indeed, Christians want to say that the Son never came into being in time, but rather has always been Son to the Father.

Surely this Father - Son relationship is quite different from what Muslims allege Christians hold, the taking of a son by God in a physical sense. Fourthly, Abū Qurra attempts to develop the idea of God's wisdom as a personification of God as a parallel to the Father- Son idea. If God's wisdom is inseparable from his nature then this is a model for understanding the inseparability of the divine nature in Father and Son.

These four apologetic moves are Abū Qurra's recorded contribution to dialogue on Christology. As a Chalcedonian bishop, it is not surprising that he defended Chalcedonian Christology. While he was ready to give detailed criticism of faulty Christologies in his writing for Christians, in his apologies for Muslims he expounded Chalcedonian Christology without arguing against alternative Christian views. The burden of his apologetic Christology for Muslims was not so much exposition and defence of received tradition, but more a defence of Christology mounted on Islamic principles. Thus in the three apologies for Muslims, there is no discussion of varieties of Christological positions held by Christians. Muslims were not asking questions about differences between Christian views, so what was essential debate in his Confession of the Orthodox Faith, is irrelevant to his apologies for Muslim. He was trying to find openings in Muslim thought for the presentation of Christ as he saw him. His contemporary Abū Rā'iṭa, with whom he debated concerning Christology, took this method to a more sophisticated level in his apologetic writing for Muslims. Chapter four will expound and analyse his contribution.

Chapter Four

The Christology of Habīb ibn Khidma Abū Rā'iṯa in Dialogue with Muslims

Habīb ibn Khidma Abū Rā'iṯa

Habīb ibn Khidma Abū Rā'iṯa was a Jacobite theologian associated with Takrit to the north west of Baghdad. He was a contemporary of Abū Qurra, with whom he claims to have debated face to face.[1] He was named in The Chronicle of Michael the Syrian as a participant in a synod held in the year 828, so probably was active beyond the third decade of the ninth century.[2] The Jacobites were named after Jacob Baradaeus who became a rallying point for those who opposed the two natures definition of Chalcedon. The Emperor Justinian I had condemned one nature Christology as heresy in 536, but Empress Theodora encouraged the survival of one nature Christology under the enthusiastic leadership of Jacob who "travelled widely ordaining monophysite clergy."[3] The one basic difference between Chalcedonians and Jacobites was over the understanding of the Incarnation. The former held to "one hypostasis in two natures; unity on the level of the hypostasis; difference on the level of the physis."[4] Jacobites held to the unity of hypostasis and physis; the one physis was equivalent to the hypostasis of the Incarnate Word.[5]

---

[1] Abū Rā'iṯa opens his *Reply to the Melkites on the union (of the divine and human in Christ)* with a reference to a debate between himself and Abū Qurra that he wishes to follow up in writing. See 'Al-radd `alā al-malkīya fī-l-ittihād', in *Die Schriften des Jacobiten Habīb Ibn Hidma Abū Rā'iṯa,* (ed.) G. Graf, *CSCO* 130 (Louvain: 1951), 65-72). See S.T. Keating's discussion of this debate in 'Habīb ibn Khidma Abū Rā'ita al-Takrītī's 'The Refutation of the Melkites concerning the Union [of the Divinity and Humanity in Christ]' (III), in *Christians at the Heart of Islamic Rule,* (ed.) D. Thomas, (Leiden: 2003), 39-54.

[2] See J-B. Chabot, *Chronique de Michel le Syrien: Patriarche Jacobite d'Antioche* 4 vols. (Paris: 1899-1910), vol. 3, 50.

[3] A.S. Atiya, *A History of Eastern Christianity* (London: 1968), 182.

[4] A. Grillmeier, *Christ in Christian Tradition,* vol 2:2 (London: 1995), 507.

[5] *Ibid.,* 504. The Jacobites were inheritors of the 'Word-flesh' Christology of Alexandria, represented especially by Athanasius (c.296-373), who held that the human nature taken from Mary was like clothing that the Word put on in such a way that it did not alter the character of the Word. "As Aaron remained the same and did not change by assuming the high priest's dress ... so the Lord did not become

Abū Rā'ita did not come from a Greek speaking Christian community like Abū Qurra. Sidney Griffith has pointed out that the Jacobite Mesopotamian community used Syriac and he believes that this was Abū Rā'ita's native language.[6] However, it is significant that like Abū Qurra, Abū Rā'ita wrote in the language of the Muslim rulers. No longer were the received ecclesiastical languages sufficient for theological work. Indeed Arabic was a necessity not just for communication with Muslims but also between Melkites and Jacobites, since it was in Arabic that Abū Rā'ita argued with Abū Qurra in his *Reply to the Melkites on the union* (of divine and human in Christ).[7] This dialogue with Abū Qurra is concerned with problems raised by the differences between Jacobites and Melkites over the precise nature of the Incarnation. Abū Rā'ita wrote a longer *Reply to the Melkites* in the form of a letter.[8] These two documents give insight into the Arabic used by a Jacobite to express Christological concepts in an intra-Christian context.

Abū Rā'ita also wrote about Christology for a Muslim audience. His Christological views are briefly outlined in *A Demonstration of the Christian Religion and the Holy Trinity*, which surveys what Christians believe about a wide range of issues.[9] A much more detailed account of Christology is given in his *Letter on the Incarnation*, which is written in the form of answers to forty-four questions posed by Muslims on the Incarnation.[10] The extant Christological writing of Abū Rā'ita is fuller than that of Abū Qurra, and the very extensive set of replies to Muslim questions in his *Letter on the Incarnation* has no parallel in the available work of Abū

another by taking the flesh, but remained the same and was clothed in it." [Athanasius, "Against Arius" 2:8, text in H. Bettenson, *The Early Christian Fathers*, 281]. The Word then is the thinking, feeling, and willing centre of Christ. Athanasius does not seem to make room for a genuine human mind in Christ after the union of Word and flesh. The Alexandrian tendency to eliminate a human mind in Christ was turned by Apollinarius (310-c.390) into a full blown 'one nature' Christology. "We confess that the Word of God has not descended upon a holy man … but that the Word himself has become flesh without having assumed a human mind." [Apollinarius, "Letter to the Bishops at Diocaesarea" 2, text in J. Stevenson, *Creeds, Councils, and Controversies*, 96]. The logical conclusion of the Word-flesh union was that the Word is the life of the body and that "the body as such cannot be accorded the character and title of a *physis*." [A. Grillmeier, *Christ in Christian Tradition* vol 1 (London: 1975), 328].

[6] See S.H. Griffith, 'Habīb ibn Hidmah Abū Rā'ita, a Christian *mutakallim* of the First Abbasid Century', *OC* 64 (1980), 161-201, 165.

[7] Abū Rā'ita, 'Al-radd `alā al-malkīya fī-l-ittihād', in Graf, 65-72.

[8] Abū Rā'ita, 'Radd `alā al-malkīya', in Graf, 105-130.

[9] Abū Rā'ita, 'Ithbāt dīn al-nasrānīya wa ithbāt al-thālūth al-muqaddas', in Graf, 131-159.

[10] Abū Rā'ita, 'Al-risāla fī-l-ittihād', in Graf, 27-64.

Qurra. The method of comparing Abū Rā'iṯa's writing for Christian and Muslim readers will be followed here, as it was in the previous chapter, to find out to what extent Abū Rā'iṯa developed his Christology in dialogue with Muslims. Therefore the two works addressed to Melkites will be studied before turning to his writing for Muslims.

Reply to the Melkites on the Union of Divine and Human Natures in Christ

At the outset of this reply, Abū Rā'iṯa refers to a meeting between himself and Abū Qurra in which differences about the correct way to describe the Incarnate state of the Messiah were discussed, and declares that he intends to state why Jacobites cannot subscribe to Melkite Christology.[11] Since only one member of the Trinity becomes flesh, that is the eternal Word, it must follow that the eternal Word is the source of thought, will and action after the union between the Word and the flesh. Melkites are therefore mistaken when they claim that there remain two natures after the union, which would imply that there were two sources of thought, will and action in Christ. If there were two natures they would split Christ into two actors, sometimes functioning on the basis of the divine nature and sometimes on the basis of the human nature.

He summarizes his view of the Incarnation in the following way,

> "It was the will of the Father, Son and Holy Spirit that one of them became Incarnate (*tajassada*) that is to say became human (*ta'annasa*). The eternal Son, the everlasting Word of God the Father became Incarnate of the immaculate virgin Mary. His Incarnation was without change in his substance (*jawhar*) and without any alteration to his state. He was a unity of the divine Word and the physical body, a rational personality (*nafs*); one person (*shakhs*); one substance (*jawhar*); consisting of divinity and humanity."[12]

Abū Rā'iṯa believes that the substance (*jawhar*) of the Second person of the Trinity cannot be divided by the addition of a human nature. To defend this conviction he appeals to the unity of mind and body in human beings. We do not claim that humans have two natures, but we say that the human mind controls the activity of the body. Likewise we must surely affirm that the divine substance controls the activity of the human body of the Messiah. "Just as a human being is a unity composed of mind and body so the Messiah is one substance (*jawhar*) and one hypostasis (*qunūm*)."[13] He asks

[11] Abū Rā'iṯa, 'Al-radd `alā al-malkīya fī-l-ittiḥād', 65.
[12] *Ibid.*, 70.
[13] *Ibid.*

Abū Qurra how Melkites can claim that Christ is a unity when he has two distinct natures? Does not the Chalcedonian duality of natures rob the eternal Word of his dignity if he has to make way for thoughts, decisions or actions that arise from his so-called human nature? This debate with Abū Qurra is underlined by a second piece of writing by Abū Rā'iṯa addressed to an unnamed Melkite correspondent that is considerably longer than his reply to Abū Qurra.

Reply to the Melkites

He begins by rehearsing the decision of the Council of Ephesus (in 431) to anathematize the teaching of Nestorius that Christ had two natures (*jawharain*) and two hypostases (*qunūmain*). He believes that the Melkites' more moderate view must come under the same condemnation, since they too hold to two natures (*jawharain*) albeit in one hypostasis (*qunūm*).[14] Abū Rā'iṯa does not regard the Council of Chalcedon of 451 as authoritative, and this accords with the normal Jacobite rejection of Chalcedon as a betrayal of the Council of Ephesus. The basic error of Chalcedon was to allow talk of a second nature alongside the divine nature in Christ, since if Christ had another nature in addition to his divine nature then the divine nature must be enlarged by the human. This would result in a new definition of the Trinity. In the Trinity, the three hypostases are within one divine substance, so to grant the eternal Word a human nature alongside his divine substance would entail adding human nature to the Trinity as a fourth hypostasis.

> "The hypostases (*aqānīm*) are the substance (*jawhar*) itself, and the substance is the same as the hypotases from the aspect of the 'one' and the 'three.' If the hypostases are not the same as the substance then the human nature becomes a fourth member of the Godhead."[15]

According to Abū Rā'iṯa, the Melkites have undermined the Trinity by their definition of the Incarnation. They define the Trinity as "one nature in three hypostases", but their use of 'nature' to describe the Incarnation conflicts with the meaning given to 'nature' in their definition of the Trinity. Jacobites do not accept such a change of use for 'nature', because Christ can only have the divine nature that is inherent in the Trinity, and not another type of nature that is inherent in humanity.

It appears that Abū Rā'iṯa was more likely to have difficulty in dialogue with Muslims than Abū Qurra, since his miaphysite view made no room for genuine human thought and action in Christ. To Muslims who encountered

---

[14] Abū Rā'iṯa, 'Radd `alā al-malkīya', 107.

[15] *Ibid.*, 116.

his Christology, Christ must have appeared to be a divine visitor like an angel rather than a human being. The Muslim insistence on the humanity of Christ posed a serious obstacle for Jacobites in a way it did not for Melkites. To his writing for Muslims we now turn.

Demonstration of Christianity and the Holy Trinity

This treatise is written as a series of responses to Muslim questions on a range of Christian convictions.[16] There are two questions about the Incarnation: why should God need to do it, and why can God not save humanity without doing it. In answer to the first question, Abū Rā'iṯa appeals for intellectual humility, since the Incarnation is too difficult for our small minds to grasp. As for the second question, he concedes the Islamic conviction that God is powerful enough to save whoever he wills. His Muslim brother knows that there is common ground between them in the fact that God sent messengers to bring humanity to obey God. However, the Muslim wants to know how Abū Rā'iṯa can speak about God becoming human. "Messengers and preachers sent by God are not equivalent to what you (Christians) mean by the Incarnation (*tajassud*) of God, or by his becoming human (*ta'annus*)."[17] Abū Rā'iṯa concedes the distinction. The coming of God himself to save humanity can only be described as an act of sheer mercy.

The Muslim then wonders how God can come without undergoing change in his nature. How can God "experience pain and death when he always lives and can never die".[18] Abū Rā'iṯa makes a distinction between human and divine attributes in the one divine substance of Christ. "There was a union of the divine personality with a human one, without change to either of the two ...They became one substance (*jawhar*)."[19] However, the one substance retains distinctive functions deriving from the original divinity or humanity. "He is truly divine and truly human; he retains these two attributes (*ṣifatain*). In his divinity he always lives and does not die or even feel pain; but in his humanity he does die and feel pain."[20] Abū Rā'iṯa seems to be making room for human experience in Christ. Despite not having a human mind, Christ has human feelings. Perhaps Abū Rā'iṯa believes that Christ can feel pain without a mind, and that 'rationality' can exist in a 'mindless' human flesh. This interpretation seems to be borne out by his description of the way the human mind and body operate "as a

[16] Abū Rā'iṯa, 'Ithbāt dīn al-naṣrānīya', in Graf, 131-159.
[17] *Ibid.*, 149.
[18] *Ibid.*, 150.
[19] *Ibid.*
[20] *Ibid.*, 151.

combination of two substances (*jawharain*); a personality which is rational and spiritual, along with a body which senses, perceives, feels pain and dies."[21] The body receives sensations from without, but does not have a mind to act on them. The Word is the only source of action.

Evaluation

The two questions on the Incarnation are indicative of Muslim anxiety that Christians impose unnecessary restrictions on God by their insistence that the divine united with the human. God's freedom to act must be limited by a human body and the whole idea of Incarnation is beside the point in terms of human salvation, since God saves whoever he wills without any external constraint. There is no doubt that these were real questions for Christians to answer in the ninth century. In this treatise only the second question is dealt with, but Abū Rā'iṯa answers the first question at some length in his *Letter on the Incarnation*, which will be studied in the following section.

In answering the question about the purpose of the Incarnation Abū Rā'iṯa appeals to the conviction common to Muslims and Christians that God sent messengers to save humans from going astray. However, the Muslim questioner is aware that Christians see Christ as more than a mouthpiece for divine truth. The key difference between Muslims and Christians lies in the Christian belief that Christ alone among the messengers is divine as well as human. Thus the Muslim turns to the impossibility of the divine being affected by human pain and death. While this treatise need not be a transcript of an actual debate between Abū Rā'iṯa and a Muslim, there is little reason to doubt that such questions were being asked of Christians by Muslims in the early ninth century.

Abū Rā'iṯa deals with the challenge by denying that the divine in Christ was affected by human suffering and death. This is essentially the same answer given by Abū Qurra to the question whether the death of Christ nullified his divine character, but in different terminology. For Abū Qurra the human nature suffered, but this did not affect Christ's divine nature.[22] Abū Qurra wrote of two natures in Christ, while Abū Rā'iṯa described two attributes in Christ's one nature. Both the Melkite and the Jacobite affirmed a duality in Christ, which enabled them to separate the experience of suffering and death from the divine character in Christ, and so both Melkite and Jacobite agreed that God did not experience either suffering or death as a result of the Incarnation. Nevertheless, from the point of view of Muslim

---

[21] *Ibid.*

[22] See the discussion of Abū Rā'iṯa and Abū Qurra on the death of Christ by Rissanen, *Theological Encounter of Oriental Christians with Islam during early Abbasid Rule* (Åbo: 1993), 188f. Rissanen makes the point that both apologists held that only the humanity of Christ died and that his divinity was not affected by his death.

readers, this separation of the divine from the human in order to achieve immunity from weakness and death must have seemed decidedly illogical and cumbersome. To Muslims, the logic of Islam was so much more obvious in that God's transcendence is at all times inviolable, and the simplicity of Islam commended the complete segregation of the divine and human. This was certainly the reaction of the Muslim philosopher Abū `Īsā al-Warrāq in his detailed critique of Christian theology later in the ninth century.[23] This summary defence of the Incarnation is given a much fuller treatment in his *Letter on the Incarnation* addressed to a Muslim audience, in which Abū Rā'iṯa attempts to show that the Incarnation is not as illogical as Muslims may think.

Letter on the Incarnation

This letter, which contains forty-four questions and answers on the Incarnation, takes up almost thirty pages in Graf's edition of Abū Rā'iṯa's writings.[24] Here, Abū Rā'iṯa not only gives a reasoned account of Christian convictions, but also challenges his questioner by a form of cross-examination, asking the Muslim reader whether the Qur'ān actually supports Christian beliefs about Christ. This apologetic method is similar to Timothy's challenge to al-Mahdī over the interpretation of *sūra* 19:33,[25] but not to Abū Qurra, who never directly quotes from Islamic Scripture. Although these forty-four questions would not actually have been asked by Muslims in the order presented, they do represent the kind of debate that was taking place in the early ninth century. Timothy's debate in the late eighth century shows that this style of dialogue was already established as a pattern for Christian-Muslim engagement. The intricacy of the argument in the early ninth century shows that the level of debate had become more sophisticated. This can be seen in the fact that Abū Rā'iṯa and `Ammār al-Baṣrī both produced exceedingly detailed answers to multiple questions on the Incarnation.[26] Abū Rā'iṯa's *Letter on the Incarnation* and `Ammār's *Book of Questions and Answers* represent the best of the apologetic writing on Christology in the early centuries of Islamic rule in the Middle East.

The forty-four questions cover the following topics; questions 1-6, the relationship between the Incarnate one and the Trinity; questions 7-12, the relationship between God and the humanity of the Incarnate one; questions13-18, the necessity for God to become Incarnate; questions 19-21, the supposed death of God by crucifixion; questions 22-24, the human

---

[23] See chapter six for a review of his writing on Christianity.
[24] Abū Rā'iṯa, 'Al-risāla fī-l-tajassud', in Graf, 25-64.
[25] See chapter two:24f.
[26] for `Ammār's contribution see chapter five.

body of the Incarnate one as a possible addition to the attributes of God; questions 25-29; the problem of change in God posed by the Incarnation; questions 30-31, the difficulty of God becoming embodied; questions 32-34, the exact nature of the Sonship of the Messiah; questions 35-40, the restriction on God implied by the Father/Son analogy; question 41, the seeming contradiction between belief about the Messiah and his own words in the gospels; and questions 42-44, the problem of the will of God and the death of the Messiah.

Questions 1-6. The Relationship between the Incarnate One and the Trinity

1. Is the Incarnate one divine or human? The Incarnate one (*al-mutajassid*) is God become human (*muta'annis*).
2. How can the Incarnate one be one of the three hypostases (*aqānīm*) and not all three at the same time? He is the Son, the eternal Word of God, not all three hypostases (*aqānīm*).
3. Does the Incarnate one act on the basis of the Incarnation? The Incarnate state is the means whereby the Incarnate one acts.
4. Who controls the actions of the body of the Incarnate one? The Word of God controls the actions of the body of the Incarnate one.
5. Does the body never act independently? The Word took a body (*al-kalimatu akhadhat li-hā jasadan*) in such a way that the body never acted independently of the Word.
6. Did the Word become Incarnate independently of the other members of the Trinity? In terms of creating and willing they work together, but in terms of appearing only the Word acts.[27]

EVALUATION

Much of this language is similar to the three pieces of writing by Abū Rā'iṯa already reviewed, but there is a new expression *akhadhat* which recalls Abū Qurra's *ittakhadha*. These two forms of the same root have a similar meaning, 'to take', suggesting that Abū Rā'iṯa like Abū Qurra found the concept congenial in dialogue with Muslims. Like Abū Qurra, he only uses the notion of the Word 'taking' a human body in dialogue with Muslims and not in his writing addressed to Christians. There he writes of the Word becoming Incarnate rather than taking a human body. Christians did not need to speak of the Word 'taking' a body when discussing Christology among themselves. The need to speak this way seems to have arisen in dialogue with Muslims most likely because Muslims used the term when insisting that God did not take a son in debate with Christians.

Abū Rā'iṯa appeals to Muslim discussion of God's attributes in answer to question 6, After replying that the three members of the Trinity work

[27] Abū Rā'iṯa, 'Al-risāla fī-l-tajassud', 27-29.

together in creating and willing, but that only the Word appeared in flesh he asks the Muslim,

> "Don't you define God as knowing, willing and performing? If so, then does God know what his will is or how he will perform it? If you say that he does, then he knows that the resurrection will take place and it is his will which he performs ... You may then say that God's knowledge is not exactly identical to his will or his performance because he knows what he does not will, evil deeds; and he also performs what he does not will, allowing evildoers to enter paradise ... This is exactly what we claim about the Incarnation; one of the hypostases became Incarnate without the other two yet all three are one nature."[28]

Abū Rā'iṯa joins in current Islamic debate over how the actions of God relate to his knowledge and will to support the Incarnation of only one of the members of the Trinity. The apparent lack of co-ordination in the action of the Trinity is comparable to the apparent discord between the knowledge of God and the performance of his will. Both Christians and Muslims have to deal with a similar difficulty in describing what God does. Both attempt to reconcile seeming contradictions in God's actions. This is a clever move by Abū Rā'iṯa showing that logical consistency is not as easy for Muslim belief in the unity of God as might be claimed. A united God appears to be divided against himself over the administration of mercy to humans who don't deserve reprieve. Christians could mount a defence of the rationality of the Incarnation by pointing out the irrationality of Islamic description of God's work. Neither side in the debate then was immune from the charge of inconsistency. But this worked to the advantage of Christians in the early ninth century who were facing the accusation that the Incarnation was in principle an inconsistent idea, since Muslims could hardly claim that they were entirely consistent in their exposition of divine activity.

Questions 7-12. The Relationship between God and the Humanity of the Incarnate One

7. If the Incarnate one became Incarnate by leaving his original state for the water of the womb have you not made the latter essential to the Incarnate one? The body is not part of the nature of the Word any more than heated material is part of the nature of fire, or a human body part of the human personality.
8. Do you claim that God dwelt in the body? God dwelt in the Incarnate state.
9. Is this indwelling not a limitation on God? It is not the sender (*mursil*), but the sent one who indwells the body.

[28] *Ibid.*, 29.

10. If something dwells in something else is it not enclosed in it? Just as light is not enclosed in the sun nor the personality in the human body neither is the Word enclosed in the body
11. How could the Word become Incarnate without limitation? When the sun's rays light up the ground the sun is not limited to that spot, so the body is not a limiting factor for the Word.
12. Is there a difference between the body of the Incarnate one and other bodies? They are similar in that they are part of creation, but different in that there is a union of the Word and the body.[29]

EVALUATION

Abū Rā'iṭa uses the analogy of the human mind and body in the context of dialogue with Muslims as he did in dialogue with Melkites, but in different ways. For Melkites the analogy shows that the Word did not unite with a human mind. For Muslims the analogy demonstrates that the sender of the Word remains untouched by the identity of the Word with the human body. These two different uses of the mind/body distinction show the versatility of Abū Rā'iṭa as an apologist, able to relate a miaphysite conviction in quite separate ways to Christian and Muslim contexts. Muslim difficulty with the Incarnation lies in the restriction placed upon God by his indwelling a human body. Abū Rā'iṭa's argument that the sender of the Word is unrestricted by the indwelling of the Word in a human body is an attempt to meet this problem by demonstrating that divinity can touch humanity without being absorbed by it in such a way as to lose transcendence. Of course this distinction between the sender and the sent may not have carried weight with Muslims, since for them the latter had to be human and not divine. Nevertheless, here is a Christian attempt to give Islamic ideas a Christian meaning in order to convey the Incarnation in terms that a Muslim could understand.

Questions 13-18. The Necessity for God to Become Incarnate

13. Why should God become human? God became human to release humans from punishment for disobeying him, and to return them to their original condition.
14. Why did God create Adam and his descendents? He had created Adam in the first place out of his goodness and kindness.
15. Was God not good and kind until he created? It is his character to be always good and kind, but he wanted to display his goodness after Adam fell into sin.
16. Could God not redeem humanity without becoming human? God can do what he wants. However, simply forgiving Adam's

[29] *Ibid.*, 30-35.

descendants for sin was not enough. If any fault remained in the human personality God could not demonstrate his complete goodness, and therefore, to fully renew his creation he had to become human to show his goodness.

17. Is not death evidence against your view of salvation? There are two kinds of death; natural death and death caused by sin. The body dies a natural death and the personality dies a death caused by sin. Faith in God delivers us from both types of death.
18. Would not the sending of angels or pure humans be more suitable for the salvation of humanity than God becoming human? God did send human messengers such as Noah, Abraham and Moses, but few followed them, so he could not save humans by sending more angelic or human messengers. God decided that the only solution was the Incarnation.[30]

EVALUATION

The two reasons given for the Incarnation, to release humans from punishment for disobeying him and to return them to their original condition of goodness, are grounded in the Christian tradition that had its origins in the teaching of the New Testament. Abū Rā'iṯa appeals to the prophetic messengers known to Muslims to back up his case that salvation needed more than human proclaimers. The fact that few people responded to the preaching of Abraham or Moses shows that only divine indwelling in a human body would have a significant impact. Secondly, even if there had been a widespread response to the messengers, humans would have continued to act in both good and evil ways. Only a perfectly good life would remove the problem of evil, and therefore, the divine had to become Incarnate. However, the explanation of this tradition for a Muslim audience might not have made its mark. Why God 'had to' become human in order to restore wayward humanity is not really clear. Might the Muslim not conclude that according to the two basic reasons for the Incarnation it was the choice of God to become human? If so, there was no external compulsion on God so to act, no necessity for him to become Incarnate. Indeed this is a difficulty for Abū Rā'iṯa that he scarcely perceives. Making the Incarnation essential to God's administration of the world because of human failure is to introduce fundamental weakness into the plan of God for creation. Perhaps the Islamic instinct for the freedom of God would have served the argument better.

[30] *Ibid.*, 35-38.

Questions 19-21. The Supposed Death of God by Crucifixion

19. If God died how could he still rule the world? The death of Christ did not undermine God's rule over his creation, since only his body died, but his divinity did not.
20. Why do you separate his divinity from his body, nullifying the unity between them? He died a human death but it did not touch his divine state. The union of the Word with the flesh was unaffected by the flesh being put to death.
21. How is being put to death a demonstration of God's goodness? The death of Christ is the ultimate demonstration of the goodness of God because it shows the length to which he was prepared to go to save humans.[31]

EVALUATION

Here Abū Rā'iṯa gives an explanation for the Incarnation that depends on choice rather than necessity. The death of Christ shows how much God cares for humans. Nevertheless, the fact that the eternal Word is unaffected by the death of his human body produces the protest that this sunders the union between divine and human in Christ. The protest of al-Mahdī is heard here too, showing how Muslims in the ninth century were insisting on the same difficulty.[32] Timothy's answer to al-Mahdī reappears in the writing of Abū Rā'iṯa and Abū Qurra, who were united in arguing that only the human body of Christ died, and that divinity could not die on the cross. While these three apologists differed over the correct language to describe the relationship between the divine and human in Christ, there is little to choose between them over their description of the death of Christ. At first sight this is strange. Should not the miaphysite Abū Rā'iṯa have more difficulty explaining the death of Christ than the diophysites Timothy and Abū Qurra? If the miaphysite insists that Christ is the eternal Word at all times and in all experiences, and that he does not have two minds, then how can the eternal Word escape the experience of suffering and death? It turns out that he did not in fact experience death. Only his human body died. However, this is a decidedly weak argument completely denying the reality of human suffering in Christ. Surely, the diophysite claim that the human mind suffered and died is a distinct improvement, even though it does not solve the problem of a radical split in the character of Christ at the point of death. A Muslim would no doubt conclude that Christians could not possibly affirm unity between the divine and human in Christ while arguing that only the human experienced death. Neither diophysites nor miaphysites had a solution to this dilemma.

---

[31] *Ibid.*, 39-42.

[32] For al-Mahdī's accusation that the union was broken at the death of only the human and not the divine nature of Christ see chapter two:24.

Questions 22-24. The Human Body of the Incarnate One as a Possible Addition to the Attributes of God

22. Is it possible for an attribute of God to add to his nature? No, it is not.
23. Is not the body of the Incarnate one an addition? Yes, but not in number. Before he became Incarnate The Word was a unity, and after his Incarnation he was still a unity.
24. How can the body not be an addition to the Word when there was a time when he did not have a body? The body does not add to the Word who remained a unity after the Incarnation. This is similar to how we understand a human being. We do not talk about the body being an addition to the human spirit.[33]

EVALUATION

Muslim anxiety centred on associating with God that which was not appropriate, so the charge levelled against Christians was that the human body was being 'associated' with the divine in an inappropriate way. Abū Rā'iṯa uses the human mind/body relationship to deny the charge. Certainly his one nature Christology comes to his aid here, since by not giving a human mind to Christ he is able to argue that the human body is not a threat to the divine mind that controls it. In effect, the human body cannot add anything of importance to the Word, since it is only a vessel for the divine personality. But it is precisely here that the true humanity of Christ is at stake, for a mindless human body is simply an empty shell for the Word to fill. Thus in gaining immunity for Christ's divinity he has sacrificed his humanity. It was theoretically possible for miaphysite Christians to protect God from associating with potentially wayward human nature, but the Christ that emerges is practically divorced from being human in any normative sense.

Questions 25-29. The Problem of Change in God Posed by the Incarnation

25. How can you deny that something which has been lit up and has light increased in it has changed from its original state? Surely light does not change the body itself or add anything to its original condition.
26. Is the Word limited by anything? The Word is not limited by anything but rather everything is limited by the Word.
27. Is the Word in everything? Certainly. He is supreme over everything.

---

[33] Abū Rā'iṯa, 'Al-risāla fī-l-tajassud', 43f.

28. Did all of the Word become Incarnate or only a part of the Word? God is supreme over all his attributes, so all of the Word became Incarnate.
29. Does this not mean that the body is in everything and that nothing remains in the Word which is not Incarnate? Abū Rā'iṯa asks the Muslim about God sitting on his throne. Abū Rā'iṯa: Do you not say that God is in heaven and on his throne? Show us whether all of God is in heaven and on the throne or only part of him. The Muslim: We do not describe God in part here or in part there. He is in heaven and on the throne and everywhere. Abū Rā'iṯa: Then heaven is in everything so that nothing remains in heaven that is not God. The Muslim: Our expression "God is in heaven and on the throne" means that he is Lord of heaven and Lord of the throne. Abū Rā'iṯa: You believe that God appears in heaven and on the throne but he is not in them. The Muslim: God is in them, he doesn't just appear in them. Abū Rā'iṯa: Then God is limited by his creation. The Muslim: God is in them by appearing on them. Abū Rā'iṯa: You agree with us that God can be in an aspect of his creation without being swallowed up by it.[34]

EVALUATION

The paradox of the Incarnation is now addressed in all its sharpness. Christians claim that the eternal Word was limited to a particular human body, while at the same time they believe that The eternal Word was still fulfilling divine control over the creation. The Muslim concludes that Incarnation cancels out divine rule. Abū Rā'iṯa makes an appeal to Muslim discussion of the throne texts in the Qur'ān in his answer to question 29, and concludes that the Muslim agrees that God can be in an aspect of his creation without being swallowed up by it. This discussion about the throne of God by Abū Rā'iṯa and Abū Qurra shows how important the analogy was in dialogue with Muslims in the early ninth century.[35] While Muslims could point to the Christian dilemma of limiting God to a human body, Christians could point to the Islamic paradox of God being limited to a throne. The use of Muslim debate about God's session on his throne enabled Abū Rā'iṯa to turn from defence to interrogation. Discussion between Muslims about whether sitting on the throne limited God in any way allowed Christians the opportunity to argue that if Muslims can believe that God is not limited by sitting on the throne then Christians are right to believe that the eternal Word of God is not limited by indwelling a human body. Finding interpretive keys in Islamic thought was vital to Christian apologetics in a period when Christians were on the defensive and

[34] *Ibid.*, 45f.

[35] For Abū Qurra's appeal to the analogy see chapter three:33-35.

struggling to stem the flow of nominal Christians turning to Islam. This appeal to the throne texts may have been helpful in the struggle to defend the integrity of the Incarnation in the face of a simpler Islamic understanding of the activity of God.

Questions 30-31. The Difficulty of God Becoming Embodied

30. How can God have a human body that is not appropriate to his nature? The human nature of the Incarnate Word was not human in the ordinary sense. The Word took flesh from the woman and became united with that flesh.
31. How does that which does not have a body become Incarnate? We do not know how the process took place. Just as nobody knows how God creates, or how the human spirit indwells flesh, so nobody can know how the Word united with human flesh.[36]

EVALUATION

Abū Rā'iṯa declines to say how the eternal Word united with the flesh taken from Mary. Abū Qurra wrote of the eternal Word purifying the flesh from Mary before uniting with it, but Abū Rā'iṯa does not follow him. Nevertheless, the thrust of Abū Rā'iṯa's response is similar. If Muslims find human nature demeaning for God to associate with, then the problem of unsuitability may be solved if the human nature arising from Mary is uniquely suited to divine indwelling. Yet the Muslim reaction to such uniqueness must surely have been to ask how Christ was at all like the rest of humanity. Abū Rā'iṯa was disadvantaged by his one nature Christology from giving a satisfactory answer.

Questions 32-34. The Exact Nature of the Sonship of the Messiah

32. Where does Christ get his sonship from? The sonship of the Messiah has to do with his birth outside of time, he is not son in a physical sense.
33. Mary gave birth to him in time, so how can you claim that God did not take a son (*lam yatakhudh ibnan*)? We do not describe the Messiah as the Son of God in the Incarnate condition in which he was born of Mary. Rather, Son of God describes the condition in which he was begotten of the Father before time and without beginning.

---

[36] Abū Rā'iṯa, 'Al-risāla fī-l-tajassud', 47f.

34. Was the son born twice, from the Father and then from Mary? Yes, there were in fact two births of the Messiah, one from the Father and the other from Mary.[37]

EVALUATION

The Qur'ānic denial that "God took to himself a son" is dealt with here. There is a sense in which Christians can agree with the Qur'ān that God did not 'take' a son because sonship belonged to Christ from eternity. There never was a time when the Father was without the Son, so the Father did not exist alone before 'taking' a son. The Qur'ānic assertion that "God does not beget" can then be understood in the same way. The begetting from eternity need not be censured by the Qur'ānic text if the nature of begetting is not physical. What the Qur'ān disapproves of is birth in the natural sense, but Christians confess generation in a non-physical sense. Abū Rā'iṯa shares a common understanding of these Qur'ānic texts with Timothy and Abū Qurra, showing how Christians across the three main confessional divides borrowed apologetic arguments from each other when dealing with the Islamic context.[38] This kind of argument is ground clearing work, but it is interesting to observe that in this treatise the discussion of the denial of sonship comes so late on in the presentation. Abū Rā'iṯa has consistently spoken of the eternal Word rather than the eternal Son up to this point, out of deference to Islamic scruples over the notion of Sonship. This is akin to the method of John of Damascus and Timothy, who preferred to talk of the Word becoming Incarnate, but not of Abū Qurra, who wrote of the Son taking flesh in conversation with Muslims. There is a clear advantage in Abū Rā'iṯa's careful avoidance of a title that would be readily misunderstood by Muslims.

Questions 35-40. The Restriction on God Implied by the Father/Son Analogy

35. Don't you believe that the Father existed before the Son? The fact that the Son is begotten of the Father does not mean that the Father is prior to the Son in time. Neither of them have a beginning.
36. Does this not contradict what is known in creation? This appears to contradict the normal process of reproduction in the created order, but remember that God need not be tied to the way of creation when he does things.

---

[37] *Ibid.*, 48.

[38] For Timothy's interpretation of sonship and begetting see chapter two:22-24. For Abū Qurra's treatment see chapter three:36-38.

37. Why tie God to your description of his activity since he only has to say "be" and it is (*kūn fa yakūn*)? We affirm that God is not tied to human action.
38. Surely you must believe that God does not do things the way people do? We affirm that God is not restricted to the way people do things. The birth of the Son is from eternity, in contrast to temporal human birth.
39. Can a father have a son without procreating? God does not need to do anything the way that creatures do.
40. If you distinguish God's actions from the actions of the created order then why talk about "father" and "son" when such language means that the father precedes the son? The Father and Son are equal, neither precedes or follows the other.[39]

EVALUATION

God's power to say "be and it is", found in *sūras* 2:111 and 3:42 of the Qur'ān, is understood by Abū Rā'iṭa to teach that God is not constrained by anything outside himself. If this is so, then the begetting of the eternal Son need not be dependent on the normal order of human procreation. While it is true that human fathers precede their sons in time, this does not apply to the begetting of the Son by the Father. The Muslim protests that the analogy is therefore useless, but Abū Rā'iṭa argues that the analogy is not nullified by its transfer from human to divine spheres. However, this different evaluation of the father/son analogy remains an unbridgeable gulf between Christians and Muslims no matter how Abū Rā'iṭa seeks to defend its validity. As far as the Muslim is concerned it would be better for Christians to drop the analogy altogether. Yet Christians could hardly give up on language embedded in the Apostolic and Patristic descriptions of Christ without losing touch with their roots.

Question 41. The Seeming Contradiction between Christian Belief about the Messiah and the Messiah's Own Words in the Gospels

41. How can you say that the Messiah is God and Lord when he said to his disciples that his father was his God [John 20:17], that his father was greater than he was [John 14:28], that he didn't know the hour [Mark 13:32], that he could not give places to people in his kingdom [Matthew 20:21,23], and when he appealed to his father in the face of death [Matthew 27:47]? All these sayings demonstrate Jesus' human nature. But it is also necessary to take into account quotations that show his divine nature. He said that he thought the same as his Father [John 14:9], that he was in his Father and his Father was in

[39] Abū Rā'iṭa, 'Al-risāla fī-l-tajassud', 49f.

him [John 10:38], that he and his Father were of one nature [John 10:30], that he was Lord of the Sabbath [Matthew 12:8], Lord of the disciples [John 13:13], and that he existed before Abraham [John 8:58].

[Abū Rā'iṯa then engages in a detailed exposition of the verses quoted by the Muslim]

i) John 20:17. "I am returning to my Father and your Father, to my God and your God." It is as if he said to his disciples - I am returning to the condition I had before I became Incarnate among you.

ii) John 14:28. "The Father is greater than I." He did not mean greater in nature (*jawhar*) because their natures are equal, nor greater in importance because they are equal in glory and honour. Rather the Father is greater in cause, but this cannot imply greater in nature.

iii) Mark 13:32. "No-one knows about that day or hour not even the angels in heaven; nor the Son, but only the Father." This is the reality of his Incarnate state in which he shares the limitations of the humanity of his disciples.

iv) Matthew 20:23. "To sit at my right or left is not for me to grant." The Messiah was not willing to make a special case for only two out of his twelve disciples.

v) Matthew 27:46. "My God, my God, why have you forsaken me." This proves that in his Incarnate state he was exactly like all other humans who experienced the fear of death.[40]

EVALUATION

This discussion of the teaching of Christ recorded in the Gospels occupies almost nine pages in Graf's edition. Abū Rā'iṯa placed considerable emphasis on interpretation of the New Testament because he was forced to do so by his Muslim questioner. It is interesting to observe the way that both Muslim and Christian seek to support their views of Christ from the Scriptures of the debating partner. Here the Muslim claims to have found evidence in the Christian Scriptures for an Islamic view of Christ. This may not be a transcription of an actual debate between Abū Rā'iṯa and a Muslim, but just such a discussion of the gospels probably took place in the early ninth century. There would be little point Christians arguing against a subordinationist reading of Christ's relationship to God unless Muslims had tried to find evidence for it in the gospels.

The four texts mentioned by the Muslim seem to show the subordination of Christ to God. Abū Rā'iṯa is at pains to point out that each of them can be interpreted from the perspective of the equality of the Son with the Father. Thus if the Incarnation of the Word is the controlling notion in the

---

[40] *Ibid.*, 51-59.

Gospel of John, then the two Johannine texts can be placed within that framework. "Going to his Father" is another way of saying that he is going back to a status of equality given up as a result of his submission to the limitations of the human body. Similarly, his lack of knowledge about the future is a feature of his taking on human characteristics during the time of his Incarnation, but this ignorance is a temporary phenomenon. Likewise the two Matthean texts demonstrate that the Son voluntarily gave up decision making about the future once Incarnate, and that he was liable to suffering in the way that all other humans are after taking a human body.

Abū Rā'iṯa appeals to the Qur'ān for support in interpreting Mark 13:32, where Christ denied knowing the hour of his coming.

> "You say that in your book God says to Moses - Give a soft reply to Pharaoh: perhaps he will remember and be afraid. In another place in your book - Perhaps your Lord will make an alliance between you and those who attack you. And - Did you say to people, take me and my mother as gods apart from God? Doesn't God attribute doubt or concealment to the human condition? So the Messiah's lack of knowledge of the hour of his coming is the result of his Incarnate condition."[41]

These texts all suggest that humans make the will of God difficult to bring about because of waywardness or even hostility. Abū Rā'iṯa does not interpret the texts individually, but simply draws his conclusion that lack of knowledge is part of what it means to be human. However, this ignorance of Christ can hardly be attributed to a human mind that he did not possess. For Abū Rā'iṯa the eternal Word is the sole intellect in the union of divine and human, so must be charged with a defective memory over future divine plans.

Questions 42-44. The Problem of the Will of God and the Death of the Messiah

42. Was Christ's death by crucifixion done with his consent? If so, there was no sin committed by those who crucified him. If not, then does not the divine become repulsive? There are two sides to his death. On one side, he did not consent to what the Jews wanted to do to him, but on the other side, he consented to death for the salvation of humanity.
43. How could he suffer willingly when he did not consent to what they did? He did not want the Jews to put him to death in the way that they wanted. This seems to be a contradiction. We ask you, "does God consent to the death of one who testifies to faith in him or not? If you say that he does, we say that that there is no sin in the unbelief

[41] *Ibid.*, 56f. The three texts from the Qur'ān are *sūras* 20:46, 60:7 and 5:116.

which puts faithful witnesses to death. If you say that he is opposed to their death, we say that God becomes despicable by allowing such injustice to happen.

44. How can you argue that God rewards liars? Your book testifies against you when it says "they slander God with their lies"[42] If this means that humans lied about God how could they do this when God does not reward them. If it is said "God is exalted far above what people do to slander him", then you agree with what we say about Christ. His divine nature is not touched by the crucifixion. The Jews did not crucify his divine nature. They tried to slander God, but he is exalted far above their slander.[43]

EVALUATION

The Muslim is concerned finally with the contradiction between God's will being achieved and the Christian insistence on the death of Christ. Abū Rā'iṯa accepts the apparent contradiction is a difficulty for the Muslim, so his way of resolving the problem is to appeal to the voluntary nature of Christ's death. If Christ gave up his life to save others then the will of God was not frustrated by those who put him to death. It may appear that humans defeated Christ by putting him to death, and that they defeated God's will in this way. However, God's will was achieved by the death of Christ. The Jews claimed to have defeated Christ, and in a sense they did defeat the human body of Christ. But they were unable to destroy the divine nature of Christ. So the Jews made false claims about the results of the crucifixion. Abū Rā'iṯa again uses his awareness of Muslim thought to answer Muslim questions about Christianity. Just as it is incorrect in Islam to believe that God rewards those opposed to him, so Christians should not be thought by Muslims to hold that those who put Christ to death are congratulated by God for performing his will. Though he does not refer to the denial of the crucifixion in the Qur'ān, Abū Rā'iṯa seems to suggest that this denial applies to the killing of the divine Word rather than the human body. While this interpretation has appealed to a few Muslims it has not succeeded in becoming widely accepted.[44]

Conclusion

Abū Rā'iṯa's Letter on the Incarnation is a more thorough treatment of Christology in dialogue with Muslims than any so far surveyed, and is an almost exhaustive scrutiny of Christian claims about Christ from what

[42] *Ibid.*, 62. See *sūras* 4:53, 5:102, 10:61, 70 and 16:117

[43] *Ibid.*, 60-63.

[44] See chapter one:10.

appears to be a skeptical Muslim point of view. While the Demonstration of Christianity dealt with only one Muslim concern, whether the Incarnation changes God's nature, the Letter on the Incarnation opens up eleven areas of Muslim unease about Christology. When these questions are compared with those posed by Melkites in the treatises addressed to them by Abū Rā'iṯa, it becomes apparent how the Islamic context radically changed the way Christology had to be discussed.

Abū Rā'iṯa handled two issues in his debates with Melkites. Firstly, he denied that Christ needed to have a human mind in order to be fully Incarnate. The danger lying behind this Melkite claim was the potential to split Christ's actions into two groups, some divine and others human. Only if Christ had a divine mind could such a split be avoided. Secondly, the Melkites were in danger of adding a fourth member to the Trinity by insisting on a human mind in Christ alongside a divine one. Neither of these questions arises in his writing for Muslims.

The eleven debating points in the *Letter on the Incarnation* are based on problems that a Muslim has with divine interaction with the world. A concern to maintain the transcendence of God underlies the Muslim questioning. Thus the first set of questions establishes whether Christ is divine or human, not a point of contention among Christians. The second group of questions asks why the Trinity did not become Incarnate, only a problem for a Muslim unitarian view of God. These questions were not raised in intra-Christian debate on Christology, and they demonstrate the radical shift in Christological discourse brought about by Islamic encounter with Christian theology. The same can be said for the other types of question raised. Anxiety about limitations placed on God by indwelling a human body, or about God's rule of the world being disrupted if Christ suffered death, or about adding a human attribute to God's nature, is symptomatic of a fear of reducing the greatness of God felt by Muslims but not by Christians. Other questions relate to the goodness of God. Can God's forgiveness be tied to the Incarnation without restricting his goodness? The death of Christ on the cross can hardly speak of a God who protects the innocent. For Christians, but not for Muslims, the Incarnation and atonement were the very demonstration of the love of God for human beings.

Muslims who could have read the New Testament would have found evidence of a human Christ who seemed quite different from the eternal Word who was Second person of the Trinity. Christians were now forced to defend the way their understanding of Christ had developed from Scriptural beginnings. Abū Rā'iṯa interprets texts which seem to support a human Christ as evidence of the Incarnate condition of the eternal Word. Christ is ignorant of the future because he has given up divine knowledge in his Incarnate state in order to share in the life of his disciples, and he is afraid of death just like all humans since his Incarnation resulted in his experience of human frailty. But here is the heart of the problem for Abū Rā'iṯa's Christology. He accused Melkites of splitting Christ into two by insisting on a union of divine and human minds, holding that unity in Christ can only be maintained if the divine mind alone is active. However, he seems to allow the divine mind to become like a human mind in order to make sense of apparent human weakness in the gospel accounts of Christ. In other words, Christ in practice does think the way humans do, and thus the gap between one nature and two nature Christologies virtually disappears. Abū Rā'iṯa speaks of two attributes (*ṣifatain*) in one divine substance (*jawhar*),[45] enabling him to allow room in Christ for human feelings and perceptions, even if he only decides and acts from his divine nature. However, knowledge and ignorance can hardly be attributed merely to receptive perception, but must be the functions of a thinking, deciding and acting mind. Muslim insistence on the humanity of Christ placed one nature Christology under intense pressure to acknowledge the reality of human mental processes in Christ, and thus to come closer to the Chalcedonian definition of Christ's two natures.

A comparison of his writing for Melkites with his apologetics for Muslims reveals two linguistic developments for the Islamic context. Firstly, he explains the duality of human and divine in Christ by using the idea of attributes. Christ has two attributes, divine and human. Muslims speak of the attributes of God such as knowing and willing, and Christians speak of Christ having attributes. Abū Rā'iṯa does not use this language in dialogue with Melkites, for whom he writes of one divine nature in a human body. For Muslims he explains this intra-Christian discussion by referring to the language Muslims were familiar with in explaining the nature of God. Thus if Muslims think about God as having more than one attribute, they may be able to understand how Christians think of Christ as having a human body and a divine mind. He can apply the concept of attributes to Christ because he holds that Christ is essentially divine, and so the eternal Word carries the attribute of divinity from his eternal state into his Incarnate state and adds another attribute as a result of taking human flesh. How the human attribute coheres with the divine is left as a mystery.

Secondly, he uses the verb *akhadha*, with its Qur'ānic allusions, to describe the process of Incarnation in the Muslim context but not the Melkite one. Like Abū Qurra, he writes of the eternal Word 'taking' flesh from Mary. While Muslims may fear that Christians hold that God took to himself a son, in reality it was the Word who took flesh from Mary, so the eternal Word is the actor, not the product. The eternal Word is not the passive recipient of divine activity, but the one who does all the creative work himself. This is an attempt to reclaim the denial of the Qur'ān that God took a son by turning the negative statement into a positive one with a

45 Abū Rā'iṯa, 'Al-risāla fī-l-tajassud', 51.

different subject of the verb, which should have indicated to Muslims that Christians could agree with the denial.

Several of the appeals to Islamic convictions to support his Christology are noteworthy. Firstly, the eternal character of the Word is supported by the Qur'ānic dictum that God only has to say - "be and it is". Muslims should not tie God to typical reproductive processes. If God can create by speech, then the Father can beget his Son without recourse to typical reproductive processes. Secondly, he shares with Abū Qurra references to God's session on his throne in support of God's ability to be in part of his creation while ruling over all of it. In the same way God is Incarnate in Christ while upholding the universe. Thirdly, as for the death of Christ compromising the power of God over evil, Muslims have their own difficulties in this area. Humans slander God's name but he is not ultimately damaged by it, because human evil does not touch him. So the death of Christ does not undermine God's power since only the human body dies. The cross does not damage God. These appeals to Islamic convictions are more penetrating in the writing of Abū Rā'iṯa than that of Abū Qurra. The use of Islamic beliefs enabled him to show that Christian belief about the Incarnation is not entirely incompatible with Islamic belief, even if he was probably unable to show any necessary connection between the Incarnation and Islamic thought.

Finally, though his Christology in dialogue with Muslims is a faithful defence of the miaphysite tradition for which Abū Rā'iṯa stood, he develops a very thorough apologetic for the possibility of Incarnation that had not been part of the traditional intra-Christian Christological debates that had run for centuries. While Abū Qurra fields a few questions raised by Muslims about the divine becoming human, Abū Rā'iṯa attempts an encyclopaedic survey of all the issues Muslims raise on the topic. His answers show a patient seriousness with questions that Christians take for granted, and provide a model for Christians in any age in their dialogue with Muslims.

Abū Rā'iṯa was not alone in developing an extensive apologetic on Christology in the early ninth century. The following chapter will examine a similar type of writing by `Ammār al-Baṣrī, a Nestorian theologian who was probably a younger contemporary of Abū Rā'iṯa and Abū Qurra.

Chapter Five

The Christology of `Ammār al-Basrī in Dialogue with Muslims

`Ammār al-Basrī

`Ammār al-Basrī came from the Nestorian church, named after Nestorius who had been anathematized at the Council of Ephesus in 431 for refusing to confess that Mary was mother of God. This movement thrived outside the Roman Empire after the expulsion of Nestorians by Emperor Zeno beteen 474 and 491.[1] The details of `Ammār's life are not known, but he was a contemporary of the Muslim scholar Abū l-Hudhayl al-`Allāf (d. c. 840) who wrote a "refutation of `Ammār the Christian in his reply to the Christians" according to the *Fihrist* of Ibn al-Nadīm.[2] `Ammār was therefore engaged in apologetic writing for Muslims in the early ninth century. The fact that he wrote in Arabic signals a development in Nestorian apologetic writing from the late eighth century when Timothy's

---

[1] See A.S. Atiya, *A History of Eastern Christianity,* 252. Nestorian Christology grew out of the Word-human nature Christology of Theodore of Mopsuestia [c. 350-428], who held that the Word assumed not only a body but also a human mind. Since sin arises in the mind it was essential for the Word to unite with a complete human nature in order to abolish sin in humanity as a whole. Thus Christ is both fully divine and fully human. "He who assumed is by nature the same as David and Abraham, whose son he is." [Theodore of Mopsuestia, "Eighth Catechetical Homily, 1", in H. Bettenson, *The Later Christian Fathers,* 167.] Nestorius applied the two natures Christology of Theodore to a dispute over the correct way to speak of Mary's relationship to Jesus. As Bishop of Constantinople, Nestorius had to mediate between some who called Mary the mother of God and others who insisted that she was only mother of Christ's human nature. Nestorius suggested "that she should be called mother of Christ, a term which represented both God and man, as it is used in the gospels." [Nestorius, "Letter to John of Antioch", in A. Grillmeier, *Christ in Christian Tradition,* vol. 1 (London: 1975), 451.] However, his refusal to allow Mary to be called mother of God led to his exile in 436 after the decision of the Council of Ephesus in 431 that Mary should be given the title "Mother of God". Followers of Nestorius later refused to accept the definition of Chalcedon in 451, which held to one hypostasis in two natures, preferring to think of the two natures as two hypostases. See A. Grillmeier, *Christ in Christian Tradition,* vol. 2:4 (London: 1996), 504.

[2] See B. Dodge, *The Fihrist of al-Nadīm, a Tenth Century Survey of Muslim Culture,* vol. 1 (New York), 388.

debate with the Caliph al-Mahdī held in 781-2 was first written in Syriac and then translated into Arabic.[3] The Nestorian community was using the language of the ruling power by the beginning of the ninth century.

The two extant works by `Ammār are apologetic treatises. His *Book of the Proof* covers the key areas of controversy between Christians and Muslims with most attention paid to explaining the Trinity and the Incarnation.[4] `Ammār's *Book of Questions and Answers* deals with the Christian understanding of Revelation, the Four Gospels, the Trinity and the Incarnation.[5] This latter work is dedicated to the Caliph, most likely al-Ma'mūn, who ruled from 813 to 833.[6]

The Book of the Proof

The Book of the Proof deals with the Christian beliefs that were controversial for Christians living among Muslims, the authenticity of the Bible, the Trinity, the Incarnation, the death of Christ, the sacraments, and the afterlife. `Ammār writes in a dialogical style offering a defence of Christianity in the light of Muslim interrogation. However, the addressees are Christians rather than Muslims since Christians are "we" and Muslims "they" throughout the book. "The author quite obviously considers the pamphlet to be a compendium of ready reference for Christians who are involved in religious controversy with Muslims on a day to day basis."[7]

Handling Texts from the Qur'ān that Deny the Incarnation

The proof concerning the Incarnation begins with an interpretation of two Qur'ānic texts that appear to deny the possibility of the divine uniting with the human in the way that Christians believe. These are *sūra* 72:3, "Our Lord is highly exalted, he did not take a female companion nor did he take a son", and *sūra* 112:3, "God does not beget nor was he begotten". On the basis of 72:3 Muslims think that Christians believe that God "took up residence in Mary's womb thus restricting his essence (*dhāt*) within her."[8]

---

[3] See the discussion in chapter two:21f.

[4] `Ammār al-Basrī, 'Kitāb al-Burhān', (ed.) M. Hayek, in *`Ammār al-Basrī: Apologie et Controverses* (Beirut: 1977), 19-90.

[5] `Ammār al-Basrī, 'Kitāb al-masā'il wa-l-ajwiba', in Hayek, 91-266.

[6] See M. Hayek, '`Ammār al-Basrī. La Première Somme de Théologie Chrétienne en Langue Arabe, ou Deux Apologies du Christianisme', *Islamochristiana* 2 (1976), 69-113, 73.

[7] S.H. Griffith, '`Ammār al-Basrī's *Kitāb al-Burhān:* Christian *Kalām* in the First Abbasid Century', *Le Muséon* 96 (1983), 145-181, 155.

[8] `Ammār al-Basrī, 'Kitāb al-Burhān', 56.

Christians should reply that this is to confuse eternal and temporal categories. The sonship of Christ is eternal not temporal so there is no real difficulty with the language of begetting if it is understood in an eternal context. After all, Muslims do not interpret names given to God such as 'knowing' and 'wise' according to the way humans are knowing or wise. Rather they understand human knowledge and wisdom in the light of divine knowledge and wisdom. "The names adhere to God in their true sense, and are given to us from him on a temporary basis, so that they belong to him eternally."[9] Thus Christian names such as 'Father' and 'Son' should be interpreted as adhering to God eternally.

The second text from the Qur'ān, *sūra* 112:3, safeguards God from imperfection according to Muslim thought. The Christian can argue that in the created order only the simplest aspects of creation fail to beget, and that human begetting reflects most closely the begetting of the eternal Son by the eternal Father. Muslims accept that God is described in human terms such as 'merciful' and 'angry', which imply that he feels pain. However, Muslims do not ascribe imperfection to God as a result, because they believe that he is free from the weakness associated with such feelings. Likewise Christians should argue, "why don't you Muslims accept that fatherhood and sonship can be imputed to God without any implication of imperfection."[10]

EVALUATION

`Ammār's treatment of *sūra* 72:3 is significantly different from the way his fellow Nestorian, Timothy, replied to al-Mahdī's quotation of the same text. Whereas Timothy simply denied the accusation that God had taken a wife and had a son, `Ammār refers to a current Muslim view of the text that understands the denial to be about the restriction of God's essence (*dhāt*) in a human being. This difference marks a development in Islamic interpretation of the Qur'ān, from al-Mahdī's assumption that the text denies God begetting as such, to the belief that the text opposes a restriction on God implied by the begetting of a son.[11] The early ninth century was therefore a period during which Muslims were interpreting the Qur'ān in more philosophical ways, and engaging Christians in a philosophical debate. `Ammār rises to the occasion with his references to Muslim interpretation of two of the attributes of God, knowledge and wisdom. If Muslims can distinguish between human and divine knowledge and wisdom, then they ought to be able to distinguish between human and divine begetting. The former is bound by limitations but the latter is not. The fact that `Ammār's appeal to Muslim interpretation of God's attributes

[9] *Ibid.*, 59.
[10] *Ibid.*, 62.
[11] For al-Mahdī's argument see chapter two:22f.

is found in Abū Qurra's treatise *God has a Son* shows the level of interaction between Christian theologians from different Christian communities in search of arguments to defend commonly held beliefs.[12]

The second text is interpreted by Muslims to protect the perfection of God, which would be undermined by a relationship between Christ and God described in filial and paternal terms. `Ammār appeals to the kind of divine attributes that could imply weakness and imperfection in him, such as 'mercy' and 'anger'. If Muslims are able to understand these attributes as being free from weakness then it follows that Christians should be allowed to do the same with the terms 'Father' and 'Son'. A similar argument is also found in Abū Qurra's treatise *God has a Son*, confirming the point already made about the sharing of apologetic approaches among Christian theologians from different communities.[13] Debate among Muslims about the attributes of God provided fertile ground for Christian apologists in the early ninth century. While the Mu`tazila and the Traditionists were engaged in a struggle to determine the nature of the attributes, Christians were able to join in the discussion to their advantage. For if God could be described in terms of activity normally associated with humans then there was scope for distinctively Christian terms to be as valid as those found in the Qur'ān. The weakness of this approach lay in the fact that the Qur'ān appeared to rule out the very attributes that Christians wished to apply to God, namely begetting and fatherhood. However, this was not to rule out Christians making use of the difficulties Muslims had with the interpretation of divine attributes, since they were entering into territory familiar to Muslim intellectuals as equals rather than inferiors.

Four Reasons for the Incarnation

Turning to reasons why God should appear in human form, `Ammār first of all argues that the appearance of God in the flesh is the best form of revelation, since it was not really adequate for God to send prophets to declare his message. It was God's ultimate plan to reveal himself to humanity in the Messiah, so that none would be in any doubt about the character of God. "He appeared to human beings in human flesh (*fī bashar min-hum*) and spoke to them about himself revealing his authority and power to them."[14] Secondly, God condescends to the human need to see the

---

12 See chapter three:36-38 for Abū Qurra's argument that God's attributes of hearing and wisdom do not imply that human hearing and wisdom are the same, and therefore it follows that divine begetting is not the same as human begetting.

13 See chapter three:36-38 where Abū Qurra argues that the title 'Father' should be acceptable to Muslims since anthropomorphic titles attributed to God such as seeing or hearing do not demean him.

14 `Ammār al-Baṣrī, 'Kitāb al-Burhān', 62.

divine nature expressed in the fact that people make images of the divine in their search for him. Then, thirdly, if God will judge humanity is it not proper for those being judged to see their accuser? Since God cannot appear to us directly he "veiled himself with human nature" (*jawhar al-insān*).[15] Fourthly, by being in a human body (*fī jasadi min-hum*) God has given humanity the opportunity to rule creation not only in time but also in eternity.[16] `Ammār concludes this section with a brief discussion of the union of divine and human in Christ. Even though Christians have different ways of describing the union, they are united in confessing that God became Incarnate. "They agree that the Creator appeared in a body like theirs ... but they disagree over how to describe the body; some say it is one hypostasis (*qunūm*) and others that it is two hypostases (*qunūmain*)."[17]

Evaluation

These four arguments seek to validate the Incarnation as profitable for humans. Firstly, human ability to see God himself in Christ in terms of authoritative speech and powerful deeds would remove any doubt that God was truly active in the world. In other words, sending human messengers was never going to be ideal to secure faith and obedience from humans, even though God had used that form of revelation over a long period of time. This argument is a direct challenge to Islamic notions of revelation, which are bound by the transcendence of God in the giving of revelation as speech, safeguarding the character of God from contamination or limitation in his relationship with humanity. That `Ammār makes this case so boldly suggests that he believes Christian ideas of revelation are simply more valuable than Islamic ones, and that the opportunity for catching sight of the divine in a man is by definition the kind of revelation that nobody would refuse. This confident assertion of the superiority of the revelation of God in Christ is unique to `Ammār among the apologists of the eighth and ninth centuries, and shows how he was willing to compare Christian and Muslim thought to the disadvantage of the latter. This method applies to his second and third reasons for the Incarnation. God understands human need to visualize the divine despite the insistence of the Qur'ān that humans had gone astray precisely by making images of divine beings. God also thinks it appropriate for humans to get some idea of the appearance of the judge they all one day will meet, even though he has to hide his face from view, despite the fact that Muslims regard God as unseen to the human eye. `Ammār seemed to think that such arguments would find a ready audience among Muslims, but this was unlikely in reality. Transcendence is breached

---

[15] *Ibid.*, 69.
[16] *Ibid.*, 72.
[17] *Ibid.*, 79.

in each of these arguments in terms simply unacceptable to Muslims, so that it must have been difficult for them to take these propositions seriously.

Dealing with the Muslim Denial of Christ's Death on the Cross

Muslims accuse Christians both of introducing weakness to God and of humiliating Christ by holding that Christ was put to death at the hands of his enemies. The first accusation is made in terms of *sūra* 19:90, "The sky is ready to burst, the earth split and the mountains fall down," which is interpreted by Muslims to imply that Christians slander God in holding to the crucifixion of Christ.[18] `Ammār suggests that Christians counter this supposed slander by arguing that the death of God's messengers is not necessarily a sign of weakness on God's part. For example, John the Baptist suffered a terrible death but Muslims do not impute weakness to God for allowing it to happen. The basic problem with the cross is the type of death it signifies. Muslims seemed to find it impossible to incorporate the defeat of a messenger of God into their understanding of prophethood. This was one of the points made by al-Mahdī to Timothy in his criticism of the crucifixion, and now, a generation later, `Ammār is aware of the force of this position for Muslims.[19] So any appeal to the death of a prophet, which suggested defeat of God's purposes, would most likely have failed to convince. Still, `Ammār thinks that this Islamic premise ought to be challenged by the story of John's killing as recorded in the gospels. John the Baptist's death is mentioned in the Qur'ān, but there is no information about the manner of his passing.[20] Whether the testimony of the Christian Scriptures would have had much persuasive power is doubtful.[21]

The second accusation, that the story of the crucifixion demeans Christ himself, can be dealt with by pointing to the subsequent honouring of Christ by God as a result of Christ's resurrection and ascension. Then Christians can argue that the victory of Christ over the power of death had incalculable consequences for humans, since by conquering death and rising to life Christ opened the way for humanity to overcome death and rise to eternal life.[22]

---

[18] *Ibid.*

[19] Al-Mahdī believed that "Jesus was honoured by God who did not deliver him into the hands of the Jews so that they could kill him." See chapter two:25.

[20] See *sūra* 19:15, "Peace on him (Yaḫyā) the day he was born, the day he dies, and the day he is raised alive".

[21] Nevertheless, the twentieth century Qur'ān commentator Yūsuf `Alī accepts the historicity of the New Testament account of John's death as an explanation of *sūra* 19:15, even though he does not in consequence accept the historicity of the gospel story of Christ's crucifixion.

[22] `Ammār, 'Kitāb al-Burhān', 80f.

EVALUATION

`Ammār does not quote the denial of the crucifixion in *sūra* 4:157, "They did not kill him, they did not crucify him." Why open the advice to Christians on answering Muslim questions about Christ with two outright denials of his status as begotten of God and Son of God, and not end with the rejection of the cross? The fact that none of the Christian apologists surveyed here from the eighth and ninth centuries mentions the content of *sūra* 4:157 provides a clue to the answer. Christians felt unable to counter the Qur'ānic opposition to the cross in a direct way, but were compelled by the strength of Muslim sentiment to talk about the cross indirectly. Timothy came closest to a direct counter argument by suggesting that the mention of the death of Christ in *sūra* 19:33 supported the gospel version of Christ's death and resurrection, but he refrained from saying that *sūra* 4:157 was wrong.[23] Muslim rule meant that there were limits to the kind of argument Christians could employ in debate with Muslims.

`Ammār's approach is to tackle the subsidiary issues of the demeaning of the characters of God and Christ felt by Muslims to be implied in the crucifixion. Here was more congenial territory for apologetic argument, since `Ammār could develop the paradox of humiliation leading to exaltation, which was the original Apostolic interpretation of the death of Christ in the New Testament. The Islamic anxiety about protecting God's messengers from shameful defeat could become the foundation for the greater truth that defeat by human enemies turned out ultimately to be the occasion for God's victory. Therefore, Christ is honoured precisely because he undergoes death to raise up fellow humans to life, and in the process he accepts dishonour to bring honour to many. This approach is unique to `Ammār among Christian apologists of the eighth and ninth centuries, and certainly provides a way of dealing with the honour and shame theme central to Islamic perception of God's messengers.[24] Still, the question remains how Muslims would have received this argument. The basic stumbling block of the denial of the cross would probably have prevented them from accepting a paradox that included the crucifixion.

The Book of Questions and Answers

In this work `Ammār deals with questions raised by Muslims about the existence of God and his creation, the four gospels, the Trinity and the Incarnation. The final fourth section answers fifty-one questions about the

[23] See chapter two for Timothy's use of *sūra* 19:33.

[24] For a twentieth century Christian attempt to deal with the shame of the crucifixion see *The Life of Christ* in chapter ten.

Incarnation but occupies a third of the work.[25] The format is similar to the forty-four questions answered by Abū Rā'iṯa in his *Letter on the Incarnation*, but is a much more substantial piece of writing. Both Abū Rā'iṯa and `Ammār al-Basrī were from Syriac speaking Christian communities, which had a history of theological writing in a question and answer style. According to Sidney Griffith, "The practice of composing books of questions was a conventional manner of scholarly composition in Nestorian academic circles."[26] While Abū Rā'iṯa and `Ammār composed questions and answers on the Incarnation, they did not adopt an identical answering approach. Firstly, Abū Rā'iṯa explicitly refers to the Qur'ān on occasion but `Ammār never does. Secondly, `Ammār's answers are often independent of Abū Rā'iṯa's, even though the questions are similar. Thirdly, `Ammār's style is less direct than Abū Rā'iṯa's. The latter addressed his questioner as 'you', but `Ammār refers to the Muslim questioner in the third person as 'he', which may indicate that, like *The Book of the Proof*, *The Book of Questions and Answers* was primarily designed to assist Christians in defence of their faith. Therefore the questions raised by the anonymous Muslim are organized to suit an orderly exposition and do not represent actual debate, but rather typify the kind of issues that Muslim intellectuals raise when in discussion with Christian theologians.

The fifty-one questions are grouped according to the following themes: questions 1-10, the union between the divine and human in Christ; questions 11-14, the embodiment of God; questions 15-20, the way God is affected by the Incarnation of the Word; questions 21-26, the choice of Mary's son: why not another human being or angel; questions 27-31, how the work of Christ affects others; questions 32-35, the purpose of Christ's suffering; questions 36-42, the historicity of the crucifixion and resurrection; questions 43-46, the relationship between Christ and the Trinity; and questions 47-51, the salvation Christ brings.

Questions 1-10. The Union between the Divine and Human in Christ

1. [Question one has been lost but part of the answer is extant] `Ammār begins with a definition of the union of the divine and human in Christ which asserts that "the eternal Word and the temporal created human being became one Messiah ... who is the union of two natures (*jawharain*)."[27]

[25] `Ammār al-Basrī, 'Kitāb al-masā'il wa-l-ajwiba: al-maqāla al-rābi`a', in Hayek, *Apologie et Controverses,* 178-265.

[26] S.H. Griffith, '`Ammār al-Basrī's *Kitāb al-Burhān:* Christian Kalām in the First Abbasid Century', 152.

[27] `Ammār al-Basrī, 'Kitāb al-masā'il wa-l-ajwiba', 179.

2. Is Christ eternal or temporal? Before the union one can speak about the eternal Word but not about Christ. "The Messiah can only be named after the eternal nature (*al-jawhar al-azalī*) became Incarnate (*yatajassad*) by uniting with created human nature."[28]
3. Are the two natures (*jawharain*) united? Yes, They are united in Christ. "The two natures (*ṯabā`ain*) or the two hypostases (*qunūmain*) are united."[29]
4. In what way is Christ a unity of two natures? He is a unity of divine and human hypostases (*qunūmain lāhūtiyan wa nāsūtiyan*).[30]
5. Does the human nature not affect the divine? No, just as coal receives heat from fire but does not impart blackness to it, so the human nature does not affect the divine.
6. Was the human nature in the virgin's womb before the uniting of the divine with a human body? The virgin conceived Christ as a union of two natures.
7. Who was the Son of God, the one who existed before the Incarnation or the one conceived in the virgin's womb? "The Incarnate Christ is the Son of God, equally in his eternal nature (*bi-jawhari-hi al-azalī*) as in his temporal nature (*bi-jawhari-hi al-zamanī*)".[31]
8. Did only one or both natures eat and drink and suffer? From his human nature Christ ate, drank and suffered, not from his divine nature.
9. Do you not hold that Christ has two births, one from eternity and the other in time? "We don't say that Christ had two births but that he was begotten (*mawlūd*) from the Father outside of time, and born (*wilād*) of his mother in time".[32]
10. How is the nature that is created in time called Son of God? The eternal Son decided that human nature (*jawhar al-ins*) should share in his sonship. "He became Incarnate, uniting with human nature as a garment for his divine nature (*libāsan li-lāhūti-hi*)."[33]

EVALUATION

`Ammār shares with Abū Qurra and Abū Rā'iṯa the root *tajassud* to describe the Incarnation. Along with Abū Rā'iṯa he uses the idea of the human nature as a garment for the divine nature. Once in this opening section he refers to the humanity of Christ as a temple (*haykal*), but `Ammār generally prefers the image of clothing to a temple. This use of

[28] *Ibid.*, 180.
[29] *Ibid.*, 181.
[30] *Ibid.*
[31] *Ibid.*, 187.
[32] *Ibid.*, 192.
[33] *Ibid.*, 193.

garment imagery leaves the impression of a human nature in Christ that is passive, a conclusion understandable for the miaphysite Abū Rā'iṯa but less helpful for the diophysite `Ammār. The image gives little room for a human mind in Christ, a concept central to the two nature Christology of Theodore of Mopsuestia.[34] In terms of its usefulness in an Islamic context the garment analogy would probably have suggested to Muslims that the Christian Christ was a divine being clothed in a human body, rather than a union between divine and human natures.

The Nestorian belief in the union of two hypostases (*qunūmain*) does seem to pose problems in the light of the fact that the three hypostases (*aqānīm*) of the Trinity are also described by the same root (*qunūm*). Answers to questions 3 and 4 refer to Christ as a union of divine and human hypostases (*qunūmain*). However, the answer to question 46 speaks of Father, Son and Holy Spirit as three eternal hypostases (*aqānīm*). It is not surprising that Abū Rā'iṯa complained that if the Nestorian terminology is followed then the human nature of Christ looks like a fourth hypostasis in the Godhead.[35] This inconsistent use of terminology shows the weakness of the Nestorian notion of two hypostases in Christ, which function alongside the two natures. Chalcedonians as well as miaphysites were justified in criticizing Nestorian over-elaboration in the description of the union. Muslims would have found grounds for their allegation that Christians were irrational in their belief in the Incarnation since the language they used lacked consistency.

`Ammār's answer to the Muslim anxiety about contamination of the divine after union with human nature is similar to that of Abū Qurra and Abū Rā'iṯa. If the eternal Son always has the initiative after his union with human nature then it is possible to defend the integrity of the divine. Despite his insistence on a union of divine and human natures, `Ammār does not hold that they function in a united way. Weakness, pain and death touch only the human nature, while the divine is exempt from any blemish caused by such experiences. As a result the Muslim questioner need not fear that the integrity of the divine is undermined by the Incarnation. All three ninth century apologists agree on this point. No matter which way they define the union of divine and human in Christ, they each assert the immunity of the divine from contamination in any form. This, of course, was the key problem for Muslims in the Incarnation of the divine, so it is hardly surprising that there is a shared apologetic argument to deal with the apparent loss of transcendence in an embodied divinity.

34 See the opening footnote of this chapter for Theodore of Mopsuestia.

35 See chapter four:47.

Questions 11-14. The Embodiment of God?

11. How is it possible for the divine nature to clothe itself with human nature without becoming limited by it? In the same way that the sun gives light to part of the earth without in any way being limited to that space. "He took human nature as a temple to dwell in" but he is not limited to that place.[36]
12. [the question is missing] We do not speak of God's body. "God the Word became human (*allāh al-kalima ta'annasa*)."[37] This is not to be understood in the same way as we think of a child becoming a man in a natural process of change. Rather, the becoming human is like a man becoming dressed or taking up arms, or putting on a turban.

    "He did not become (*sāra*) a turban or weapons, or armour. Likewise we say that God the Word became embodied (*tajassada*); became human (*ta'annasa*). In other words, he brought into being (*ahdatha*) a body (*jasadan*) and clothed himself with it (*labisa-hi*). He created (*khalaqa*) a human being (*insānan*) and put it on (*tadarra`a-hu*)."[38]

    Christ is a union of God the Word with this human nature created by him.
13. Why did he want to have a human nature? To unite humanity with himself.
14. Why do you speak of God's temple but not his body? It is not the temple of God but rather the temple of the eternal Word. The Father and the Spirit did not become incarnate, so it is not appropriate to speak of God's body.

EVALUATION

The answer to question 11 uses the analogy of the sun lighting up the earth without being confined to it in the same way as Abū Rā'ita does, which perhaps enables the Muslim to grasp that God may interact with his creation without becoming restricted by the connection.[39] `Ammār's answer to question 12 does not refer to the eternal Word "taking" human nature as Abū Qurra and Abū Rā'ita do. Instead, he says that the Word brought into being (*ahdatha*) a body, or created (*khalaqa*) a human being. Whereas Abū Qurra and Abū Rā'ita may have been sensitive to Islamic convictions that only God creates, and therefore emphasized that the Word fashioned a pure body out of that which already had been created, `Ammār applies to the

---

[36] 'Kitāb al-masā'il', 194.
[37] *Ibid.*, 196.
[38] *Ibid.*, 196f.
[39] See chapter four:53.

eternal Word full creative powers from nothing.[40] While Christ created (*khalaqa*) a real bird from a clay model in *sūra* 5:110 of the Qur'ān, he did not make the bird from nothing. So, although `Ammār uses the term *khalaqa* for the action, the meaning goes beyond that found in the Qur'ān when applied to Christ's creative work, and suggests a power that belongs to God alone. This was an unnecessary complication for a Muslim audience, and shows the wisdom of his two ninth century colleagues in using the notion of 'taking' what already was there.

`Ammār shares with Abū Qurra and Abū Rā'iṯa the conviction that the human nature of the Messiah was different from that of other humans. In this way all three apologists distanced God from mingling with human sin. However, this very safeguarding of God from contamination may have left Muslims with the impression that Christians did not think that Christ was a normal human being. This reaction would probably have been reinforced by the use of clothing and temple imagery by `Ammār.

`Ammār takes the opportunity in the answer to question 12 to show that only Nestorian Christology satisfies Islamic suspicion that the Incarnation implies the embodiment of God. He criticises miaphysites for failing to distinguish the divine and human in Christ by speaking of "one nature and one hypostasis" (*jawharan wāḫidan wa qunūman wāḫidan*). This can only result in the body of the Messiah being the body of God. He also believes that the Chalcedonian insistence that Mary is the mother of God also entails the embodiment of God. The name 'God' in the Chalcedonian statement applies not only to the Messiah but also to the Father and the Spirit. Therefore the followers of Chalcedon are guilty of speaking of the body of God or saying that Mary gave birth to God. He appeals to Scripture for support, because Matthew and Luke speak of the birth of the Messiah not the birth of God. Therefore only the Nestorian position safeguards God from embodiment. The argument that Miaphysites and Chalcedonians are bound to hold that God is embodied appears to give the Nestorian an advantage in dialogue with Muslims. For it is `Ammār who can most easily say that only the Word of God is embodied. Abū Rā'iṯa may hold that the sent one not the Sender indwells the body, but if Christ is only a divine hypostasis in a human body then divinity has to be directly linked to human flesh.[41] Abū Qurra is bound to lead Muslims into confusion by adhering to the formula "Mary is the Mother of God".[42] The advantage of the Nestorian view was that a Muslim would be less likely to think that there was a direct association between God and human nature.

---

[40] See chapter three:34-36 for Abū Qurra's and chapter four:58 for Abū Rā'iṯa's contributions.

[41] See chapter four:52.

[42] See chapter three:31.

Questions 15-20. The Way God is Affected by the Incarnation of the Word

15. [The question is not complete, but begins by asking how the divine nature could unite with human nature while at the same time being united with the other two members of the Trinity] Just as the rays of the sun give heat without being separated from the sun, so the Son could unite with human nature without being separated from the Father and the Spirit.
16. Why did the Father and Spirit not become human rather than the Son? Since human nature is not eternal, it would not be appropriate for the Father to enter the temporal in the same way as the Son has done. Likewise the Spirit cannot become embodied and remain the eternal Spirit.
17. How can you prove that the Son became Incarnate? The prophecy in Isaiah 7:14 about a virgin giving birth to Emmanuel shows both that the Messiah had the same human nature as Mary and that he had the divine eternal nature. The four gospels show the same unity in the Messiah of the human and divine nature. Matthew 1:1 declares that Jesus Christ had a human lineage, but in 8:18-34 Christ cast out demons by divine power.
18. Did the union between divine and human not result in a new kind of human being? When the Word of God took human nature as "a body, a temple and a dwelling place", (*jasadan wa-haykalan wa-mahallan*) he gave to it his authority but not his eternity or his spiritual nature.[43]
19. How can the divine nature be unaffected by this union? We do not know how the divine united with the human. This is analogous to creation. We do not know how God creates.
20. Why did the Incarnation happen if God does not perform futile actions? The condescension of God towards his creation is demonstrated exactly in the enfleshment of the Word and not otherwise, for by the Incarnation God grants sonship to all humans by means of one particular human (*al-shakhsa al-wāhida al-insiyya*).[44]

EVALUATION

`Ammār uses two traditional arguments in this section. Firstly, the Trinity is explained by the analogy of the sun, its rays and the heat it produces,[45] and secondly, the divinity of Christ is established from the prophets and the

---

[43] 'Kitāb al-masā'il', 213.

[44] *Ibid.*,215.

[45] See the *Anonymous Apology* for a similar application of this analogy in chapter two:19.

gospels of Christian Scripture.[46] This is the first of many appeals to Biblical evidence for the Incarnation by `Ammār, which shows that, despite Muslim doubt about the trustworthiness of Christian Scripture, Christians found it hard ignore the source of their theology in defending the Incarnation.[47] A third argument, shared with Abū Rā'iṭa, relies on Muslim agnosticism concerning the way God acts.[48]

> "If we Christians ask Muslims how God creates, they say that they do not know how ... Likewise there is no reply to any question about how the divine became human (*tajassada illāh*) or how the human body united with the incarnate one (*al-mutajassid*) in the state of sonship (*al-bunuwwa*)."[49]

If Christians may be interrogated on the logical inconsistency of the divine becoming human, then by implication Muslims ought to be willing to be questioned about the way God works. Christians may have difficulty explaining the union of the divine and the human in Christ, but then Muslims are not able to explain the manner of God's creative work. There is an equality of ignorance between Muslims and Christians in understanding the processes of God's actions. Certainly, this is a useful apologetic stance, which takes the discussion back to first principles. Human knowledge of God is based on revelation, with the result that what humans know is dependent on what he has made clear to them. Both Christians and Muslims have knowledge of the results, but not the method, of God's actions.

Questions 21-26. The Choice of Mary's Son: Why not Another Human or an Angel?

21. Why did the Creator not become incarnate in everybody? He chose one person through whom the rest would be honored.
22. Why did he not choose an angel rather than a human being? Angelic appearance would not touch humanity except from the outside.
23. How did he choose the particular human being to unite with? He chose him on the basis of "his righteousness and his purity" (*birri-hi wa tahārati-hi*).[50]
24. If he was pure before entering the womb how can it be just for other humans to be deprived of a similar purity? Some individuals have

[46] See also the extensive series of Biblical texts quoted in the *Anonymous Apology* supporting the divinity of Christ in chapter two:18-20.

[47] See Abū Qurra's use of Biblical evidence in chapter three:39f. Abū Rā'iṯa was least dependent on Scripture quotation among the three ninth century apologists.

[48] See chapter four:52 for Abū Rā'iṯa's version of the argument.

[49] 'Kitāb al-masā'il', 214f.

[50] *Ibid.*, 218.

indeed been made pure before birth such as Jeremiah according to Jeremiah 1:4, "before I took you from the womb I purified you". But the majority of humans only gain purity from the Incarnation.

25. How can you prove that he is better than any other? If God had found another more righteous he would have chosen him.
26. Was it possible for him to lose his purity after becoming human? It was possible, but he did not lose his purity.

EVALUATION

`Ammār's answer to question 26 involves a discussion of what is meant by sinlessness. If it means being prevented from sinning by God's decree then that does not apply to Christ, because he had to obey God's will like any other human being. There was no special protection for Christ from the temptations to rebel and go astray. This use of the continued testing of the obedience of Christ to affirm his true humanity sets `Ammār apart from Abū Qurra and Abū Rā'iṯa. While all three insist on the purity of Christ at the point of union between divine and human natures, only `Ammār stresses the importance of the lifelong process of maintaining that purity. `Ammār's Christ is one who had to prove his worth before God. This Nestorian definition of the human nature of Christ as that which the rest of humanity shares is without doubt closer to a Muslim perception of him. Though Abū Qurra held to a fully human nature in Christ, he did not allow for the human mind in Christ to entertain the possibility of sinning, but maintained that the divine mind was in control.[51] According to *sūra* 5:116f of the Qur'ān, Christ was interrogated by God over whether he had asked his followers to worship himself and his mother apart from God, showing that the Qur'ānic Christ was judged capable of sinning. The purity of Christ in the Qur'ān was not beyond scrutiny, and although he denied the allegation vigorously, the questioning shows that Christ had to maintain the purity given to him at his conception. As a result, a Muslim reader of all three apologists may have been more able to identify `Ammār's Christ as truly human rather than the Christ of Abū Qurra and Abū Rā'iṯa who seems not to have faced the testing of his purity.

Questions 27-31. How the Work of Christ Affects Others

27. How does the merit of Christ relate humans to God? Imagine a king who wants to do the best for his people by identifying with them as fully as possible, and so has a son who is born among them. The son still inherits the kingdom of his father with all the authority that goes with it, but the son is one of the people. Since he stems from his father and from the people, the latter are caught up in the inheritance

[51] See chapter three:31f.

of the kingdom. "In the same way the Incarnate one by taking a human body relates humanity to his divine inheritance by taking humanity into that which belongs to God."[52]

28. Could the Creator take back the gifts of authority and power conferred on the Incarnate one? No, because after the union of divine and human there can be no separation.
29. How can you claim that there can be no separation between the two natures when only the human nature experiences pain and death? The unity of the divine and human means that divine power and authority is truly united with human weakness. There is no "separation or distance between them."[53]
30. Was the outcome of the union not already decided before it took place? Just as a son who inherits from his father needs to prove his faithfulness to his father throughout his life, so the human nature has to prove by action that it is worthy of the union with the eternal. Scripture supports this idea of testing. Only after the resurrection is Christ given all authority in heaven and on earth, according to Matthew 28:18.
31. Does this text not say that he was only given divine authority at that point and not before? In Matthew 11:27, Jesus claims that his Father has given everything to him as proof that he possessed divine power and authority before the resurrection. However, the full exercise of that authority had to wait for the outcome of his obedience to death.

EVALUATION

The parable of the king having a son raised among his people is an innovative interpretation of the Incarnation, which illustrates `Ammār's fourth reason for the Incarnation in the Book of the Proof.[54] Humans are enobled by the condescension of the son who is one of them in order to lift them up to share in God's kingdom. This is a worthy attempt to disclose the value of the Incarnation to the rest of humanity by stressing the fact that the presence of the son guarantees life with God. Given that Muslims were not free to depend on another for salvation, the offer of help from the son would possibly be both a sign to them of the distance between Christians and Muslims, and an attractive aspect of the Christian story.

`Ammār's answer to question 29 turns on the way that divine attributes function in Christ. Some divine attributes, such as eternity, are not communicated to the human nature of Christ, whereas other divine attributes, such as power and authority, are shared with the human nature. At death the eternal nature of Christ is unaffected, but the power and

---

[52] 'Kitāb al-masā'il', 222.
[53] *Ibid.*, 224.
[54] See above, 71.

authority of Christ are reduced to impotence. In some sense the divine attributes shared by the human nature are affected by a temporary defeat before being restored at the resurrection. This is a more satisfying solution to the problem of the death of Christ impacting the divine nature adversely than the one given by Abū Rā'iṯa, who held that, though the death of Christ did not at all affect his attribute of divinity, there was no separation between the attributes of divinity and humanity. `Ammār manages to show why there was no separation between the two natures in the death of Christ.

`Ammār drives home the point that an untested Christ is without value either to God or humanity. Whereas Abū Qurra and Abū Rā'iṯa leave the impression that the divine nature in Christ was never seriously disturbed by testing, `Ammār holds to a genuine dialectic between the two natures in Christ. The human nature could have ruined Christ if he had allowed it to lead him astray. The greatness of Christ lay in his ability to submit to God's will in all circumstances, and this is what qualifies him to transfer merit to those who fail to submit to God. While the potential for true union between the divine and human was there from conception, actual union of will and action had to happen under extreme conditions in the life of Christ.

Questions 32-35. The Purpose of Christ's Suffering

32. Why did he have to suffer even to death if he possessed divine glory and authority? Like a prizefighter who has to use up all his strength to defeat an opponent, Christ was willing to submit himself even to death to defeat death on behalf of others. Like a doctor who wants to demonstrate his ability to heal by swallowing some poison before administering medicine to a patient, "Christ chose to rescue humanity from wrongdoing and from slavery to Satan by submitting to death in order to raise to life those subject to death."[55]
33. Did not Moses and David and other prophets experience the resurrection without Christ offering himself for them? Moses told Israel what their Lord expected of them. Christ announced to Israel that he had come to save them from the results of their failure to fulfil what Moses brought to them.
34. Could he not have preached the resurrection without having to die and be raised himself? Yes, but people would not believe in the resurrection without visible proof. So he died and rose again to "place firmly in their hearts the promise of their resurrection."[56]
35. But then wouldn't it be better to be raised up without having to be put to death by his enemies? "If he died on his bed as others do and

[55] 'Kitāb al-masā'il', 229f.

[56] *Ibid.*, 233.

then rose up alive it would leave grave doubt in people's hearts."[57] But if he consents to death at the hands of his enemies and then is raised up, he can vanquish any doubt in his ability to overcome death.

EVALUATION

While Abū Rā'iṯa also argues that the death of Christ shows the lengths to which God goes to rescue sinful humanity, `Ammār's analogies are original and compelling. The prizefighter exhausts himself in victory just like the divine power in Christ which gives way to abject weakness, and the doctor poisons himself in the pursuit of a drug which might heal others, just like Christ who willingly drinks the cup of death to bring life to others. These illustrations go to the heart of the Christian sense of the love of God shown in the self-giving of Christ, and give a true exposition of the value of the Incarnation in terms that a Muslim would understand. If the end result of the Incarnation is the defeat of weakness, sin and death, then the Incarnation goes beyond a doctrine that might seem to be denigrating to God's honour, to a belief that provides assurance of success for humans in their struggles. Such illustrations would probably have had a more immediate impact on Muslims than Abū Rā'iṯa's more formal argument.[58]

`Ammār's concentration on the resurrection is strikingly different from the apologetics of Abū Rā'iṯa and Abū Qurra. `Ammār alone argues that Christ's resurrection enables others to rise from the dead. The Muslim query about whether Moses and David experienced the resurrection is probably based on the notion of resurrection found in the Qur'ān, where believers are granted resurrection to bliss. `Ammār's answer focuses not so much on the possibility of resurrection for believers, but on the assurance that Christ's resurrection gives to those who believe. Muslims believed in the possibility of resurrection but that only God knew who actually would be raised. `Ammār's confidence in the promise of resurrection is a notable apologetic position, because the possibility of personal resurrection to life is now strengthened by the firm promise of Christ that those who believe will be raised to life. Here again the value of the Incarnation is made clear, that the self-giving of Christ releases humans from the grip of death into life. Muslims would no doubt have understood why Christians held to the Incarnation, even though they may not have thought the idea to be true to their comprehension of God's transcendence.

[57] *Ibid.*, 234.

[58] For Abū Rā'iṯa's argument see chapter four.

Questions 36-42. The Historicity of the Crucifixion and Resurrection

36. How could it be possible for Christ to let his enemies put him to death like a criminal? By allowing them to crucify him, he demonstrated, to all those who witnessed his death, the grace that would flow from that death.
37. Then why did he not come down from the cross alive instead of being buried in the ground? Isn't that what those who crucified him suggested when they said, "save yourself and come down from your cross and we will believe in you?"[59] Just as the Children of Israel tested God in the wilderness and were punished for it, so those who crucified Christ were putting God to the test and deserved not to be placated but punished. In any case there had to be no doubting whatsoever about the fact of his death.
38. How is it that a crowd witnessed his crucifixion but only twelve of his followers met him raised alive? Just as God does not reveal himself to unbelievers, so Christ only appeared to those who had faith in him. If he appeared to the same people who had crucified him, they would quite likely say that it was the work of Satan to deceive them. The only alternative to appearing to a small number of believers would have been to appear to the whole of humanity, nation by nation, but this was clearly impossible. Christ chose to reveal his divine glory through those who witnessed his resurrection.
39. If Christ sent those who witnessed his resurrection to the nations to perform miracles in his name, why was it not sufficient for the apostles only to witness his death? In that case doubt might rise up in the minds of the apostles, but since the enemies of Christ saw that he really died, then the apostles could be assured that he both truly died and truly rose from death.
40. If Christ decided to die to save others from divine punishment, then why should the Jews who killed him not receive a reward for putting him to death? The Jews did not have the same intention as Christ; he wanted to save others, but they wanted to destroy him. The only possibility of salvation for them would follow repentance for their crime.
41. Did not the Messiah ask God to forgive the Jews who had put him on the cross when he said, "Father forgive them for they don't know what they are doing?" If the Jews were offered forgiveness by Christ how can they be punished? When Jesus sought forgiveness for people, he sought it for those who did not know what they were doing, but the Jews who wanted Christ killed certainly knew what they were doing.

[59] 'Kitāb al-masā'il', 236.

42. If they saw his miracles and understood his teaching, why did the Jews kill him? The Children of Israel had defied the prophets of God before so there was no reason why they could not rebel against Christ in a similar way.

EVALUATION

`Ammār's section on the crucifixion is much more detailed than Abū Rā'iṯa's, and is focused on the intentions of Christ rather than how the crucifixion could be God's will, which preoccupied Abū Rā'iṯa.[60] `Ammār sees Christ as the willing subject of the cross, who decides to give himself for the salvation of others. Thus the Jews who sought to kill Christ were in one sense defying God, but in another sense were only doing what was always possible for the people of God to do. In this way `Ammār deals with the Qur'ānic denial of the cross. The Jews were quite capable of that kind of thing, and God allowed them to achieve it because Christ willingly submitted to it. However, `Ammār allows the Muslim to uphold the denial of the death of Christ on the cross by finding possible support for it from the gospels. So the Muslim questioner quotes from Matthew 27:42, where the crowd challenge Christ to come down from the cross. The significance of the quotation for a Muslim would lie in the possible match between the assumption in the suggestion and the teaching of *sūra* 4:157 in the Qur'ān. For if Christ had come down from the cross alive, then the Qur'ānic statement "they did not kill him" would be upheld. By allowing a detailed comparison between *sūra* 4:157 and Matthew 27:42, `Ammār enables a Muslim to engage in comparative exegesis of texts, in the hope that the latter may come to a new interpretation of the death of Christ.

`Ammār deals directly with Muslim doubt about the value of the testimony to the crucifixion and resurrection in the gospels, which neither Abū Rā'iṯa nor Abū Qurra do. This may be explained by the apologetic approach of `Ammār, who makes more use of New Testament sources than his two contemporaries. His rather elaborate four points defending the paucity of witnesses to the resurrection can be seen as an attempt to offer a thorough defense of the few witnesses to the event. Muslims were all too aware that the evidence for the death of Christ hung on the truth telling of a few people who were keen to promote the story.[61] His argument that even the enemies of Christ witnessed his death is designed to head off this complaint. Nevertheless, debate about what actually happened to Christ at the end of his life still could come to grief over interpretation of texts.

---

[60] See chapter four:63f for Abū Rā'iṯa's presentation.

[61] See the remarks of al-Rāzī in chapter one:9 that the only way to combat the Christian story was to question the veracity of the witnesses.

Questions 43-46. The Relationship between Christ and the Trinity

43. How could Jesus command his disciples to baptize people in the name of the Father, Son and Holy Spirit? Isn't this text "evidence of the corruption" (*taḥrīf*) of the message of Jesus by Christians?[62] Christ also said that he had descended from heaven and that he existed before Abraham, so he claimed a relationship of equality with his Father.
44. Why does he speak of the Spirit rather than simply the Father and the Son? While there is a place for a dual relationship between Father and Son that is not the whole reality of the Trinity.
45. How could Christ send the Holy Spirit, the Paraclete, to the apostles when the Spirit is the Creator, the Father and the Son included? When Christ said he would send the Holy Spirit, the Paraclete, to his disciples, he meant that the miracles they would perform in his name could only be done in the power of the Spirit and that "the three eternal hypostases (*al-aqānīm*) were equal in authority and in nature."[63]
46. What is the meaning of the statement that Christ sits at God's right side interceding for others? Does God have a right side to sit at? Why should the Messiah intercede for others? First of all, the 'right side' shows that he has the authority of God. Secondly, his power to intercede is based on the fact that only Christ among humans is perfectly righteous. In fact his sacrificial death intercedes for sinners by "annulling the sin of Adam in the descendents of Adam through his righteousness and purity."[64]

EVALUATION

`Ammār's discussion of the Trinity in the gospels is significantly different from Abū Rā'iṯa's debate on the relationship between the eternal Word and the other members of the Trinity, since the latter is concerned with the way the second person of the Trinity functions in relation to the other two, whereas`Ammār deals with the meaning of Trinitarian language in the New Testament.[65] `Ammār allows the gospel accounts to be scrutinized by the Muslim who wonders how much the Trinity features in them, which gives him the opportunity to show that the Trinity was Christ's teaching. The Trinity, therefore, is not an axiom of theological reflection unrelated to the teaching of Christ himself, but is expressly taught by him.

In posing question 43, the Muslim asks whether Jesus has been reported accurately when he refers to the Trinity in Matthew 28:19, and whether the

---

[62] 'Kitāb al-masā'il', 249.

[63] *Ibid.*, 252.

[64] *Ibid.*, 255.

[65] For Abū Rā'iṯa's presentation see chapter four:51.

text is not basically corrupt. This is a fascinating insight into the kind of research Muslims were doing in the early ninth century into Christian scripture. Certainly there would be no call for Christians to go looking for New Testament texts that gave evidence of corruption of a supposed original reading. While the Qur'ān usually accuses Jews of corrupting their scriptures, here is testimony to the charge of corruption being made of Christian texts too. Presumably the discovery of the content of the gospels by Muslims lent urgency to the need to extend the corruption charge to these Christian scriptures as well. `Ammār does not deal directly with the accusation of corruption against the authenticity of the sayings of Christ in the New Testament. He had already answered fourteen questions on the accuracy of the gospels in the Book of Questions and Answers before the fifty-one on the Incarnation.[66] His basic conviction on the authenticity of the saying of Jesus which includes the Trinity is that it is consistent with many other sayings that presuppose the Trinity even if they do not explicitly endorse it in so many words. Therefore the text is not corrupt when read alongside corroborating texts from the fourth gospel in particular. Of course a Muslim could simply reply that these other texts confirm the charge of corruption.

Questions 47-51. The Salvation Christ Brings

47. If Christ brought forgiveness for the sin of others how is it that sin has been so widespread since the time of Christ? In reality Christ cancelled the effects of the sin of Adam on the rest of humanity. Death became the universal experience of humanity as a result of Adam's sin, but Christ's righteous character undid the effects of death for all others. He made void the power of death and made possible the gift of eternal life for others.
48. If Adam was created to die before he sinned and he and his descendents were raised from death before Christ's coming, why did they need Christ's righteousness? God intended to grant life without end to the first man, but Adam's sin deprived his descendents of life without end, so Christ became the means by which people of any generation might attain life without end.
49. If this is so then why have people kept on dying since Christ's coming? The experience of death is not removed, but the reality of eternal life is given within the experience of death.
50. Even if all this may be granted, does it not simply show that Christ was only a servant among servants, as "he is called in your books?"[67] It is true that the prophet Isaiah refers to the servant of

---

[66] 'Kitāb al-masā'il', pages 127-146.
[67] 'Kitāb al-masā'il', 259f.

God carrying the sin of the people; but this way of speaking is not used by Christ, who calls himself 'bread', 'a door', 'the way', 'light', 'life' and 'resurrection'. However, the Messiah uses the title 'servant' not of himself, but of people enslaved to sin. When Isaiah the prophet spoke of the servant of God carrying the sin of others, he was looking forward to Christ taking away sin from those enslaved to it. This is what Christ himself said he had come to do, when he told the apostles to eat bread and drink wine in memory of his death.

51. If you claim that there is no eating and drinking and other pleasures in the life to come is this life not preferable to such a future life? There is no pleasure in food and drink when hunger and thirst cannot be satisfied. The bodies in the new life will not be subject to the same desires as in this life.

EVALUATION

`Ammār and Abū Rā'iṯa both answer questions concerning the way Christ removes sin inherited from Adam. `Ammār focuses on the opportunity for eternal life opened up by Christ for Adam's descendents, whereas Abū Rā'iṯa emphasizes the necessity for God to show his goodness in the Incarnation as a result of Adam's fall involving his descendents in evil.[68] This difference is in line with `Ammār's special interest in the resurrection in his answers to questions 32 to 35. `Ammār answers a question about the possible use of the title 'servant of God' for Christ, which fits a Muslim perception of him. `Ammār concedes that Christ is given the title by others but does not use it himself. He argues that Muslim preference for such language should not disguise the fact that Christ calls himself names that imply a much more exalted status. In other words Muslim language to describe Christ is valid in a limited sense, but must be supplemented by the testimony of the gospels.

Conclusion

`Ammār shares with Abū Qurra and Abū Rā'iṯa similar vocabulary to describe the Incarnation, by using *tajassada* and *ta`anassa* for the manner in which the eternal Word becomes human. Like Abū Rā'iṯa he understands the eternal Word to have fashioned a human nature for himself from the human issue from Mary. However, the human nature created by the eternal Word can be compared to a temple in which God dwells, or a turban that adorns the divine head, or even weapons that he takes up. These metaphors inherited from Nestorian tradition suggest that the human nature of Christ was somehow external to his divine consciousness, and that the thinking,

[68] For Abū Rā'iṯa's argument see chapter four:53f.

feeling and willing of Christ was solely the divine nature at work at the heart of the human clothing, but they are at variance with `Ammār's insistence on the testing of Christ's obedience to the will of God. Unlike Abū Qurra and Abū Rā'iṯa, `Ammār argues that the purity of Christ is not guaranteed by the creation of a sinless human nature before the union of the divine and human natures. Rather, the sinless Incarnate one had to prove his obedience to the divine will right to the end of his earthly life, since only at the end could he be pronounced pure of any kind of wrongdoing. There is a paradox in a truly human experience of testing and the use of the metaphors of temple, turban and arms that hardly allows for any real human experience for Christ. If the human nature was merely an inanimate shell for the eternal Word then why would the latter need to be tested for submission?

In the end, the theme of testing is more significant in the Christology of `Ammār than the clothing or temple metaphors, for he painstakingly argues for the unfolding obedience of Christ as if disobedience was a real possibility. Indeed it is this struggle to obey the will of God that gives `Ammār's Christ a real human nature, despite the metaphors that imply the opposite. `Ammār then wishes to make room for a human Christ within a set of metaphors that are inadequate for the task. He sees the human mind interacting with the divine mind in Christ, which leaves the metaphors far behind. The apologetic value of the testing of Christ would have been considerable, since the fact that Christ is tested by God would have enabled Muslims to recognize a human Christ in `Ammār's presentation more readily than in any of the others from the eighth and ninth centuries. Even his fellow Nestorian, Timothy I, did not argue for the continued testing of Christ in his debate with al-Mahdī. One of the serious difficulties with the Incarnation for Muslims lay in the notion that the eternal Word was the thinking, feeling and willing centre of Christ, because such a notion robbed him of humanity. Since `Ammār allowed for a dynamic interchange between divinity and humanity in the life experiences of Christ, his presentation was an advance on the apologetic alternatives on offer in the early ninth century.

`Ammār's three analogies for the purpose of the Incarnation in the Book of Questions and Answers are excellent means of communication with Muslims. The parable of the king having his son born among his people who then brings the people into his father's inheritance shows the loving identification of God with humans that the Incarnation seeks to uphold. The prizefighter who exhausts himself in defeating his opponent, and the doctor who takes poison before giving it to his patient, show the lengths to which God is prepared to go to rescue humans from death, the key idea behind the death of Christ. These stories expound the importance of the Incarnation and the atonement in imaginative ways that would probably have made a favorable impression on Muslims. Other analogies that `Ammār uses may not have hit their target. The second and third of his four reasons for the Incarnation in *The Book of the Proof* were more likely to offend Muslims by challenging their belief in the strict transcendence of God. The idea that since humans tend to make images of divine beings God condescended to their level through the Incarnation, and the picture of God making himself visible to those he would judge out of compassion for them, would probably be understood by Muslims to make God a promoter of idolatry.

`Ammār's presentation of the death of Christ is original and compelling in three respects. Firstly, in *The Book of the Proof* he argues that the humiliation of Christ, so unacceptable to Muslims, can be mitigated by the honour he is given by God as a result of his defeat of death. Therefore the shame of his crucifixion is outweighed by the glory he is able to grant to other humans whose death is transcended as a result of the cross. Muslims may have been able to perceive that someone who lays down his life in a shameful fashion could give honour to others in the process, and so be praised for seeking the greater glory of others. Secondly, his distinction between divine attributes related to Christ's human nature and others that are separate helps to hold together the divine and human natures of Christ at his death. If eternity is not imparted to the humanity of Christ then it is not lost at death as Muslims may think must be the case. On the other hand, if God's power and authority are imparted to his humanity then these are lost at the point of death. There is a temporary loss of these divine attributes between the time of death and the resurrection of Christ in God's power and authority. This is a distinction unique to `Ammār, which goes a long way to answering the question also asked in the writing of Timothy, Abū Qurra and Abū Rā'iṯa, how it is that the divine nature can die, without losing control of the created world. Whereas the other three apologists simply deny that the divine dies and that only the human experiences death, `Ammār shows that some aspects of divinity can cease to be part of Christ at death. However, the fundamental characteristic of God's nature, his eternity, is unaffected by death. This dialectical Christology is much more flexible in an Islamic context than the more rigid separation of divine and human found in the apologetics of Timothy, Abū Qurra and Abū Rā'iṯa.

Thirdly, his emphasis on the resurrection of Christ as a guarantee that death can be overcome for others is unique among eighth and ninth century apologists. The weakness of any theoretical offer of life beyond death lies in the lack of assurance that it will actually happen, but this is not the case for those who believe that Christ went through death into a new life. Here is the evidence that others can follow him after death into life. Such an indirect challenge to Muslims to see if they have similar evidence for their resurrection is met with the idea that Christ was raised without going through death, but `Ammār points out that humans need to be assured that death will not overcome them. It is altogether more reassuring for the rest of humanity if Christ did die before being raised to life. The Muslim response would probably rely on the will of God finally determining the destiny of human beings beyond this life, but here `Ammār has shown that in the resurrection of Christ there is a promise that humans can rely on.

These distinctive arguments show both that `Ammār was searching for creative ways to defend the two natures Christology inherited from his Nestorian tradition and that he was prepared to develop new ways of forming Christology in the context of dialogue with Muslims. The new developments are seen in the emphasis placed on the testing of the human nature of Christ, and in the distinctions between types of divine attributes that impacted Christ's human nature. Even if Muslims appreciated the rounded human portrait of Christ offered here, they probably were not convinced by the equation of divine attributes of power and authority at work in Christ with the actual presence of God in him. Nevertheless, `Ammār's presentation of Christ for Muslims is the most comprehensive in his epoch, offering a more detailed treatment than Abū Rā'iṯa of the issues facing Christians in their understanding of Christ in a Muslim context.

Chapter Six

The Christologies of Abū Qurra, Abū Rā'iṯa and `Ammār al-Baṣrī and Muslim Response

Two questions arising from the apologetics of Abū Qurra, Abū Rā'iṯa, and `Ammār al-Baṣrī will be explored in this chapter. Firstly, what developments in Christology can be observed as a result of engagement with the Islamic context? Secondly, what impact did these presentations of Christology have on Muslims? In answer to the first question, Sydney Griffith has suggested that Islam forced Christian theologians in the Middle East to make an intelligible case for their beliefs.[1] He sums up Abū Rā'iṯa's Christological apologetics as an attempt to support "the reasonableness or the non-contradictory nature" of the Incarnation.[2] This is an apt judgment of Abū Rā'iṯa in particular among the three apologists, but it is a verdict that can also be applied to Abū Qurra and `Ammār to a large extent. An examination of the arguments employed by the three men to demonstrate the reasonableness of the Incarnation will show to what extent this conclusion is true. If Griffith is right, then the development in the writing of Christology is to be seen especially in the justification of the notion of Incarnation as worthy of God given the prevailing conception of his nature.

The second question can be answered by studying the writing of Muslims on Christianity. Despite the fact that the refutations of Abū Qurra by `Īsā ibn Sabīh al-Murdār (d.840), and of `Ammār by Abū l-Hudhayl (d.c.840) are no longer extant, it is possible to discover the views of other Muslims about the Incarnation.[3] The criticisms by several ninth and tenth century Muslim authors of Christological affirmations made by Christians provide an indication of the impact of Christian apologetics in the period. These writers are al-Qāsim ibn Ibrāhīm al-Ḫasanī al-Rassī (d. 860), `Ali ibn Rabbān al-Ṯabarī (d. 855), Abū `Īsā al-Warrāq (d. 861), al-Nāshi' al-Akbar (d. 904), and Muḫammad ibn al-Ṯayyib al-Bāqillānī (d. 1014).[4]

[1] S.H. Griffith, 'Ḫabīb ibn Hidmah Abū Rā'iṯah, a Christian *mutakallim* of the First Abbasid Century', *OC* 64 (1980), 161-201, 161.

[2] *Ibid.*, 192.

[3] These refutations by leading Mu'tazilite scholars are mentioned in B. Dodge, *The Fihrist of al-Nadīm, a Tenth Century Survey of Muslim Culture,* vol. 1, 388 & 394.

[4] There are two other Muslim commentators on Christology who are not expounded here. Abū `Alī al-Jubba'ī (850-914) gives a brief summary of the three main Christologies without offering a critique. The tenth century writer `Abd al-Jabbār

The Christology of Abū Qurra

Developments in the Language of Christology

Abū Qurra's Christological summaries show similarities and differences between his Christology in dialogue with other Christians and his Christology in dialogue with Muslims. The Christological summary in his *Confession of the Orthodox Faith* written in the context of dialogue with other Christians may be compared with the one in his *Treatise on the Atonement* written in the context of dialogue with Muslims.[5] Two similarities are striking in the Muslim context. Firstly, Christ is called 'the eternal Son' in dialogue with Muslims as much as in debate with Christians. Use of the term 'son' would surely have been understood by a Muslim as a direct denial of the Qur'ānic assertion that God had no son, but Abū Qurra did not resort to calling Christ by the more Qur'ānic title 'word'. Secondly, Christ is 'begotten of God before time' in both summaries, but the term 'begotten' would probably be understood by Muslims as a challenge to the Qur'ānic denial that God begets. It appears then that Abū Qurra did not attempt to redesign the language of his Christology at these points in order to accommodate Qur'ānic conceptions of Christ. Three differences seem to be intentional changes for a Muslim context. Firstly, he drops the concept of 'hypostasis' when writing with Muslims in mind. In the *Confession*, he says that the eternal Son "formed for his hypostasis a living body", whereas in his *Treatise on the Atonement* he writes that the eternal Son "took a body, making it like himself". For Muslims he spells out the mechanics of the Incarnation in a way that he could take for granted in the Christian context. For Christians he writes of the eternal Son forming a body to accommodate both human and divine natures, but for Muslims he describes the entry of the eternal Son into Mary's womb to extract a human body from her in order to shape it into his own likeness. Abū Qurra then appears to be interpreting inherited theological language in the Muslim context so that technical terms do not impede understanding.

Secondly, Abū Qurra does not describe two natures in Christ when writing for Muslims, so setting aside the key element that defined the Christology of his own community in favour of terms that would communicate clearly to Muslims what all Christians believed about the Incarnation. Thirdly, in his search for language more understandable to Muslims, Abū Qurra appears to have used the expression 'took' in the light of the Qur'ānic denial that God took to himself a son. Here he asserts that it is the Son who took to himself a human body. The idea of the eternal Son

---

gives a fuller account of Christology, but seems to be dependent on Abū `Īsā al-Warrāq for his information and provides no fresh evaluation of his own.

[5] See chapter three.

'taking' a human body was not a traditional way of describing the Incarnation in Christian theology. At the beginning of his *Treatise on the Incarnation* Abū Qurra has the Muslim use the verb in his very first question, "How can the Son who is divine want to take a body in which he will suffer?"[6] He represents the Muslim using the language of "taking a body" rather than the usual Christian language of "becoming human". Abū Qurra probably believed that such a shift in language facilitated dialogue with Muslims. Whether Muslims actually used this manner of speaking is debatable, but putting such a question on the lips of his fictitious Muslim enabled Abū Qurra to communicate the Incarnation in a way that Muslims might find more acceptable. These three changes in language are modest and leave most of the traditional Chalcedonian terminology in place. Abū Qurra's aim seems to have been to modify that tradition where he could without losing its essential elements when addressing a Muslim context. More important for him were arguments supporting that tradition based on Islamic patterns of thought.

Arguments for the Incarnation

Abū Qurra used three arguments to demonstrate the reasonableness of the Incarnation. The first of these is based on the Qur'ānic picture of God seated on his throne which allows Abū Qurra to show that there are situations where it is appropriate for the divine to interact with the created world.[7] Discussion among Muslim scholars in the early `Abbasid period about the anthropomorphisms of the Qur'ān provided Abū Qurra with an opportunity to engage in an Islamic debate as a Christian. If the Mu'tazila thought that nothing could be learned from the anthropomorphisms of the Qur'ān about the nature of God, and if the Traditionists held that it is not possible for us to know how God sits on a throne and is present elsewhere at the same time, then Abū Qurra offers a third interpretation which could be more satisfying.[8] If the Incarnation is true then it becomes a key to interpret God's relationship with the created world, because God restricted himself to a human body while at the same time leaving himself free to be elsewhere ruling the world. According to Abū Qurra, this Christian reading of God's session on a throne is ultimately more satisfactory than any interpretation offered by Muslims because it allows us to say that this is

[6] Abū Qurra, 'Treatise on the Incarnation', in Bacha, 180.

[7] His *Treatise on the Incarnation* is a sustained defense of the reasonableness of the incarnation based on the implications of God's session on his throne.

[8] For a good summary of Islamic debate on Qur'ānic anthropomorphisms in the early ninth century see the introduction to B. Abrahamov, *Anthropomorphism and Interpretation of the Qur'ān in the Theology of Al-Qāsim ibn Ibrāhīm* (Leiden: 1996), 1-18.

how God works in his world. There is a solution to the apparent paradox of God limiting himself to a particular place, and it is to believe that God is at one and the same time limited and unlimited. But only the Incarnation gives this solution. Only the fact that the divine becomes limited to the human body without becoming trapped there allows this third way of reading the throne texts. By engaging with Muslim forms of argumentation he forced intellectual Muslims to take him seriously as an equal, and offered an apologetic that worked as long as Muslims themselves debated the interpretation of anthropomorphisms.

The second argument defending the Incarnation is that the body indwelt by the divine nature was perfectly adapted for the purpose so that no imperfection could cross over from the human to the divine. Abū Qurra has the Muslim raise the issue of impurity. "It is undeniable that God sits on the throne but he does not take up residence in the body. The throne is pure but the human body is not suitable for God."[9] Here is the heart of the problem for Muslims. The purity of God must be preserved at all costs, but Incarnation automatically destroys purity. The logic of transcendence must be maintained in the face of Christian denial. Abū Qurra seeks to defend divine enfleshment by taking 'impurity' out of the discussion. He alludes to the Qur'ānic belief in the purity of Christ expressed in *sūra* 19:19 as a basis for his argument that in the case of Christ there is no suspicion of impurity in his nature. His own interpretation of that purity is that the Holy Spirit cleansed the human body taken from Mary before the eternal Son united himself with it, and so God himself guaranteed the purity of the human body by his own action. This is a very significant argument in the light of *sūra* 19:19, because it offers to Muslims a way of seeing human flesh as fitting for God's indwelling. If Gabriel announced to Mary that she was to bear a 'pure boy' then it follows that Christ was conceived without any defect. But then this purity is a perfect ground for the union of divine and human natures. Muslims cannot claim that indwelling this pure human body taints God's pure character. Therefore the Incarnation is not an unreasonable idea when it implies a union of divine and human natures. The appeal to purity could possibly have provoked Muslims to rethink their distaste for such a union, and despite their probable rejection of the Incarnation as undermining transcendence, they may have become aware of one reason why Christians believed in the Incarnation.

Thirdly, in his *Treatise on Sonship* Abū Qurra deploys another argument based on the anthropomorphisms of the Qur'ān. The treatise sets out to deal with the Muslim suspicion that Incarnation implies physical begetting on God's part. The opening question of the Muslim is, "how can God give birth in the light of the fact that a man only has offspring after intercourse

[9] Abū Qurra, 'Treatise on the Incarnation', in Bacha, 183.

with a woman?"[10] Abū Qurra's answer is a counter-question, "if you accept that God can be called the One who hears and the Wise, why can't you accept that he can be called the Father?"[11] He appeals to the Mu'tazilite interpretation of the divine attributes in this question, since if they are correct in supposing that God does not actually have ears with which to hear, then Christians are correct in holding that God does not actually have a child in the normal way. Christians are not guilty of attributing physical fatherhood to God. They speak of fatherhood and sonship in a non-physical sense because the relationship of father and son exists outside time and space. Therefore God cannot have given birth to a son in the sense that human fathers do, since the Son lives forever with the Father. The logic of the Incarnation is dependent on the definition of God as Father of the Son from all eternity. Muslim acceptance of the validity of this argument would depend on a fresh reading of the Qur'ānic texts that denied that God begot a son, but this was probably unlikely given the outright rejection of the language of sonship in the Qur'ān.

These three defensive arguments support Griffiths' view that Christian apologists in the early `Abbasid period were concerned to uphold the non-contradictory nature of the Incarnation. Abū Qurra used debate among Muslims as a resource for Christian apologetics in order to draw attention to conceptual difficulties encountered by Muslims in their understanding of God's action in the world. A purely transcendent interpretation of the anthropomorphisms of the Qur'ān leads to the emptying of such expressions of their meaning. On the other hand, a willingness to accept that God acts in the world without a willingness to understand how he acts leads to an inability to make sense of God's character. However, Christian belief in the Incarnation provides us with a way to bring the transcendence of God into ordinary human life without sacrificing God's otherness, and it also shows how God works in his world without becoming restricted to it. Abū Qurra's three arguments are still useful for Christians who want to uphold the Incarnation in a Muslim context.

The Christology of Abū Rā'iṯa

Developments in the Language of Christology

The Christological summary in Abū Rā'iṯa's dialogue with Abū Qurra may be compared with the one in his *Treatise on Christianity* written with an

[10] Abū Qurra, 'Treatise on Sonship', in Bacha, 94. See chapter two:22 for a similar question posed by al-Mahdī to Timothy.

[11] Abū Qurra, 'Treatise on Sonship', in Bacha, 95.

Islamic context in mind.[12] Both summaries present the eternal Word as uniting with human flesh from Mary, with the result that there was one nature consisting of divine and human characteristics. Abū Rā'iṯa presents a Miaphysite Christology in both contexts. The divine and human aspects of Christ are not two natures because the human aspect cannot be equal to the divine without infringing the character of God. The divine hypostasis takes on human characteristics after the union with human personality. This divine hypostasis is equivalent to the divine nature, so Melkites like Abū Qurra are wrong to speak of nature and hypostasis as distinct.

Within the substantial agreement between the two summaries are four differences that show an adjustment to an Islamic audience. Firstly, Abū Rā'iṯa drops the expression 'the eternal Son' in the Muslim context, for unlike Abū Qurra, he seems to be more sensitive to Islamic rejection of sonship for Christ. Therefore, he uses the phrase 'the eternal Word' because he probably believes that it is less open to misunderstanding by Muslims. Secondly, there is no mention of God as 'Father' in the summary for Muslims, which further reduces the risk of misunderstanding by Muslims. Thirdly, he uses the verb 'take' in the apology for Muslims but not in the dialogue with Melkites, to refer to a divine 'taking' of a human body. Like Abū Qurra, Abū Rā'iṯa appears to be offering a reflection on the Qur'ānic teaching that God did not take to himself a son by suggesting that it was not God who took a son, but the eternal Word of God who took a human body. This sharing of the same linguistic innovation by Abū Rā'iṯa and Abū Qurra may be traceable to an earlier apologist whose work is not available today. Alternatively, one of them may have been the source of the innovation, but it would be difficult to know the direction of borrowing, given the facts that they debated with each other and that their writing cannot be dated with enough precision to judge who borrowed from whom. Fourthly, he uses the Islamic term *ṣifāt* to describe the divine and human aspects of Christ. Muslims used *ṣifāt* for the attributes of God such as hearing, seeing, knowing and willing, but Abū Rā'iṯa applies the idea to Christ. This enables him to argue that in Christ there is one divine nature which has two attributes, just as in God there is one nature with several attributes. This is Jacobite one-nature Christology being interpreted in a way that Muslims might be able to understand through the use of the language of attributes. For if Muslims were able to hold that God was one even with many attributes, then Christians could point out that they believe that the divine nature in Christ is one even when it has human characteristics. This is a significant innovation by Abū Rā'iṯa which arises out of his Miaphysite tradition but is not determined by it. Rather the new context of engagement with Islamic language provides him with the linguistic resources to develop a novel description of the union of divine

[12] See chapter four.

and human characteristics in Christ that would perhaps make sense of the union to Muslims.

These four linguistic innovations show that Abū Rā'iṯa was alert to the need for sensitivity to Islamic discourse in a more thorough fashion than Abū Qurra. They also challenge Sydney Griffith's claim that Abū Rā'iṯa had both Melkites and Muslims in view in his apologetic writing so that "we should not assume that his quarrel with these two groups, especially as it was conducted in Arabic, was aimed in two different directions."[13] This opinion is surprising in the light of his earlier statement that "the Arabic language became the catalyst for new thought models in Christian theology, especially in as much as Arabic was and is inextricably intertwined with an Islamic religious consciousness."[14] It would be more accurate to say that Abū Rā'iṯa wrote for two different audiences. In his argument with Melkites he used concepts translated into Arabic from Syriac, but in his apologetic work addressed to Muslims he removed some traditional Christological terminology that might be misunderstood and adopted some Islamic concepts that might make Christology more understandable.

Arguments for the Incarnation

In his Letter on the Incarnation Abū Rā'iṯa presents five arguments which attempt to show the reasonableness of the Incarnation to Muslims. Two of them are shared with Abū Qurra. The first of these shared arguments is the defence of Christ's sonship as being outside time, and the second is the defence of the human body as suitable for union with the divine nature by means of interpretation of the session of God on his throne.[15] The need to place the concept of 'sonship' outside time was obviously felt by all Christians in dialogue with Muslims, since the Nestorian Timothy I, the Melkite Abū Qurra, and the Jacobite, Abū Rā'iṯa used the same argument. These three Christian communities had a common understanding of the Father/Son analogy which gave them a theological unity in the face of the Islamic denial of 'son' as a true descriptive category for Christ. If the sonship of Christ was not from eternity then Muslims were right to reject it as demeaning to God's character. On the other hand, if Muslims could see that Christ's sonship is a non-physical notion, then they would have no grounds for rejecting the idea as unworthy of God.

The second argument shared with Abū Qurra is the use of the session of God on his throne to point out to Muslims that God can be in the world without ceasing to be transcendent over it. If Muslims reject any suggestion that God is confined to the throne then Christians can claim that the divine

---

[13] See S.H. Griffith, 'Ḫabīb ibn Hidmah Abū Rā'iṯa', 168.
[14] *Ibid.*, 165.
[15] Abū Rā'iṯa, 'Letter on the Incarnation', questions 32-34 and 26-29.

nature indwells the human body of Christ but is not confined to it. Whereas Abū Qurra alluded to contemporary debate among Muslims, Abū Rā'iṯa engages directly in debate with Islamic interpretation of the throne texts of the Qur'ān. "God is in heaven and on the throne" must mean that he is Lord of heaven and Lord of the throne, and that God is in heaven and the throne and does not just appear in them.[16] His much more direct challenge to Muslim interpretation of the Qur'ān would no doubt have evoked a more immediate response than Abū Qurra's less direct argument, though the conclusion of the argument would probably have been unacceptable to Muslims whichever way it was presented.

There are three new arguments put forward by Abū Rā'iṯa. The first of these appeals to Muslim understanding of the attributes of God to support the Incarnation of the second person of the Trinity. If Muslims define God as knowing, willing and performing, they have to admit that these attributes do not always function together. If God allows evildoers to enter paradise then he knows and performs what he does not will, the entry of evil people into paradise. Yet Muslims claim that these apparently contradictory attributes do not affect the unity of God. On the same basis, Christians claim that when "one of the three hypostases became Incarnate without the other two" all three remained united. Diversity in attributes does not destroy unity in nature.[17] The second novel argument in support of the Incarnation makes use of the relationship between the human mind and body to explain the way the divine and human attributes work together in Christ. Abū Rā'iṯa has the Muslim ask whether the water of the womb is essential to the divine nature as a result of the Incarnation. The reply is negative since the physical body is no more essential to the divine nature of Christ than a human body is essential to a human personality.[18] If a Muslim grants that there is a kind of duality in human beings as a result of the union of non-material mind with material body then he might be prepared to entertain the possibility that non-material divine nature has united with material human nature. It is not nonsense for Christians to believe that divine and human characteristics have united in Christ.

The third innovative argument concerns the relationship between Christ and other messengers of God. The Muslim wonders why it is not more fitting for God to send a pure human to save humanity than to become human himself. Abū Rā'iṯa concedes that God did send human messengers such as Noah, Abraham and Moses but few listened to them. God could not save humanity merely by sending more of the same, so he decided to solve the problem through the Incarnation. There were two advantages to this decision; when people saw the divine nature in human flesh they were more

[16] *Ibid.*, question 29.
[17] *Ibid.*, question 6.
[18] *Ibid.*, question 7.

able to respond to God's will, and in addition, God was able to show his goodness in a way that would not have been possible merely through messengers.[19] Here Abū Rā'iṯa appeals to the Qur'ānic sequence of prophetic messengers familiar to Muslims, but takes Christ out of the list into a separate category. This argument that Christ is superior to all other messengers flies in the face of the presentation of Christ in the Qur'ān where he is presented as one among several messengers who stand together as equals in God's sight. Abū Rā'iṯa directly challenges the clear teaching of the Qur'ān, a method he usually avoids. Acceptance of the initial premise that Christ was superior to other messengers because of his divinity would depend on a leap of faith by a Muslim that seems highly unlikely. Elsewhere, Abū Rā'iṯa tended to begin his arguments for the Incarnation with premises acceptable to Muslims before attempting to reach Christian conclusions. As a result this argument is not as useful in dialogue with Muslims as the four others surveyed.

Abū Rā'iṯa does not develop a fresh Christology in dialogue with Muslims. His apologetic strategy does nevertheless force him to argue for the reasonableness of his view of Christ in the light of Islamic convictions. Unlike Abū Qurra, he is explicit about the nature of Muslim thought, even to the point of relying on the teaching of the Qur'ān to support his own argument. The presupposition seems to be that, properly understood, a Christian view of Christ is not incompatible with Islamic conceptions of him.

The Christology of `Ammār al-Baṣrī

A Defence of Nestorian Christology

`Ammār's known Christological writing is addressed to Muslims, and if he wrote for a Christian context only, his writing is not available. It is then not possible to compare his Christology for Muslims with a Christology for Christians. However, a comparison can be made between the apologetics of `Ammār, Abū Qurra and Abū Rā'iṯa. `Ammār's description of the Incarnation differs from Abū Qurra's and Abū Rā'iṯa's in his insistence on talking of a unity of two natures in two hypostases. He acknowledges this difference in his shorter apologetic work, *The Book of the Proof*.[20] In the answers to fifty-one questions he also affirms this two natures, two hypostases view. He finds it necessary in dialogue with Muslims to show why this view is more accurate than those of the Melkites and the Miaphysites. According to `Ammār this view safeguards God from

[19] *Ibid.*, questions 13-18, especially the answer to 18.

[20] `Ammār al-Baṣrī, 'The Book of the Proof', 62.

becoming embodied. Miaphysites have to concede that God is embodied because they claim that there is only a divine nature in the Messiah. Melkites are subject to the same difficulty, since God must be embodied if Mary is God's mother.[21] Clearly `Ammār believes that a Nestorian Christology is less susceptible to Muslim objections than rival ones. `Ammār then, in dialoguing with Muslims, is conducting another debate with Christian rivals, using the Islamic context to show that Nestorian Christology is truer than other types of Christology. It is almost as if the Nestorian is grateful to Islam for providing a platform for re-instating the anathematized Nestorian teaching to its rightful place as the truth.[22]

Arguments for the Incarnation

`Ammār uses three arguments found in other apologetic writing. Firstly, he shares with Timothy I, Abū Qurra, and Abū Rā'iṯa the argument that the begetting of the Son by the Father was outside time and therefore unlike human procreation. `Ammār's version of the argument is different because he appeals to Islamic interpretation of the attributes of God to support a non-physical understanding of the Father/Son relationship. Since Muslims do not interpret the knowledge and wisdom of God according to human knowledge and wisdom, the fatherhood of God should not be interpreted according to the way humans understand fatherhood. If God's attributes are eternal and non-physical then the sonship of Christ must also be eternal and non-physical.[23] This way of putting the argument is more sophisticated than his contemporaries' versions that simply state that Christians do not understand the sonship of Christ as bound by time, and therefore has greater usefulness in dialogue with Muslims.

Secondly, in common with his contemporary apologists he holds that the human characteristics of Christ do not adversely affect the divine nature, since the suffering of Christ was endured only by his human nature. If this is difficult to imagine then he suggests the analogy of coal that is heated by fire but does not impart blackness to it.[24] This analogy is particular to `Ammār's presentation of the argument, again showing his desire to support the Christian case with ideas that might appeal to Muslims as reasonable. Thirdly, he shares with Abū Rā'iṯa the related argument that the divine nature is not limited by the humanity of Christ, but adds an analogy to help the Muslim to see the sense of the argument. The divine nature relates to

---

[21] `Ammār al-Baṣrī, 'The Book of Questions and Answers', question 12.

[22] See P.K. Hitti, *History of the Arabs* (London: 1970), 354f, for the rivalry between Nestorians and other Christians to be accepted as 'true' representatives of Christianity to their Islamic rulers.

[23] 'The Book of the Proof', 59.

[24] 'The Book of Questions and Answers', questions 5 and 8.

the human nature in the same way that the sun lights up the earth without being limited to it.[25]

`Ammār has several arguments not found in other Christian apologetic writing in the period. They are of two kinds; arguments that are based on Islamic premises, and arguments that show the value of the Incarnation once the idea is granted as possible. He has two innovative arguments based on Islamic premises. Firstly, in order to deal with the denial that God begets in *sūra* 112:3, he refers to the divine attributes of mercy and anger which imply that God suffers. If Muslims hold that, in fact, God does not suffer despite the apparent meaning of 'anger' and 'mercy', then Christians are justified in believing that the Father can have a Son without 'begetting' imputing imperfection to God in any way.[26] Secondly, `Ammār appeals to the manner of God's creative work to present the process of Incarnation. If Muslims do not know how God created the world then it is not a weakness for Christians to be ignorant about the way the divine nature united with the human nature in Christ. `Ammār's reminder that agnosticism about the actions of God is a necessary position for both Muslims and Christians has a continuing validity, though there will always be a contention between Muslims and Christians concerning divine actions deemed admissible by one side or the other.[27]

`Ammār is especially interested in showing Muslims the value of the Incarnation for faith in God, despite the fact that Islam seems to reject the idea. He has six arguments commending the Incarnation as inherently true that do not depend on premises held by Muslims. Four of them come from *The Book of the Proof*. The first of these states that since human messengers cannot show God's character, only God Incarnate can enable people to see him. Christ did exactly this when he revealed to the people of his day his divine authority.[28] This appeal to the historical Jesus of the Gospels is unusual in ninth century apologetics, which are typically focused on the developed Christology of the Christian communities of the Middle East. Secondly, God chose to become visible to people as an act of mercy, in recognition of the fact that people make images of the divine in their search for him. This is sheer condescension by God who knows that the weakness of humans needs to be taken into consideration in the process of revelation and salvation.[29] Here `Ammār probably has made too strong a connection between God's choice to become visible in Christ and the supposed need of humans to see God, because Christians normally affirm

---

[25] *Ibid.*, question 11.

[26] 'The Book of the Proof', 62.

[27] See the debate on such admissibility between Kenneth Cragg and Ismā'īl al-Farūqī in chapter eight:136-138.

[28] 'The Book of the Proof', 65.

[29] 'The Book of the Proof', 67.

the former but not the latter. Moreover, in the context of dialogue with Muslims this argument is flawed, since it seems to suggest that the desire to visualize God is acceptable to him, an idea which the Qur'ān flatly opposes.

The third argument is related to the second in that `Ammār again uses the notion of the desired visibility of God for human beings. This time the visibility comes at the Day of Judgment when humanity will appear before the divine judge, but since God cannot be seen directly on that day, he has chosen Christ as an appropriate means of being seen.[30] However, the idea that the human Christ is God's veil in the judgment room is less than appropriate to the argument, because it follows that God is not seen as such, but only the veil of Christ's human nature. A Muslim would rightly infer that since veils hide rather than reveal, `Ammār is actually arguing for the hiddenness rather than the revelation of the divine nature. The fourth argument has to do with the outcome of judgment for those being saved. If God gave humans authority over the rest of the created world, then he will surely give them similar authority in the eternal world. This is guaranteed by the Incarnation of the divine nature in the human.[31] The idea of believers ruling with Christ in the afterlife is found in the New Testament but not as a result of the Incarnation as such.[32] `Ammār seems to be arguing that human beings can only rule as a result of the fact that the human Christ showed his divine authority, and that without the Incarnation there would be no rule for believers in the next life. However, the argument lacks coherence in the form in which `Ammār expresses it, and would therefore be hardly likely to commend the Incarnation to a Muslim.

Two further arguments for the value of the Incarnation come from *The Book of Questions and Answers*. Firstly, the Incarnation is supported by the purity of Christ from the beginning to the end of his life. While Abū Qurra and Abū Rā'iṯa both appealed to the purification of the human body taken from Mary before the union with the divine nature, only `Ammār argues that the maintenance of that purity is significant for the Incarnation to be verified. At least one other human being is said to have been pure at the point of conception, according to `Ammār, so it is not enough for Christ to be pure at the outset of his life. He quotes Jeremiah 1:4 as evidence that God purified the prophet Jeremiah in the womb, and goes on to argue that Christ could have lost his purity during his life, but, unlike the rest of humanity, he kept himself pure.[33] The implication of this testing of Christ throughout his life is that the human nature in Christ has a role to play alongside the work of the divine nature. The divine nature does not need to be tested for it is always perfect, but the human nature does need to be

---

30 *Ibid.*, 69.

31 *Ibid.*, 72.

32 See for example Ephesians 2:6 and Revelation 20:6, 21:5.

33 'The Book of Questions and Answers', questions 23-26.

tested to prove its continuing suitability as an abode for the divine nature. Here `Ammār parts company from the emphases of Abū Qurra and Abū Rā'iṯa, for whom the fact that the eternal Word fashioned a body from the flesh derived from Mary ensures the continuing purity of that human nature. This is not adequate according to `Ammār, since the human nature taken from Mary may be susceptible to failure after the union with the divine. He believes that the human nature in Christ was active in responding to the will of God, which contrasts with Abū Rā'iṯa's assumption that only the eternal Word responds to God's will. `Ammār's Christ has human struggles that Abū Rā'iṯa's seems to know nothing of. This conviction arises from the fact that Christ can only save other humans if he has gone through the same experiences as they have. The continuing relevance of this argument can be seen in the way Karl Pfander in the nineteenth century and Kenneth Cragg in the twentieth century appealed to the obedience of Christ as essential to his value for humanity.[34]

The second innovative argument in *The Book of Questions and Answers* follows on from the establishment of Christ's complete obedience to the will of the Father. The culmination of that obedience involved death on the cross to release humans from the judgment of God and to grant them eternal life. The value of Christ's death and resurrection lies in the gift of resurrection life to humanity. `Ammār's analogies of a prizefighter using up all his strength to defeat an opponent, and of a doctor swallowing poison before administering harmful medicine are interesting attempts to commend the idea to Muslims. It was not enough for Christ to promise the resurrected life to others without offering proof that it could happen, so he willingly submitted to death and resurrection to "place firmly in their hearts the promise of their resurrection".[35] This is an argument for the Incarnation that looks to the end rather than the beginning of the action, thus Incarnation is not defined merely by the commencement of a union between the divine and human natures as Abū Qurra and Abū Rā'iṯa seem to argue. Without the willing submission of Christ to death there is no guarantee that death can be overcome, and without the resurrection of Christ there can be no certainty that humans will have a life beyond this one. `Ammār's argument is based on the teaching of several New Testament texts,[36] and has often been repeated in modern apologetics for Muslims.[37]

---

[34] See chapter seven for Pfander and chapter eight for Cragg.

[35] 'The Book of Questions and Answers', questions 30-34.

[36] See for instance John 11:25f; Acts 2:31f; and 1Corinthians 15:21-23.

[37] See the use made of the voluntary death of Christ by Pfander in chapter seven, Cragg in chapter eight, and Küng in chapter nine.

Muslim Responses to Christian Views of Christ in the Ninth and Tenth Centuries

The Truth about Christ Comes from the Qur'ān

The first type of response was to appeal to the Qur'ān as the measure by which to judge Christian beliefs. This was the approach of al-Qāsim ibn Ibrāhīm al-Ḫasanī al-Rassī (d. 860) who wrote a *Reply to the Christians* possibly in the period from 815 to 826 during which he debated with Christians in Egypt. If this is the case his *Reply* is the earliest surviving Muslim writing against Christian beliefs.[38] Al-Qāsim documents the three main Christian presentations of the Incarnation by Melkites, Jacobites and Nestorians before concluding that all of them depart from the teaching of "the prophets and apostles of God".[39] He does not actually specify at what points Christian teaching on the Incarnation diverges from that of the Qur'ān, but he may have taken for granted that his Muslim audience did not need much assistance with such a critique. His intention seems to have been to provide Muslim readers with an accurate reference work of Christian thought, as can be seen in his description of the Incarnation. Melkites believe that the Messiah had two natures, divine and human, in one hypostasis; Jacobites hold that the divine nature and the human nature are one, "just as the human spirit and body are one;" and Nestorians claim that the Messiah had two natures and two hypostases.[40] These are good summaries of the three main Christian positions, even noting the distinctive mind/body analogy used only by Jacobites.

Alongside the presentation of separate Christologies, al-Qāsim notes that all three Christian communities hold a common view of the purpose of the Incarnation. "The reason for the descent of the divine Son from heaven was because of the sin of Adam, which included all of his descendents. He delivered them from the power of Satan by offering himself on the cross."[41] But this is a mistaken notion since the crucifixion did not take place as Christians believe. They may have a tradition in their scriptures that the Jews put Christ to death, but the Jews themselves did not claim to have crucified him. "The Christians gave their interpretation from their own opinions."[42] Only here does al-Qāsim refer to Qur'ānic teaching to refute Christian belief, but his underlying assumption is that Christians have

---

[38] See D. Thomas, 'The Bible in Early Muslim Anti-Christian Polemic', *ICMR* 7 (1996), 29-38.

[39] Al-Qāsim, 'Radd `alā al-naṣārā', (ed.) I. de Matteo, 'Confutazione contro I Christiani dello Zaydati al-Qāsim b. Ibrāhīm', *RSO* 9 (1921-2), 301-64, 319.

[40] *Ibid.*, 316f.

[41] *Ibid.*, 317.

[42] *Ibid.*, 319.

developed their beliefs about Christ as a result of poor scriptural foundations. They are wrong about the facts of Christ's death and their concepts of Incarnation are a product of their imagination.

Christian Scriptures do not Support the Incarnation

A second type of critique made by `Alī ibn Rabbān al-Ṯabarī (d. 855) and al-Nāshi al-Akbar (d. 904) was to separate developed Christology from that found in the Bible in order to show that Christian thought had forsaken its roots. `Alī al-Ṯabarī claimed to have been a Christian for seventy years in his *Reply to the Christians*, which must have been written sometime around the middle of the ninth century.[43] The fact that he had been a Christian most of his life is seen in his familiarity with the Bible on which he bases his criticism of Christology. He has two particular points to make; the Bible presents a human rather than a divine Christ, and the father-son terminology found in the Gospels has been radically changed by developed Christological formulations into something it was not intended to mean. In support of his first point al-Ṯabarī quotes from the Messianic prophecies of the Old Testament, such as Psalm 8, where the Messiah is clearly expected to be a human being without any hint that he might be divine.[44]

His second point is that Christological writing has taken father-son language in the New Testament out of context. In the Gospels the term 'father' is used as a metaphor in the same way that clan leaders and aged people are called father by those who are not their children. Similarly, the term 'son' is figurative like the sons of leaders who are not their actual children. However, Christian tradition has corrupted this understanding of the father-son analogy, "because Christians hold the literal truth of these names."[45] They want to hold that the Father is a parent while being beyond the process of creation, and they claim that the Son is born before time. But these are self-contradictory positions that do not arise from the Gospel accounts from which the terminology is taken. Worse still, developed Christology has made the Son equal to the Father in a way that is both a false interpretation of the Gospels and logically incoherent.

> "To say on the one hand that the Son is like his Father in his eternity, and on the other that he is not like his Father because he is born, is to deprive the words [father and son] of any meaning ...If the Father and Son are

---

[43] `Alī al-Ṯabarī, 'Radd `alā al-naṣārā', (ed.) I-A. Khalife and W. Kutsch, *MSJ* 36 (1959), 113-48, 119.

[44] *Ibid.*, 146.

[45] *Ibid.*, 147.

> equal in power and eternity then what authority remains for the Father over the Son?"[46]

Al-Ṯabarī is able to make great play over the removal of the father-son analogy from typical figurative use by Christian doctrinal formulations. How could Christians have gone from a metaphor for the lordship of God over the submitted Christ as found in the Gospels to a divine paternity of a divine offspring occurring beyond space and time? Sadly for al-Ṯabarī, Christians have ended up being unable to separate the divine from the human in their thinking. The only solution for them is to go back to the human Christ in their scriptures.

Al-Nāshi' al-Akbar also contrasts the Christologies of the ninth century with the portrait of Christ in the Gospels in order to show how Christians have forsaken their roots. He blames Christians for superimposing Greek philosophical categories on the language of the Gospels.

> "Whoever looks at the evidence of the Gospel will come across the saying of the Messiah – 'Consecrate the people in the name of the Father and the Son and the Holy Spirit'. There is no evidence here as to whether the Messiah is eternal or contingent, or whether he has one essence or not. These Greek philosophical expressions which have been adopted by Christians would not occur to those who examine the Gospel where Jesus (*`Īsā*) says – 'I am going to my Father and your Father, my Lord and your Lord', and makes himself the same as them."[47]

In other words Christians are guilty of reading into the father-son analogy ideas that simply don't belong to the original image in the Gospels. A straightforward interpretation of these sayings of Jesus leads to the conclusion that he referred to God as his father and himself as God's son in deferential terms. The father is Lord, so the son is submitted to his father. The son turns out to be on the same level as those to whom he is speaking, rather than on the same level as God. Subsequently, Christians have re-interpreted the sonship as equality of status with the father via the alien concept of eternal sonship imported from Greek thought. Al-Nāshi` quotes Melkite and Jacobite Christological formulas to illustrate the distance between them and the Gospels. Melkites believe that the Messiah has two natures, eternal and temporal, in one hypostasis, whereas the Jacobites hold that the Son joined with the human and became one nature, "God the Word who is Jesus".[48] When compared with the figurative language of Jesus in the Gospels such formulae seem to bear no relation to the true intent of Jesus to be submitted to his Lord and to lead others in that submission. The simplicity of the Gospel accounts has been abandoned by Christians who

---

[46] *Ibid.*, 148.
[47] Al-Nāshi' al-Akbar, *Kitāb al-Awsāt fi-l-Maqālāt,* (ed.) J. van Ess, (Beirut: 1971), 82.
[48] *Ibid.*, 80.

have elaborated Jesus into a divine being through complex ideas borrowed from the wrong sources.[49]

Arguments for the Incarnation are Incoherent

A third type of response was to deny the validity of the apologetics put forward by Christians to defend the Incarnation as reasonable. Abū `Īsā al-Warrāq (d. 861) and Abū Bakr Muḥammad ibn al-Ṭayyib al-Bāqillānī (d. 1014) argued that the analogies used by Christians to explain the Incarnation were inadequate for the task because the notion of the union of the divine with the human was basically incoherent. Abū Īsā stands out among the Muslim authors of his time for his thoroughness in handling Christian material. In his *Refutation of the three Christian sects* he surveys in great detail the Christologies of the Melkites, Jacobites and Nestorians, pointing out inconsistencies in their use of language to show that Christians were incapable of making sense of their beliefs about Christ. His main criticism of the language used by Christians has to do with terminology for the humanity of Christ. He observes that Nestorians and most Jacobites claim that the eternal Son united with "a particular human being", but that Melkites hold that the eternal Son united with "the universal human" nature shared by all humans "in order to save everyone." The Melkites believe that if the Son "had united with one human being then he could only have intended to save this individual and not everyone."[50] However, he notes that despite this observation, Nestorians, Jacobites and Melkites are not consistent in the way they describe the humanity of Christ. "They all tend to apply the explanations loosely, interpreting the human nature as a human being and vice versa."[51] This lack of precision in the use of language is confirmed by the terminology for the Incarnation found in these Christologies. "Sometimes they say the Word became human (*ta`annasa*) and some of them say the Word became embodied (*tajassada*)."[52]

Abū `Īsā lists seven metaphorical explanations given by Christians of the union of the divine Word with the human body; firstly, the Word united with the human body in the sense of mixing and mingling with it; secondly, the Word took the body as a temple; thirdly, the Word took the body as a garment; fourthly, the Word dwelt in the body; fifthly the Word appeared in

---

[49] See similar Muslim argumentation answered in the apologetics of Abū Rā'iṯa and `Ammār, as well as the basic agreement of John Hick with such arguments in chapter nine, though with no awareness of these authors.

[50] Abū `Īsā al-Warrāq, 'Radd `alā al-thalāth firāq min al-naṣārā: al-juz' al-thānī, al-radd `alā al-ittiḥād', ed. D. Thomas, *Early Muslim Polemic against Christianity*, Cambridge, 2002, 87.

[51] *Ibid.*

[52] *Ibid.*

the body without indwelling it; sixthly, the Word appeared in the body like a seal in clay, without being transferred to the clay itself; seventhly, the Word appeared in the body as a face appears in a mirror without being part of it.[53] Of these seven analogies only the idea of indwelling is used by Abū Qurra and Abū Rā'iṯa. `Ammār has indwelling as well as the temple and garment analogies. As far as Abū `Īsā is concerned the amount of disagreement between Christians tells against the coherence of the idea of union between divine and human natures. Such internal inconsistency does not encourage Muslims to take Christology as a source of true information about Christ. Abū `Īsā seems to list the variety of Christian perspectives in order to show how much more rational is the teaching of Islam. If Christian faith in Christ corresponds with a Muslim view then Christianity has little to teach that is not confirmed by Islam. Where Christian teaching about Christ differs From Islamic teaching it is likely to be faulty. This can be illustrated by his criticism of the death of Christ. If the divine nature died then Christians worship a dead god, and if only the human nature died then the Messiah did not actually die, "because the human alone was not the Messiah". Whichever argument is put forward by Christians "causes the collapse of the uniting".[54] The logic of transendence is transparent to any sane thinker, confirming the rational excellence of Islam.

Abū Bakr al-Bāqillānī provides a critique of two more analogies used by Christians to explain the Incarnation. The first of these appeals to the session of God on his throne. "There are those who say that the Word indwells the human nature without being confined to it, just as the Creator descends on his throne without being confined to it. This is irrational, because the Creator is not on his throne in the sense that he indwells it."[55] Al-Bāqillānī points out that any use of God's contact with his throne as an analogy for the contact of the Word with the human body is illegitimate because Christians claim an indwelling of the Word. The parallel is simply not there in the session on the throne, for God cannot be thought by any stretch of the imagination to be within his throne in the way that the Word is supposed to be in the human body. Both Abū Qurra and Abū Rā'iṯa had appealed to the session of God on his throne as a helpful analogy for the Incarnation, but al-Bāqillānī demonstrates the gap between the Christian affirmation of divine embodiment and the Islamic conviction that God transcends that which he has created.

The mind-body analogy is also criticized for failing to provide what Christians really argue for. "The idea that the mind is the essence of the person and yet is not affected by the body is futile."[56] When applied by

---

[53] *Ibid.*, 88.
[54] *Ibid.*, 119.
[55] Al-Bāqillānī, *Kitāb al-Tamhīd,* (ed.) R.J. McCarthy, (Beirut: 1957), 88.
[56] *Ibid.*, 90.

Christians to the Incarnation the analogy does not work since they want to maintain that the Word was basically unaffected by the body. The mind-body analogy was used by Abū Rā'iṯa because he believed that in fact the human body did not influence the human mind, but this understanding of human psychology lacked cogency for Muslims like al- Bāqillānī.

Both of these analogies are inadequate for the task to which Christians put them because they attempt to support the union of the divine with the human, a notion which is completely impossible. Al- Bāqillānī dismisses these apologetic moves as incapable of achieving what Christians desire because the basic belief in the Incarnation is irrational in the first place.

Conclusion

The developments in Christology are mainly seen in the presentation of arguments to commend the rationality and value of the Incarnation as understood within the traditions of the three authors, Abū Qurra the Melkite, Abū Rā'iṯa the Jacobite, and `Ammār the Nestorian. Abū Qurra and Abū Rā'iṯa shared a common concern to argue for the Incarnation on Islamic grounds, even to the extent of using the same Islamic conceptions as premises of their arguments. They both appealed to the session of God on his throne, familiar to Muslims from the Qur'ān, as a way of defending the reasonableness of divine union with a human body. `Ammār was more inclined to present arguments that showed the value of the Incarnation as a means of the revelation of God, but he did also develop some distinctive arguments based on Islamic ideas. There were some developments in the language of Christology, especially in the writing of Abū Rā'iṯa, who used the concept of attributes to describe the divinity and humanity of Christ when addressing a Muslim audience. However, Abū Qurra and `Ammār were less inclined to adopt Islamic terminology, preferring to explain the meaning of their Christological traditions in ways that might be intelligible to Muslims.

The response by Muslim authors illustrates the way such arguments were received. Ultimately the Christian case for the Incarnation is perceived to be a poor building on any Islamic foundations suggested. Nothing in Islam allows for the union of the divine with a human body, and the use of divine anthropomorphisms in Islam to make room for Incarnation is not admissible. However, the fact that al-Bāqillānī took the trouble to refute such arguments in the second half of the tenth century shows that Muslim intellectuals felt the force of the Christian case made over a century before. This may suggest that arguments based on Islamic premises can have a continuing usefulness to Christian apologists. Muslim reading of the Gospels to deny the divinity of Christ put Abū Rā'iṯa and `Ammār on the defensive, but they were convinced that the divinity of Christ was clearly portrayed there. Perhaps these ninth century discussions of the Gospels have less relevance in modern times in the light of critical Gospel scholarship, but the issues surrounding scriptural roots for developed Christology raised by `Ammār's presentation of a tested Christ have a continuing importance.

What does remain relevant to the twenty first century is the attempt to show the coherence of the Incarnation on Islamic terms. For modern Christians who continue to uphold the Incarnation, the models provided by these three ninth century apologists still have value. Their careful distinction between the transcendence of God and his immanence in Christ can be usefully employed today among Muslims who fear that God may be tarnished by too close an identification with humanity. If Christ was able to defeat sin throughout his life and conquer death through new life as `Ammār argued, then no shame attaches to the divine nature that was in him. Muslims need not reject Incarnation if transcendent majesty is preserved.

Chapter 7

New Beginnings in the Nineteenth and Early Twentieth Centuries

Between the Ninth and Nineteenth Centuries

In between the ninth and twentieth centuries lies a period of increasing distance between Muslims and Christians. By the end of the ninth century Muslim intellectuals had abandoned debate with Christians on the grounds that everything that can be known about revealed truth was contained in Islam, and that Christian conceptions of revelation were not only inadequate but subversive to the truth of the oneness of God. Christians in the Islamic world continued to decline in numbers as many born into Christian families converted to Islam. Such a demographic shift meant that the self-confidence of the Christian communities also declined, as the distance between Muslim and Christian intellectuals grew wider. The arrival of the Mongols in the Middle East after 1259 led to the systematic oppression of Middle Eastern Christians, which became particularly intense under Tīmūr Lang from 1394 to 1405 when Christians in the Mesopotamian region who did not convert to Islam were hunted down.[1]

Christians beyond the Muslim Empire looked on Muslims as a military threat for many centuries. European Christians typically saw Islam as the Antichrist seeking to engulf Christian Europe just as once the Christian Middle East had been overrun. The few European Christians who attempted to understand Islam did so from an antagonistic base. Not until the academic study of Islam in the eighteenth century did Europeans approach Islam from a more reasoned and sympathetic point of view. Missionaries to the Muslim world from Europe began to debate with Muslims in terms of the academic study of Islam, and this culminated in twentieth century Christian theologians attempting to do theology on a global rather than a western level. The encounter of Christians from beyond the Muslim world with Islam has been difficult, but as the twenty first century opens, there is a more lively concern to be Christians in an Islamic context than ever before. Muslims have continued to hold Christians responsible for undermining the unity of God, and relatively few have sought to debate with Christians on the Incarnation and atonement.

---

[1] See A.S. Atiya, *A History of Eastern Christianity,* 276.

Between the creative period of the late eighth and early ninth centuries and the suppression of the post `Abbasid era, Christian dialogue on Christology with Muslims hardly developed in novel directions. A notable exception, however, is the contribution from the twelfth century made by Paul of Antioch, Melkite Bishop of Sidon, who quoted extensively from the Qur'ān in support of the Gospel accounts of Christ in his *Letter to the Muslims*. For instance, he was able to accept the Qur'ānic denial of the death of Christ on the cross by arguing that the Qur'ān meant that the divinity of Christ was untouched when his human nature died.[2] However, the letter does not match the earlier apologetic writing of the ninth century for arguments commending the Incarnation.

During the Medieval period, the European Christian encounter with Islam was coloured by the sense of threat posed by possible Muslim invasion. Those who attempted to understand Islam did not engage in the kind of apologetic used by Middle Eastern Christians, but sought to directly criticise Islam in the light of Christian truth. Ramon Lull (1232-1316), who visited North Africa on a number of occasions to debate and preach, produced a treatise three years before his death for Christian merchants doing business in the Muslim world. He advised his readers that Muhammad had misunderstood what Christians believed about the Trinity, the Incarnation, the crucifixion, and the resurrection. Other aspects of his teaching corresponded to Christian truth; God is creator, Christ is the Spirit and Word of God, Christ is born of the Virgin Mary, he is exalted and alive in heaven, and he is the worthiest man of all time. While acknowledging that Muhammad was not wholly in error, the notion that he had misunderstood Christian teaching was to become standard in subsequent Western writing on Islam until the modern era.[3] Ricoldo of Montecroce (c.1243-1320) worked in the Baghdad area with Tartars. His polemic against the authenticity of the Qur'ān, entitled *Confutatio Alcorani*, represents a still more critical approach to Muslims. The Qur'ān repeats the teaching of Arius who regarded Christ as the noblest of God's creatures but not as divine. He suggests that Christians defend the Incarnation by arguing that no limit ought to be placed on God by human reason, so the Incarnation is possible for the Almighty.[4]

---

[2] Paul of Antioch, *Letter to the Muslims,* (ed.) P. Khoury, (Beirut: 1964), 73.

[3] See D. Urvoy, 'Ramon Lull et L'Islam', *Islamochristiana* 7 (1981), 127-146, 135. Lull grew up among Spanish Muslims and was familiar with the work of several Muslim writers including ibn Hazm, al-Ghazālī, The Brethren of Purity, and ibn Masarra from the tenth century and ibn Sab`īn from the thirteenth century. He may also have been aware of the two twelfth and thirteenth century Andalusian Muslim writers, ibn Rushd and ibn al-`Arabī.

[4] See J.W. Sweetman, *Islam and Christian Theology* vol. 2:1 (London: 1955), 118-122.

Nicholas of Cusa (1401-1464) made the greatest effort in the West to read the Qur'ān sympathetically. He wrote *De Pace Fidei* in 1453 in the aftermath of the fall of Constantinople to Muhammad II, confident that despite differences between Christians and Muslims the truth would win out in the end. His *Cribratio Alkorani* was written at the request of Pope Pius II probably in 1461. While not aimed at a Muslim audience, it does attempt to show that the Qur'ān contains a Christian view of Jesus. In the tradition of John of Damascus whom he had studied, he argues that the title 'Word' given to Jesus in the Qur'ān must imply his divine nature. "Since He is the Word of God sent from Heaven, then assuredly He is of the same nature as God who sends (him). For since the Divine Word is the Word of God, we cannot say that it is something other than the most simple God."[5] He is innovative in dealing with the supposed denial of the crucifixion. While the Qur'ān denies that the Jews killed Christ it leaves open the possibility that Pilate had him put to death.

> "It is not denied that the Jews could be perpetrators of the killing of Christ, even though they did not (really) kill him. Therefore, in the whole of the Koran there is no denial that Christ was crucified; rather Pilate, not the Jews, could have carried out this crucifixion in the way stated by the gospel."[6]

Nicholas seems to have been the first to suggest this way of reading *sūra* 4:157. However, he did not engage in debate with Muslims to test out his approach.

The arrival of Jesuits in Northwest India in the sixteenth century provided a new opportunity for engagement with Islam. They were able to hold discussions with the Mughal Emperor Akbar on a variety of topics including the Incarnation and crucifixion of Christ. They appealed to the Qur'ānic title 'word from God' for support for the divinity of Christ and to the intimation in the Qur'ān that Christ died for support for the death of Christ as recorded in the Gospels.[7] However, it was not until the nineteenth century that European Christian mission was able to produce apologetic work that addressed Muslims in terms of their own scholarly tradition. By then, developments in the study of Islam by European scholars had become available for apologetic use. The fruit of this knowledge can be seen in the writing of Karl Pfander (1803-1868), whose training in Islamic studies in

[5] Nicholas of Cusa, *Cribratio Alkorani* vol.1:12:59, in J. Hopkins, *Nicholas of Cusa's De Pace Fidei and Cribratio Alkorani* (Minneapolis: 1994), 5.

[6] *Ibid.*, 2:14:129, in Hopkins, 103.

[7] See J.S. Hoyland and S.N. Banarjee, (trans.) *Commentary of Father Monserrate S. J. on his Journey to the Court of Akbar* (London: 1922), 59f. and 180. See also P. Jackson, 'Jesuits at Akbar's court', *Salaam* 16 (1995), 100-113.

Switzerland enabled him to engage in debate with Muslims by quoting Muslim scholars to support Christian interpretation of the Qur'ān.[8]

Karl Pfander's *The Balance of Truth*

Karl G Pfander, a Pietistic Lutheran from Germany, joined the Basel Mission to work among Muslims on the northern border of Persia.[9] His presentation of Christianity entitled *The Balance of Truth* was published in Armenian in 1831, Persian in 1835, and Urdu in 1843, after he moved to India in 1841. Pfander wrote the work to fill a gap in literature for the Muslim audience he encountered in preaching around Shusha in the Caucasus and on trips within Persia. He subsequently rewrote the work in the late 1840's utilising fresh studies on Islam by European scholars as well as Islamic writing available *in situ*.[10] Few of his missionary contemporaries had read the Qur'ān or Islamic writing. Henry Martyn was one who had, but he had dedicated his energy to Scripture translation before his death in 1812 at the age of 31.[11] Pfander was attempting to communicate the Christian faith in terms a Muslim might understand, rather than simply repeat the theological terminology he had learned in Europe.

The Balance of Truth first addresses the authenticity of the Old and New Testaments since Pfander had discovered that this was the most important point of contention in discussions with Muslims. If he could persuade his reader of the trustworthiness of Christian Scripture then the Trinity and the Incarnation which he goes on to expound, would be firmly grounded. Pfander declined to debate these doctrines in isolation from their origin in revelation. His was not a philosophical approach that sought to show the reasonableness of the Trinity or the Incarnation on a priori grounds, since as a Pietistic Lutheran he was inherently suspicious of natural theology. His presentation of Christian claims about Jesus follows a detailed argument showing that the *Torah* and the *Injīl* had not been corrupted by Jews or Christians. Pfander's Protestant background shows through in his opening emphasis on the Apostolic conviction that Christ died to save sinners. To support this he ranges widely over the New Testament teaching on the Atonement.

---

[8] See A.A. Powell, *Muslims & Missionaries in Pre-Mutiny India* (London: 1993), 135f.

[9] See the survey of Pfander's life and work by J.S. Moon, 'From Carey to Zwemer. Karl Pfander', *BCIIS* 1 (1967), 46-57.

[10] Pfander mentioned that he had used material provided by the British Islamist William Muir, who was in India at the time, along with books by Gustav Weil on the early history of Islam, and the *Hadīth* collection of Majlīsī published in Teheran in 1831. See Powell, 147f.

[11] See J. Sargent, *Life and Letters of the Rev. Henry Martyn* (London: 1862).

The Sinlessness of Christ

The introductory section shows an important aspect of Pfander's method. The Old Testament prediction of Jesus' birth from the virgin Mary is backed up by *sūras* 21:91 and 66:12. Later he pays close attention to these Qur'ānic statements using references from commentaries on the Qur'ān in order to demonstrate that the Qur'ān teaches the sinlessness of Christ.

> "The Qur'ān accuses the other prophets of sin but does not once accuse Jesus of sin; rather it testifies that he is innocent. *Sūra* Maryam 19 says on the lips of the angel who announced him to his mother – 'I am your Lord's messenger to announce to you a pure boy'. Baiḏāwī said this means purity from sin or growth to goodness or progress towards goodness from year to year. Bukhārī and Muslim said that the following *Ḫadīth* agrees with this verse; 'Satan has pierced the side of every newborn son of Adam with his finger except 'Īsā son of Mary.'"[12]

Pfander's appeal to the Qur'ān commentator al-Baiḏāwī (d.c. 1290) and the *Ḫadīth* collectors al-Bukhārī (810-870) and Muslim (d. 875) marks a new stage in Christian apologetic writing for Muslims. He presents evidence from Islamic sources to back up Christian claims about Jesus. This approach to apologetics is an intensification of the eighth and ninth century use of the Qur'ān to support Christian belief, since it allows the apologist to back up a Christian reading of the Qur'ān with Islamic scholarship. In this context, the confirmation of the sinlessness of Christ by the renowned commentator al-Baiḏāwī establishes the credibility of Pfander as a serious debater who seeks appropriate evidence for his points. The quotation of a sound tradition from the collections of al-Bukhārī and Muslim shows that Pfander was aware of the importance of the *Ḫadīth* in the interpretation of the Qur'ān in the Islamic Persia and India of his time. In fact, the tradition is even more valuable than the commentary, since Christ is picked out as uniquely free from the taint of evil among humans, giving the apologist the opportunity to challenge the common assumption that all the prophets were sinless.

> "There are many sayings of Muḫammad showing that he asked for forgiveness and repented of sin. Among them are these sayings, 'I ask God's forgiveness and I repent seventy times a day' and 'Repent to your Lord for I tell you that I repent to God the Almighty and Sublime a hundred times a day'."[13]

---

[12] K.G. Pfander, *Mīzān al-Ḫaqq* (Rikon:) 179f. This is a reprint of the Arabic translation published in Beirut in 1877. W.S. Tisdall edited an English version in 1912 with revisions to the original text of Pfander.

[13] *Ibid.*, 180.

Muslims would not be able to take refuge in the theory that such sayings are unsound since they appear in al-Bukhārī and Muslim. Pfander softens any accusation of Christian bias by sticking rigidly to impeccable Islamic sources to reinforce his central claim of the unique status of the Messiah among God's prophets. The new knowledge gained from Islamic literature provided apologists with the opportunity to move beyond the stereotyping of Muhammad long familiar to European thought. Now Christ could be rescued from an inferior status to Muhammad by reference to the sayings of the Prophet. If Muhammad himself claimed to have needed forgiveness and yet taught that Jesus was without fault then the Christian case is made by the Prophet of Islam.

Having achieved his aim of isolating Jesus as the only sinless prophet according to the *Hadīth*, Pfander enters into a lengthy explanation of the Biblical view that sin needs atonement, and that such atonement can only be made by a pure sacrifice according to the *Torah*. Only Jesus Christ is capable of acting as that perfect sacrifice and this is foretold in the *Torah* itself. As for the gospels, they are supported by the Qur'ān in their portrait of Jesus' ministry. "He performed amazing miracles, he healed the sick, cast out demons, gave sight to the blind, hearing to the deaf, cleansing to the leper, and made the cripple walk. Read *sūra* 3:42."[14]

Pfander cannot claim similar Qur'ānic testimony for the death and resurrection of Jesus. This silence of Islamic testimony considerably weakens his case for the importance of Jesus as a pure sacrifice. However, his exposition does emphasise the self-giving of Jesus and the fact that the Jews handed him over to the Roman governor.

> "Jesus once told his disciples that he would bear suffering not out of compulsion but willingly out of love for people that he might give them eternal life. The Messiah allowed the Jews to seize him, to mock him, to hit him and hand him over to the Roman judge, Pilate the governor of Judea, to whip him and crucify him."[15]

Pfander possibly hopes to show first of all, that Jesus voluntarily went to his death on behalf of others. If that is granted then the injustice of the death of God's prophet is mitigated. Secondly, he points out that the Jews, while wanting to kill Jesus, handed him over to the non-Jewish governor of their country. Pfander may have hoped that this explanation would fit in with the Qur'ānic assertion that "they certainly did not kill him", interpreting 'they' as the Jews. However, Pfander does not spell out how he reconciles the gospel accounts of the death of Jesus with the seeming denial of death by crucifixion in the Qur'ān. It is here that his method breaks down. Why quote the Qur'ān when the text favours a Christian

---

[14] *Ibid.*, 213.
[15] *Ibid.*, 214.

interpretation, but fail to indicate when the Qur'ān appears to contradict it? Surely his reader would be frustrated with Pfander's unwillingness to discuss the Qur'ān's opposition to Jesus' death by crucifixion in *sūra* 4:157.

Christ's Divinity

Pfander then deals with the divinity of Christ, recognising Muslim difficulty with the concept of sonship.

> "The name given to the Messiah, (in John 3:16 and 4:9), 'Son of God', has been a stumbling stone on the path of many Muslims because they believe that this name goes beyond the acceptable limits imposed by the Qur'ān, since the Qur'ān denies that God took a partner or a son. But the gospels call the Messiah 'Son of God' *ibn Allāh* not *walad Allāh*, the difference between *ibn* and *walad* is clear because the word *ibn* is often used metaphorically whereas the word *walad* is only used literally."[16]

Pfander shows awareness of the impasse caused by the emphatic opposition of the Qur'ān to 'son' language by his decision to move swiftly to a much longer exposition of the Messiah as 'Word of God'. By drawing on Messianic prophecy from the Old Testament and the use of the title in the Johannine writing of the New Testament he concludes that "it is obvious to the informed Muslim that the Qur'ān agrees with the *Torah* and the *Injīl* in calling the Messiah 'Word of God'."[17] According to John, the Word existed with God before space and time and then became human. He was fully human yet free from sin. The meaning of the title is expressed in the way the Son relates to his Father. "As a human being he prayed to God his Father and fasted. But he showed his divine nature when he called God his Father in the sense that he was connected to him as a son is connected to his father and that he was sent from God as a son is sent from his father."[18] The title 'Word' gives the meaning to the title 'Son' by showing that the relationship between God and Christ is an identity of thought and intention and speech.

Pfander anticipates a negative response from his reader who is concerned about the confusion between divinity and humanity in the Incarnation. "If the question is asked – 'How is it possible to unite the divine and human natures?' We reply – 'How is it possible to unite in a human being spirit and body?'"[19] Pfander is clear that the union of the two natures is not to be understood as "the changing of one nature into another or a mixing or

[16] *Ibid.*, 219.
[17] *Ibid.*, 222.
[18] *Ibid.*, 223.
[19] *Ibid.*, 224.

mingling of them."[20] How the union may be described positively is governed by our inability to comprehend the way in which God works. We have a limited intellectual capacity and depend ultimately on the fact that God has revealed the union of divine and human natures in Scripture. Thus we must believe in the fact of Incarnation even though we cannot fully understand the manner of union between divine and human nature.

The value of the union of divine and human in the Messiah is the certainty this brings to his redeeming power. "This union of divinity and humanity in the Messiah accomplishes the goal of the eternal God to lavish on people his abundant grace, saving them from destruction, sin, and slavery to Satan."[21] Here Pfander returns to the theme of Christ's sacrificial death on behalf of others, which is central to his Christology. At this point he tackles the Muslim objection that human sin can be forgiven without the work of Christ.

> "Some have objected to this asking – 'Is it not possible for God to save people from the punishment of hell by the exercise of his unlimited authority, and to show his mercy to those who he wants to be merciful to, without the way of salvation set out in the *Injīl*? Is it not God who says to anything he wishes – 'Be! and it is'?"[22]

Pfander catches the mood of his Muslim reader very well in these two questions. While the Christian claims the Incarnation to be possible, surely the greater possibility is for God to deal directly with humans. A Muslim might respond that when it comes to weighing different possibilities it is necessary to allow the greatest measure of freedom in portraying God's actions, since the Qur'ān shows that God can bring things into being by a mere word of command. The elaborate story of the Incarnation and atonement is therefore a less than credible account of his work. Pfander's understanding of Muslims is clear, but his reaction to these questions is to insist on the validity of the Biblical demand for pure sacrifice for sin, and to insist that God chose Jesus to be the ultimate sacrifice. This story has ultimate value for us because by means of God's choice to display his nature in Christ he showed his love for people by "taking away their suffering."[23] Christianity offers a way for sinners to find acceptance with God that does not make light of their wrongdoing. Only the atonement made by Christ adequately combines God's justice and his mercy. What then of the frequent Qur'ānic testimony to the mercy and compassion of God? Pfander declines to compare New Testament thought with that of the Qur'ān at this point. His method is certainly consistent in that he only

[20] *Ibid.*
[21] *Ibid.*, 225.
[22] *Ibid.*, 226.
[23] *Ibid.*

quotes the Qur'ān to back up Christian teaching and not when Christian positions seem to be challenged.

By now the reader of *The Balance of Truth* could well raise the logical problem of the supposed death of God. Pfander is alive to this difficulty, and leans on the distinction between the two natures in Christ to deny that God died on the cross. "God does not die, indeed it is not possible for God to die, but the Word of God, when he became human, was able to taste death on account of his human nature."[24] This traditional answer does not receive scrutiny from Muslim conviction. For instance, Pfander does not raise and answer the questions – in what way is the Word of God connected to the human Jesus? And why do Christians insist on the union of divine and human natures if the union fails at such a crucial juncture?

Evaluation

Pfander's Christology is inherited from his Lutheran background. The definition of the Council of Chalcedon governs the language that he uses to describe the union of the divine and human natures in Christ. The essential Christian message is the salvation of the human race from the consequences of sin by the union of the eternal Word with human nature. The Incarnation was essential to the rescue operation, but the sacrificial death of Christ was central to the rescue itself. Only a pure sacrifice sufficed to cleanse humans from guilt. Without the death of the sinless Christ there can be no assurance of pardon for anyone, but since he has laid down his life for others they can receive the benefits of his sinless character. Luther's emphasis on the exchange of Christ's righteousness for our unrighteousness is at the heart of Pfander's presentation.[25]

Pfander seeks not to develop a new Christology but to present a received view in a way that Muslims might accept. He tries to back up the perfect obedience of Christ from Islamic sources to get his reader focused on the key idea of Christ's character. Similarly, he appeals to those sources to deny to any other messenger of God the same perfection. Muhammad taught that only Jesus among the prophets was untouched by Satan, so Muslims must hold that Christ is unique in his obedience to God. If Islamic sources testify to the truth of the Christian message at this point then the

---

[24] *Ibid.*, 230.

[25] The idea of the exchange of Christ's perfect obedience for our disobedience was characteristic of Luther's reformed theology. See, for example, his sermon on "Two Kinds of Righteousness" from 1519, in which he expounds his new reading of the New Testament. "Through faith in Christ his righteousness becomes our righteousness and all that he has becomes ours; rather he himself becomes ours ... This is the righteousness given in place of the original righteousness lost in Adam." *Luther's Works* vol.31 (ed.) H.J. Grimm, (Philadelphia: 1957), 298f.

rest of the Christian case ought to follow. The sacrificial death of Christ should make sense to Muslims once they understand the need for sacrifice to remove the guilt of sin. The love of God should be clear to them once they see that he has gone to such lengths to forgive them.

Reaction to Pfander's apologetics can be seen in a public debate held in Agra in 1854 between Pfander and Rahmatullāh al-Kairānawī, who saw himself as a defender of Islam, and who challenged Pfander to deal with the status of the Bible, the Trinity, the Prophethood of Muḫammad, and the status of the Qur'ān.[26] The status of Christ would most likely have been considered under the heading of the Trinity, but in fact the debate did not proceed beyond the first topic. By using the insights of Christian Biblical scholarship, Rahmatullāh had Pfander bogged down in the details of Scriptural exegesis which tended to support the contention that the Gospels were riddled with contradictions that could not be made to cohere.[27] The order of issues for debate corresponds to the order of topics in *The Balance of Truth*, demonstrating that Christology was not a primary subject for discussion.

The debate introduced a new dimension to dialogue between Christians and Muslims. Pfander had not read Strauss's *The Life of Jesus* before the debate and had been largely unaware of critical European gospel scholarship that had been engaged in the task of separating the Christ of history from the Christ of the faith of the Church. It would now be difficult for Christian missionaries to avoid the work of Christian scholars in the way that Pfander had, because Muslims could produce literature liberally quoting the findings of such scholarship. The future path of dialogue on Christology was now established, but Pfander did not himself embark on it.[28]

Ibrāhīm Lūqā's *Christianity in Islam*

Pfander's method of using Islamic sources to defend Christian belief was taken much further by an Egyptian Coptic priest, Ibrāhīm Lūqā, in the

[26] See Powell, 221-5; and C. Schirrmacher, 'The Agra Debates of 1854', *BHMIIS* 13 (1994), 74-84.

[27] *Ibid.*, 248-255. Rahmatullāh had consulted *The Life of Christ* by the radical German scholar D.F. Strauss, which had been published in an English edition in 1846. Rahmatullāh went on to write a widely disseminated critique of the Bible entitled *Iẕhār al-Ḫaqq*, which was first published in Arabic in 1867.

[28] See how Kenneth Cragg attempts to hold together a critical reading of the gospels with the developed traditions of the Church in chapter eight, and how Hans Küng and John Hick use gospel scholarship to fashion their different portraits of the historical Jesus in chapter nine.

following century. His *Christianity in Islam*, first published in 1938, was into its third printing in 1967 when it was banned by the Egyptian authorities.[29] Lūqā's treatment of Christ takes in the whole of the Qur'ānic portrait, paying particular attention to the way well known commentators understood the Christ of the Qur'ān, with the aim of demonstrating that Christian teaching is not incompatible with that of the Qur'ān. His adoption of Pfander's apologetic method shows that not only Western missionaries were inclined to try to read the Qur'ān in a Christian way. The difference between the two men lies in their approach to Islamic sensitivities. Whereas Pfander was prepared to show that Muḫammad lacked sinlessness, Lūqā avoids any direct criticism of the Prophet. The title of his work reveals his goal because Christianity in Islam is an apt description of what he is attempting to achieve. Chapters 1 and 2 deal with the trustworthiness of the Old and New Testaments, and Chapter 3 with the Trinity. In the fourth chapter he turns to the Messiah. This is basically the same format as Pfander's *The Balance of Truth* since Lūqā also recognises the importance of establishing the authenticity of the sources of Christian faith in the face of Muslim allegation of the corruption of the Bible.

The Titles of Christ in the Qur'ān

The section of the study devoted to Christology opens with the surprising claim that what Christians believe about Christ is also testified to by the Qur'ān. "The Messiah is truly God and truly human: this is the authentic Christian teaching about the person of the Messiah and it is also what the Qur'ān teaches about him."[30] So it is clear from the outset that Lūqā is attempting to show that the Qur'ān teaches the divinity of Christ, and that Muslims have failed to grasp this key point. This might seem an impossible task after so many centuries of Qur'ān interpretation, but Lūqā is ready for the challenge. He begins his analysis of the Qur'ān with the title 'Word from God' found in *sūras* 3:45 and 4:171, quoting comments on these *sūras* by al-Rāzī, al-Baiḏāwī, and the two Jalāls noting that they understand 'word from God' to be God's speech.[31] Lūqā questions this interpretation in the light of the Qur'ānic expression "by a word from him whose name is" in *sūra* 3:45, arguing that "this word is not speech, but a person,"[32] and must share God's eternal character. "It is clear from the expression 'cast into Mary' that this word existed before being cast into Mary. Thus the Messiah

---

[29] See O Leirvik, *Images of Jesus Christ in Islam* (Uppsala: 1999), 175.

[30] I. Lūqā, *Al-Masīḫiyya fī l-Islām* (Rikon: no date), 119. This is a reprint of the original 1938 edition.

[31] The two Jalāls were Jalāl al-Dīn al-Maḫallī (d. 1459), who began writing the commentary and Jalāl al-Dīn al-Suyūtī (d. 1505), who finished it.

[32] I. Lūqā, 124.

exists eternally because he is here identified with the word of God."[33] Lūqā boldly contradicts the long tradition of Qur'ānic hermeneutics by analysing the contextual relationships of 'word', 'Mary' and 'whose name is', concluding that 'word' can only apply to the child to be born of Mary. "The Messiah is the Word of God who entered into the virgin Mary, sharing her human nature and yet at the same time possesses the nature of almighty God."[34]

Lūqā next examines the title 'spirit from him' also found in *sūra* 4:171. He quotes al-Rāzī's four possible interpretations of this phrase along with the comments of al-Baiḏāwī and the two Jalāls. Al-Rāzī mentions the following possible interpretations of 'spirit from him'; from the breath of Jibril, meaning from the grace of God; creative life force from God; mercy from God to mankind; and a spirit from the spirits, meaning a prophet from among the prophets. Al-Baiḏāwī understands that the Messiah is called 'spirit' because he would give life to the dead and to human hearts. The two Jalāls think the Messiah is given the spirit from the Almighty as a gift, and not as Christians allege to become Son of God and God. Lūqā believes the best interpretations focus on the breath of God in the Messiah, but holds that the context demands more than just breath. All the commentators overlook the fact that only Jesus is named 'spirit from him'. What can this unique title mean except that God has endowed Jesus with his own spirit, which is much more significant than breathing life into a human so that he draws breath. God puts his spirit into Mary, not to invigorate her with his breath, but to bring about a new human being, and since only Jesus among humans possesses God's spirit, only he possesses God's character.

Lūqā summarises his presentation of the word and spirit of God in Christ in a version of John of Damascus' argument that God ought not to be mutilated by the removal of his word and spirit from his essential nature.[35]

> "If God possesses spirit and word from eternity we ask - are these two qualities of the essence (*dhāt*) of God or not? If not, then alongside God there are two independent attributes and God is not one … The spirit and the word together are of the essence (*dhāt*) of God, both of them attributes (*ṣifāt*) of God, without addition or separation."[36]

In other words God has attributed to Christ his own character, and there is no sense in which human beings have attributed 'word' and 'spirit' to Christ in a way that would leave them open to the charge of *shirk*. The Qur'ān therefore testifies that Christ shares the nature of God. According to Lūqā's contextual interpretation we cannot conceive of the Messiah being

---

[33] *Ibid.*, 125.
[34] *Ibid.*
[35] For John's argument see chapter two:15.
[36] *Ibid.*, 127f.

from the Spirit of God without him having God's nature. "So he is true God from true God, eternally existing and not created."[37] Therefore the Qur'ān teaches by the very titles given to Christ that he is equal in nature to God, and any other reading of these titles does less than justice to their meaning.

Lūqā examines the title 'Messiah' in *sūra* 3:24, where "the angels said, Mary, God has blessed you with his word called the Messiah, Jesus, son of Mary", but is not impressed by most of the explanations given for this title by the commentators. They are summed up without attribution to particular commentators as, "applying to descent and legitimacy or being like a smooth coin with nothing engraved on it, or great in kindness, or anointed with oil and with blessing."[38] He believes al-Rāzī gives a better interpretation when he says that the Messiah was given that name because he was kept from sin and wrongdoing, and because Jibrīl's wing touched him at the time of his birth to keep him from Satan. Lūqā notes that al-Rāzī's view corresponds with the *Hadīth* recorded by al-Bukhārī, that Satan pierced the side of every son of Adam with his finger at the moment of birth, except Jesus, son of Mary. When Satan tried to pierce him, he pierced his garment. Lūqā concludes that Islam holds, not only to the sinlessness of Jesus, but also to the culpability of all other humans. "Islam teaches that all human beings have erred and become corrupt. It teaches that the Messiah alone is sinless and that he alone was protected from the influence of Satan, raising the Messiah above the level of humanity, and therefore teaches his glorious divinity."[39] The latter claim seems to go beyond the evidence, but Lūqā is not shy about making the case.

The Life and Death of Christ in the Qur'ān

Lūqā turns from the titles given to Jesus to the details of his life and ministry found in the Qur'ān. Of particular interest is his treatment of the miracle of birds fashioned from clay which is found in *sūras* 3:48 and 5:115. He might have been expected to pass over the story in silence since it has no support in the canonical gospels. Rather, he gives the impression of accepting the historical validity of the account and that he is prepared to receive testimony about Jesus from sources outwith the New Testament. *Sūra* 3:48 describes Jesus as creating birds from clay, and Lūqā points out that the verb *khalaqa*, to create, is only used of the action of God elsewhere in the Qur'ān. "The power to create is credited to God alone. The Qur'ān accords to the Messiah this same power, testifying clearly to his divinity."[40] Lūqā does not engage with any of the commentators on the interpretation of

---

[37] *Ibid.*
[38] *Ibid.*, 132.
[39] *Ibid.*
[40] *Ibid.*, 140.

this miracle, which is strange given his method of interacting with al-Baiḏāwī, the Jalāls and al-Rāzī. The latter plays down the significance of *khalaqa* with reference to Jesus' own power, arguing that it is God who created the birds from clay using Jesus as his means of creation, and that it is wrong to think that God transferred an attribute belonging to himself to Jesus.[41]

He moves on to the description of Jesus in *sūra* 3:40, as "highly honoured in this world and in the hereafter" quoting four commentators on the significance of *wajīhan*, 'highly honoured'. Al-Rāzī, the two Jalāls, al-Baiḏāwī and al-Zamakhsharī all agree that "highly honoured in the hereafter" means that Jesus is given the power of intercession.[42] Lūqā then refers to *sūra* 39:4, "Say, to God belongs all intercession, to him all authority over heaven and earth" and does not hesitate to draw the parallel between the powers of Jesus and the Almighty. "Islam makes it clear that intercession does not belong to humankind, and that intercession is one of the attributes of God. The ascription of intercession to the Messiah is a clear indication that Islam holds to his divinity."[43]

The apparent denial of the crucifixion of Jesus in *sūra* 4:157 is dealt with by means of paying attention to the account in the canonical gospels.

> "We do not see in this verse what others see, namely, a denial of the death of Jesus by crucifixion. What the verse says is that the Jews are lying when they say we killed the Messiah. This is because the Jews did not kill him by crucifying him. They did not in fact have the authority to do it in the days of the Messiah. The one who did it was the Roman governor since the Romans controlled the land of the Jews."[44]

Lūqā believes that the Qur'ān does not oppose the historicity of Jesus' death by crucifixion, however, he does not seriously reckon with the unanimous understanding of the commentators that the verse does deny the crucifixion. Lūqā sees his task as that of giving basic information to Muslims so that they can adjust the traditional interpretation of the text to allow for the death of Jesus.

Evaluation

Lūqā's method is to read the Qur'ān in order to align it with Christian convictions, but his reading strains Qur'ānic exegesis beyond limits

---

[41] See al-Rāzī's interpretation in chapter one:4f.

[42] Al-Zamakhsharī's commentary was written before the others. He died in 1143. Al-Rāzī died in 1210, al-Baiḏāwī around 1290, Jalāl al-Dīn al-Maḥallī died in 1459, and Jalāl al-Dīn al-Suyūtī died in 1505.

[43] I. Lūqā, 141.

[44] *Ibid.*, 143.

acceptable to Muslims. Lūqā would probably argue that though Muslims have a traditional hermeneutic of the Qur'ān, this should not preclude novel readings of texts being offered for discussion. This was the method of Christian readers of the Old Testament such as the Apostle Paul. Jews may yet object to Paul's habit of finding Jesus in the Old Testament where such exegesis cuts across the original context in an unwarranted fashion. Lūqā is carrying out the same procedure with the Qur'ān. While Paul convinced only a small number of Jews of the Messianic status of Jesus, most Christians would not condemn him for his Old Testament hermeneutic. Thus Lūqā's interpretation of the Qur'ān, while unacceptable for Muslims, may still be supported by some Christians who think that the Qur'ān can be used as a source for Christian truth.

His extensive use of well known commentators on the Qur'ān marks a fresh development in dialogue that goes beyond Pfander's limited use of them, and shows the importance for Christians of paying close attention to Islamic thought. In many respects Lūqā's work represents the fruit of a new attitude among Christians to the careful study of Islam which would become the basis for dialogue in the second half of the twentieth century. For example, Kenneth Cragg, an important European contributor to dialogue with Muslims, has continued the method of listening to Islamic scholarship while offering a Christian reading of the Qur'ān.[45]

Lūqā, like Pfander, makes no reference to modern Christian scholarship. His Christology is relatively undeveloped, and can be summed up as upholding the teaching of the Nicene creed. There is no hint of the post-Nicene distinctions between miaphysite and diophysite understandings of the Incarnation. Indeed, Lūqā is not really concerned with the issues surrounding the union of the divine and human in Christ, since he is focused on finding support for the divinity of Christ from the Qur'ān. In other words, the Christology of Lūqā neither reflects the complete traditions of the Coptic community in Egypt, nor the search for the historical Jesus within the Christ of the Church's faith going on in Europe. His avoidance of the Incarnation and the problems surrounding the son of God concept in the Qur'ān means that the most important difficulties for Muslims in Christology are not dealt with.

Muslim Reactions to Christology in the Nineteenth and Early Twentieth Centuries

Two Indian and two Egyptian writers have been chosen as representative of a variety of responses to Christian views of Jesus. The two Indian writers from the nineteenth century were both replying to Pfander, one very

[45] See Cragg's Christian reading of the Qur'ān in the following chapter.

negatively and the other much more positively. The first Egyptian writer finds the New Testament portrait of Jesus contradictory, while the second finds much to admire in that portrait. The first Indian Muslim response came from Rahmatullāh al-Kairanāwī who debated publicly with Pfander and published pamphlets and a book refuting his arguments. The second Indian, Sayyid Ahmad Khān, took a positive view of the Christian gospels, but argued that they support neither a divine Jesus nor a Christ crucified for the sin of humanity. Muhammad `Abdūh, the first of the two Egyptian writers, was one of the leading Muslim thinkers of the late nineteenth century. His criticisms of the Jesus of the Christian gospels have had a significant impact on subsequent Muslim thought. The second Egyptian, Muhammad Kāmil Husain, is much more sympathetic to the portrait of Jesus in the gospels. His openness to Coptic Christians results in an appreciation of their faith in Jesus, but a Muslim cannot look to Jesus as more than an exemplar.

Rahmatullāh al-Kairanāwī (1818-1891) published an attack on the authenticity of the Bible entitled *A Miraculous Cure, as miraculous as the Cures of `Īsā - The Burnisher of the Corruption* using Christian commentaries. His understanding of the Jesus of the four gospels is determined by the extent to which the real Jesus can be seen in them. The only parts of the four gospels that could be considered genuine are the direct words of Jesus, so he finds too much interpretation by the four writers. Jesus was supposed to have spoken Hebrew but the only documents available are translations into Greek. He concludes that the witness of the gospels is thoroughly unreliable.[46]

Sayyid Ahmad Khān (1817-1898) was influenced by the controversy between Pfander and Rahmatullāh, and like the latter, Ahmad Khān attempted to respond to the missionary impact in Islamic India by meeting Christians on their own ground. Unlike Rahmatullāh, he accepted the genuineness of much of the Bible, so that instead of perverting the *Injīl* the four gospels actually preserve it. In a three volume work, *The Mahomedan Commentary on the Holy Bible*, published between 1862 and 1865, Ahmad Khān argued that there is nothing incompatible between the four Gospels and the Qur'ān when read properly. In other words Christians have not corrupted the text of the Gospels, but have only misinterpreted the meaning of the text. Textual discrepancies found in the Gospels by Christian scholars are really insignificant. Ahmad Khān relied on similar Christian sources to those used by Rahmatullāh for his information on the Bible. The most quoted text is T.H. Horne's *Introduction*, a widely used textbook in the early nineteenth century, which presented a conservative view of

[46] See the study of *The Burnisher of the Corruption* in C.W. Troll, *Sayyid Ahmad Khān* (New Delhi: 1978), 80-83; and Troll's essay 'Sayyid Ahmad Khān on Matthew 5: 17-20', *Islamochristiana* 3 (1977), 99-105.

Scripture. Ahmad Khān also knew about radical critics such as J.W. Colenso, D.F. Strauss and F.C. Baur, but he did not follow their sceptical approach to Scripture. "There remain a few passages, that without any doubt, have not yet been brought back into correspondence with the original texts. I think in this matter there is no doubt between us and the Christians."[47]

Christians, like Pfander, are right to argue that the Gospels are largely authentic, but this authenticity is on a par with the *Hadīth* rather than the Qur'ān. The four gospels do not so much give us the words of Jesus as reports of what he said, albeit by his companions who were trustworthy men. Jesus' companions would have no good reason to falsify the message that they should worship God, but this means that an Incarnational interpretation of the four gospels is actually incompatible with the original documents. According to Ahmad Khān, the Ebionites in the early church preserved the Hebrew version of Matthew, which is more purely unitarian than the Greek version. Unfortunately the majority of Christians came to understand Jesus in a trinitarian sense. The true picture of Jesus in the gospels does accord with that of the Qur'ān, where Christ was sent by God to teach spiritual holiness. "It was necessary that a person should be born who would teach the people spiritual holiness and spiritual light. This could be done effectively only by the one who was born of the spirit only and not through any external cause."[48]

Muhammad `Abdūh (1849-1905), represents a Middle Eastern response to Christianity in the nineteenth century. `Abdūh was both a lecturer at al-Azhār in Cairo and the leading reformer in the Arab world of his day. His openness to European thought meant that like Sayyid Ahmad Khān, he was able to appreciate the presuppositions of Christendom. He also shared with Ahmad Khān a desire to integrate Enlightenment rationalism into Islam. Another area of agreement between the two thinkers was their willingness to accept that the Bible contained the authentic *Torah* and *Injīl*. Thus the life and teaching of Jesus can be retrieved to a large extent from the four gospels. In his commentary on the Qur'ān transcribed in twelve volumes by his disciple Rāshid Ridā, he held that the disciples of Jesus recorded "what they understood of all that he taught them, his commands, his wisdom, and his proclamation; and these gospels are true in our opinion."[49] `Abduh believed that Jesus spoke of God as his father metaphorically.[50]

---

[47] A Khān, *The Mahomedan Commentary on the Holy Bible* vol.1:150, in Troll, 81.

[48] *Ibid.,* vol.3:23, in Troll, 98.

[49] M. `Abdūh, *Tafsīr al-Manār* vol.2:159f, in R. Caspar and J-M. Gaudeul, 'Textes de la Tradition Musulmane concernant le Tahrīf des Écritures', *Islamochristiana* 6 (1980), 61-104, 93.

[50] *Ibid.,*vol.3:345, in Caspar and Gaudeul, 95.

Muhammad Kāmil Husain (d. 1979), was a medical practitioner in Cairo who published widely on religious subjects, and became well known for his 1954 novel on the events of Good Friday in Jerusalem, entitled *City of Wrong*, which led to an Egyptian State Prize for Literature in 1957. This dramatic account of the desire of the Jewish leaders to have Jesus crucified relied heavily on the evidence found in the four gospels. His novel is structured around the people who witnessed the events of Good Friday. The Romans are central to the plot as exercising authority at the time. The Jews want rid of Jesus, but they do not have the power to execute him. "The day was a Friday. On that day the Jewish people conspired together to require from the Romans the crucifixion of Christ, so that they might destroy his message, a decision to crucify the human conscience and extinguish its light."[51] There follows a series of portraits; Pilate and his wife, a blacksmith, a merchant, the lawyer who issued the death sentence on Jesus, Lazarus, Caiaphas, Mary Magdalene, the disciples who ran away, a Roman officer and finally a soldier. Husain stops short of portraying the crucifixion itself. Husain was asked by his English translator, Kenneth Cragg, what his attitude was to the crucifixion of Jesus recounted in the gospels, and he replied that the Qur'ānic text concerning the crucifixion is difficult to interpret with assurance. "The text is taken to mean that the Jews thought they killed Christ, but God raised him unto him in a way we can leave unexplained among the several mysteries which we have taken for granted on faith alone."[52] Husain decided to live with the paradox of faith cancelling history. He was happy to quarry the gospels for information for his novel without affirming that any of it actually happened in reality. Faith arises from what has been revealed in the Qur'ān, and Husain composed his novel within the confines of that revelation. Where story transgresses faith, then Husain is silent. When pressed on the historicity of the events of Good Friday, Husain adopted an ambiguous stance.

He returned to the historicity of the crucifixion in a later work on the philosophy of religion, *The Hallowed Valley*. Here he expounds why Islam denies the death of Jesus on the cross. The real issue is not so much whether Jesus died by crucifixion, as what Christians claim happened on the cross. Indeed the conflict between Muslims and Christians concerning the death of Christ runs much deeper than many imagine.

> "The real issue that divides lies in the fact that Christians believe in atonement and redemption, whereby men may be delivered from their sins and be declared pure and clean ... Muslims, for their part, do not enthuse about redemption. Nor do they believe in atonement for

[51] M.K. Husain, *City of Wrong* (Amsterdam: 1959), 3.
[52] *Ibid.*, note on page 222.

transgressions by dint of what befalls another who is not the transgressor. With us, no burden bearer can bear any other's burden."[53]

The real contention is therefore not about history but faith. The denial of the death of Christ on the cross is not so much a denial of history as a denial of Jesus as an object of faith. Although Husain is sympathetic to the story of Christ in the gospels, the death of Christ and the focus Christians place on its effects do not impress him as true. Kenneth Cragg, who translated Husain's writing, has attempted to respond to these concerns, and the next chapter will examine his apologetic work.

Conclusion

Pfander and Lūqā show how Christians could take Islamic convictions into their Christological writing at least in a partial way. The main attraction for them in referring to Qur'ān commentary or the *Ḫadīth* literature lay in the seeming support found there for certain Christian interpretations of Christ's person and work. Thus both Pfander and Lūqā made great play over the sinless character of Christ argued for by Qur'ān commentators and sound Prophetic sayings. The negative role of Islamic tradition was not so helpful to them. For example, neither of them engaged with the unanimous denial of the crucifixion by the Qur'ān commentators, nor the idea that Christ would break crosses on his return at the end of time found in the *Ḫadīth*. As a result, Muslim readers would most likely conclude that Islamic writing was only being used as a repository of arguments to back Christian claims and not as a source of objective truth.

The Muslim writers surveyed show a mixed attitude to Christian scripture and tradition from the generous attitude of Aḫmad Khān to the hostile approach of Rahmatullāh. However, the findings of gospel scholarship enabled both of them to separate the developed faith of the church from the teaching and practice of Jesus of Nazareth, and argue for a Christ that appeared to be much closer to the Qur'ānic portrait than most Christians cared to acknowledge. Neither Pfander nor Lūqā were ready for this reaction, since post-enlightenment gospel scholarship did not contribute to their understanding of Christology. They were essentially locked into a pre-enlightenment framework of scripture interpretation and were incapable of interacting with newer approaches to Christ.

During the second half of the twentieth century this deficit was made up by Christians who realised that dialogue with Muslims about Christ simply had to be conducted on the basis of sound interpretation of the gospels. The following chapter analyses the contribution of Kenneth Cragg, whose

---

[53] M.K. Husain, *The Hallowed Valley* (Cairo: 1977), 75f.

portrait of Christ is based on his understanding of the historical Jesus rather than the Christ of the Church's faith.

Chapter Eight

The Christology of Kenneth Cragg in Dialogue with Muslims

Getting Back to the Historical Jesus

The Christological writing of Kenneth Cragg (b. 1913) for an Islamic context spans much of the second half of the Twentieth century.[1] His approach to Christology is quite different from any of the apologists reviewed so far, since he bases his understanding of Christ on the records found in the synoptic gospels, rather than on the theology of the fourth gospel, or the New Testament epistles, or the creeds of the church. Cragg accepts the distinction, made by New Testament criticism in the modern era, between historical facts about Jesus of Nazareth and beliefs about him developed by the church. For Cragg it is essential to present to Muslims what Jesus taught and did, carefully distinguishing the self-understanding of Christ from the beliefs in Christ held by the church.

In order to present the historical Jesus to Muslims it is also necessary for Christians to begin with what Muslims already know about him from the Qur'ān. This is the only sound method of apologetics, because a Christology that does not take account of Islamic convictions about Christ will not be properly understood, let alone accepted, by Muslims. Cragg's way of using the Qur'ān is new in Christian apologetics. Eighth and Ninth century apologists appealed to Qur'ānic texts to support the possibility of the union of divinity and humanity in Christ as developed in the theology of the churches. Pfander's quotations from the Qur'ān supported New Testament belief in the sinlessness of Christ, since Pfander held the Apostolic teaching about Jesus to be central to Christology. Lūqā's use of the Qur'ān was not to support the Jesus of history but to back up the divinity of Christ presented in the Johannine writings of the New Testament and in the Nicene creed of the Patristic era. Cragg seeks to get back behind developed Christology to the kind of person the historical Jesus claimed to be.

[1] Cragg's first major treatment of Christology was in his 1956 *The Call of The Minaret*, but it was not until his *Jesus and the Muslim* of 1985 that he produced a book entirely dedicated to the subject.

The Call of the Minaret

Cragg's earliest attempt at communicating a Christian view of Jesus to Muslims was made in his first book *The Call of the Minaret*, written in 1956 while he was teaching at Hartford Seminary in Connecticut, USA. He had served as a curate in the Church of England before moving to Beirut in 1939 to teach philosophy in the American University there. The book reflects his situation as an educator of Western postgraduate scholars of Islam and is addressed to Christians who seek to relate to Muslims in the Islamic world. In the light of his own exposure to the Islamic world he encourages Western Christians to identify as much as possible with Muslims in their thinking and communicating. In terms of Christology this means that Christian talk about Jesus must be done "in terms that Muslims can understand."[2]

The ideal approach is to enable Muslims to relate to Christ in the same way that the first disciples did. They came to convictions about him after a period of time rather than all at once, and Muslims may need to be allowed some considerable time to appreciate who Jesus claimed to be. This process of understanding must begin with the Qur'ānic account of Jesus which provides a Muslim with some basic knowledge that can be enlarged from the accounts in the New Testament gospels. The rather slight data concerning the historical Jesus in the Qur'ān can then be supplemented "by all those aspects of Jesus which remain unknown to Islam."[3] A Muslim may then reach the same kind of view of Jesus that the first disciples came to on their travels with him.

But there are two obstacles arising from the Islamic conception of God that might prevent a Muslim from reaching the conviction of the early Christians that Jesus was an Incarnate saviour. The first obstacle is that God reveals through the speech of prophets and the books they brought but not in the men themselves. The Christian conception of Jesus is that he reveals God not only in his speech but also in himself. How then can a Muslim step around this rock on the path to understanding Christ? The solution lies in the Christian reminding the Muslim that the nature of God is personal for Muslims as well as Christians. On this basis it must be possible for a Muslim to see that speech implies self-revelation. Just as humans reveal themselves when they speak, so God must be showing his character when he speaks. A Christian ought to lay the groundwork for a Christian presentation of Jesus by making the argument, "if God is personal, knowledge of Him must be a personal revelation. He can never be only propositional."[4]

---

[2] K Cragg, *The Call of the Minaret* (New York: 1956), 287.
[3] *Ibid.*, 288.
[4] *Ibid.*, 290.

The second obstacle is that since God is sovereign his will is always accomplished despite any appearances to the contrary, which seems to make the Christian idea that God has come in Jesus "an unworthy thing."[5] The Christian needs to address this conception of sovereignty by asking the Muslim whether a God who never comes to deal with his wayward subjects directly is really in control. This coming of God in Jesus may be very difficult for a Muslim trained to think of God as utterly transcendent to accept, so Christians must find a way of showing that transcendent divine power and majesty is enhanced by Christ.

> "When we present Christ, we ask Muslims to believe not less but more, in the undefeated sovereignty of God ...[We] invite men to seek and find in Christ the demonstration that God is God alone, and that all contrary powers are gloriously vanquished and subdued."[6]

This conclusion can only be made after leading the Muslim to the outcome of the death of Jesus. But this means that the presentation of the life and teaching of Jesus from the gospels seems to depend on the way his disciples came to believe that Christ's death overcame forces hostile to God's rule. Cragg does not really demonstrate how a Christian should take a Muslim on the journey through the ministry of Jesus. After working out how to get the Muslim around the two obstacles on the path he goes on immediately to discuss a third obstacle, the denial of the crucifixion in the Qur'ān. This is curious when he has announced his intention to lead the Muslim the way the disciples went. The Muslim has to consider the implications of the death of Jesus before he follows the life of Jesus in the gospels, whereas Jesus' disciples were only faced with the realisation that Jesus had arrived on the scene to suffer and die after having lived with him for many months.

According to Cragg there ought to be no real difference between Jesus' disciples' and a modern Muslim's appreciation of Jesus if he intended to go to the cross right from the outset of his ministry. Jesus had come to die and anyone who approaches the gospels today cannot fail to see this, although it took his disciples time to accept the truth. As far as Jesus was concerned he was aware of

> "the inevitability of suffering and His surrender to the necessity ... From beginning to end, he resisted the temptation - in the wilderness, on the road, in the garden, even on the cross itself … to avoid the climax, to abandon Jerusalem, 'to come down from the Cross'."[7]

The Cross is the main motive for Jesus' life and ministry, so this third obstacle for a Muslim is not only to be found towards the end of the journey but very much also at the commencement. However, it may be more of a

[5] *Ibid.*, 291.
[6] *Ibid.*, 292.
[7] *Ibid.*, 296.

barrier than the first two obstacles since the Qur'ān seems to deny the historicity of the crucifixion. This rejection of the cross has "made havoc of the manifest continuity between what Jesus taught and what Jesus suffered."[8] Cragg thinks that the denial of the death of Christ by crucifixion arose from a desire to protect Christ from defeat at the hands of his enemies, based on the presupposition that prophets succeed in their mission. This fear of a failed prophet has distorted the portrait of Jesus in the Qur'ān. "In conforming Christ to its own conception of the successful Prophet, Islam has robbed Him of Himself, transformed Him into an unrecognisable Jesus."[9] In the face of such Islamic determination to have a successful Jesus, what should the Christian do? It is better not to argue, but rather to witness to the impact of the cross. "We must show what the preaching of the Cross has meant in our own lives and proclaim the discovery of power and peace which has been made by multitudes through the faith that Christ died for them."[10] However some explanation of this faith ought also to be given. Jesus forgave those who crucified him and because he forgave, forgiveness becomes possible for others. Only by bearing sin does he bear away sin. His death is an act of obedience to his Father's will as well as a demonstration of the love of God for sinful people. Finally, His death shows that suffering is essential to the nature of God.

Evaluation

Cragg expounds the significance of Jesus from an Evangelical Protestant perspective that emphasises the effect of his death for others. The teaching of Jesus held to be central by Liberal Protestants is hardly touched on here. Cragg has more in common with Pfander than Liberal gospel scholars who deny that Jesus intended to die for others.[11] His failure to acknowledge such scholarship opens his writing to the same criticism that Pfander had faced a

---

[8] *Ibid.*

[9] *Ibid.*

[10] *Ibid.*, 297.

[11] Cragg does not report and discuss the kind of gospel scholarship common in Germany that rigorously distinguished between the thinking and teaching of Jesus and the ideas and words credited to him by the early church. For example, *The Theology of the New Testament*, by the leading German scholar Rudolph Bultmann, had come out in an English edition in 1951. Bultmann believed that Jesus had been crucified but that his intention to die as a ransom for others was not historically accurate. Only after his death did the church develop the crucifixion into an intentional act of atonement. "Can there be any doubt that the predictions of the passion are all *vaticinia ex eventu*?" [R. Bultmann, *The Theology of the New Testament* vol.1 (London: 1951), 29.] From Bultmann's perspective Cragg expounds the faith of the early church but not the thinking of Jesus.

century previously, that the picture of Christ is not one that is truly representative of Christian opinion. Cragg might have argued that many distinguished gospel scholars held that Jesus did intend to go to the cross on behalf of others, but he seems unwilling to get drawn into Christian scholarly debate.[12]

However, this lack of attention to internal discussion among Christians is a serious problem for a presentation of Jesus for Muslims. In the nineteenth Century, Pfander could be excused for ignoring new interpretations of the gospels as products of the faith of the church rather than the actual teaching or activity of Jesus himself, but Cragg had been exposed to this well established tradition of scholarship in his training for Church of England ministry. The measure of the problem can be observed in a round table discussion organised by the World Council of Churches in 1976, in which Ismā'īl al-Farūqī used his extensive knowledge of Christian gospel scholarship to challenge the historicity of the life and teaching of Jesus found in the synoptic gospels.[13]

Dialogue with Ismā`īl al-Farūqī

From 1959 to 1967 Cragg had been involved in teaching at an Anglican college in Canterbury, England, and then had been appointed Assistant Bishop of Jerusalem, living in Cairo from 1970 to 1973. At the time of the dialogue he was Reader in Religious Studies at the University of Sussex, a

---

[12] British and American gospel scholars tended at mid-century to be less radical than their German counterparts. For example, leading British synoptic gospels expert, Vincent Taylor, complained of "excessive scepticism from the continent" [V Taylor, *The Life and Ministry of Jesus* (London: 1954), 26.] He held that Jesus predicted his death by crucifixion as a ransom for the sins of Israel.

[13] The debate over al-Farūqī's paper "On the Nature of Islamic Da'wah" was published in *IRM* 65 (1976), 391-409. Al-Farūqī was the leading Muslim spokesperson and Cragg the foremost Christian debater among the invited participants. Al-Farūqī had published *Christian Ethics* in 1967 and showed a fine awareness of current Christian scholarship. During the discussion of a presentation entitled "The Concept and Practice of Christian Mission" by Arne Rudvin, a Lutheran Bishop from Pakistan, who had insisted that Christian mission to Muslims was an inevitable consequence of Jesus' commission to his disciples to make disciples among all nations, al-Farūqī pointed out that Jesus himself gave no such order as the best Christian scholars had shown, but that the early church had put the command on Jesus' lips to attempt to give dominical authority for a mission to non-Jews. Therefore Jesus could not be quoted as supporting mission outside the Jewish community (*Ibid.*, 385). In this al-Farūqī was correct, since even the moderate German scholar J. Jeremias held that Jesus only commissioned his disciples to go to fellow Jews with the message of the kingdom. [J. Jeremias, *New Testament Theology* vol.1 (London: 1971), 303-10.]

post he retired from in 1978. It was not surprising that Cragg should be invited by the World Council of Churches Department on Dialogue with other Faiths and Ideologies to represent them in a debate on mission at Chambèsy, Switzerland in 1976. Cragg had established himself as the leading Christian exponent of dialogue with Muslims, not only through the widely read *The Call of the Minaret*, but also in his 1959 work, *Sandals at the Mosque*. The very titles of these books suggested an eirenic attitude on his part to Islamic convictions. Cragg was summoning fellow Christians to a serious listening exercise, and was the obvious choice for the leadership of the kind of high profile event that the WCC dialogue section had in mind. Ismā'īl al-Farūqī was also an obvious leader of the Muslim delegation at the talks. He had taught religious studies in several North American Universities, and had established a reputation as a Muslim student of Christianity.

Cragg followed his *The Call of the Minaret* method in the conversation at Chambèsy, by attempting to get the Muslim group to reassess their concept of God to make room for the Incarnation. Cragg took the lead in continually pressing the Muslims to answer his points. Al-Farūqī was the main respondent, so that eventually the table talk became a dialogue between the two men with the rest of the group reduced to being silent listeners. Cragg's opening question concerned the teaching of the Qur'ān about the relationship between the Creator and his creation. Cragg wondered whether the Qur'ān did not actually presuppose God's involvement with humanity. Here he was dealing with the first obstacle to a Christian presentation of Jesus outlined in *The Call of the Minaret* concerning the transcendent character of God. According to the transcript of the informal table talk, Cragg was unable to elicit a positive answer from al-Farūqī.

Cragg pressed al-Farūqī to accept that God has compromised his omnipotence in entrusting the created world to human management. Al-Farūqī replied that the creator of a computer is not compromised by the power of the machine he has created. Cragg retorted, "Man is not a computer ... He is a volitional being, and what is required of him is a volitional Islam ... God is involved in wrong that jahiliyyah does to him."[14] Al-Farūqī denied the involvement of God in the wrongdoing of humans.

> "I would deny accountability or responsibility on the part of God for my misdeeds ... God has given me freedom and moral responsibility ... Now if it is my will, despite all this, to disobey Him, then I am responsible and I live to bear the burden, not God."[15]

---

[14] *IRM*, 407.
[15] *Ibid*., 407f.

Cragg tried another route. The issue is really the degree of God's involvement with humanity. Islam acknowledges that God cares about people, but he shows it through speech alone. Surely compassion must be more than issuing commands. So Cragg asked, "Is there the possibility of a relationship more tragic, more compassionate? It is possible you can be found forbidding things to God in the interest of what you trust is His dignity."[16] Al-Farūqī responded by arguing that he is forbidding man not forbidding God. However, Cragg protested, "You are forbidding God the sovereign freedom of manifesting His transcendence in whatever way He chooses - which may be to condescend to man's condition in terms of incarnation."[17] Al-Farūqī had the last word, and it was a Qur'ānic one. "There is this revealed text in the Qur'ān which says - There is nothing like unto him [42:11]. It is we who must beware of what is appropriate when talking about God and about transcendence."[18]

Evaluation

Cragg concentrates in this debate on the logic of Incarnation since the character of God is at stake when presenting a Christian view of Jesus. The details of the life of Jesus are insufficient to establish his divinity, so the life of Jesus can only demonstrate Incarnation if the idea is first argued for. Cragg does not really think that the historical Jesus can establish his own Incarnate identity. Perhaps the idea of the Messianic Secret in the synoptic gospels is in the back of Cragg's mind. In Mark's gospel in particular Jesus appears to want his Messianic status to be kept in the dark, but he is constantly foiled by excited recipients of his healing ministry who cannot but tell of what he has done for them. But why cannot Jesus establish his own case? Why does Cragg insist on a priori argument about what God can and cannot do? Even if Cragg wins his argument about the possibility of Incarnation, he still has to establish that Jesus is actually the Incarnate one, which can only be done by examining the gospel accounts themselves.

Here Cragg shows that he is in the great tradition of Christian apologetics in an Islamic context. If he can persuade Muslims to rethink their view of God, then the Incarnation can become acceptable to them. In following this methodology he does not acknowledge any debt to the ninth Century writers surveyed in this thesis, but his argument is similar to the discussion of the throne texts by Abū Qurra and Abū Rā'iṭa.[19] Cragg's own evaluation of the debate points out the strategic importance he placed on the doctrine of God in discussion with Muslims concerning Christ. In a lecture

[16] *Ibid.*, 408.

[17] *Ibid.*

[18] *Ibid.*

[19] See chapters three and four.

delivered at the Pontifical Institute of Arabic Studies at Rome in December 1976, Cragg commented on the Chambèsy encounter with al- Farūqī,

> "The parties are united in holding that to speak of God as transcendent means including and excluding certain things ... both are agreed that God is most great. The problem between them is that He is differently greater. The obligation for dialogue, then, is just a longer patience and a surer realism."[20]

Patience and realism were to be tested by the advent of the 1979 Iranian revolution and the heightened atmosphere of Islamic vigour in the early 1980's. Cragg wistfully reflected on this new situation in 1983. Dialogue has to do with moving "from bigotry and towards finality". However Christians and Muslims have different sources of truth which they believe to be final. "The New Testament will be truth for Christians, the Qur'ān truth for Muslims, irrespective - in the mutual situation - of the truth of either for the other."[21] He recognises that some argue that dialogue is not likely to get beyond these two "mutually complementary and mutually contradictory Truths". He resists this conclusion because it leads to "supine tolerance", which presumably means a reduction of the concept of truth to varieties of belief that are more or less of equal value. If dialogue is about truth rather than belief, or about truth rather than truths, then it will take courage in the face "of national passion, of hemispheric tension and of spiritual alienation."[22]

Cragg reflected again on the Chambèsy encounter in a 1995 paper about al-Farūqī. Recounting the 1976 discussion, Cragg commented that his partner had "ignored the whole careful consideration as to the congenially divine".[23] He drew three conclusions from the "ignoring" of his arguments. Firstly, Christians should not be put off by such "bland dismissiveness" from the Muslim side, but should continue to set forth the logic of the intentional involvement of God in His creation. Secondly, they should not listen to non-Muslims who complain when Christians "read things Christian into things Islamic". Thirdly, non-Muslims should not tell Muslims what Islam "ought to be in regret that it is not".[24] There must be no shrinking back from "authentic" dialogue, which presses from the Christian side the question of how far the compassion of God has to go to meet the predicament of man.

---

[20] K. Cragg, "Legacies and Hopes in Muslim/Christian Theology", *Islamochristiana* 3 (1977), 1-10, 9.

[21] K. Cragg, *The Pen and the Faith* (London: 1983), 113.

[22] *Ibid.*

[23] K. Cragg, "Ismā'īl al-Farūqī in the Field of Dialogue", in Y.Y. Haddad & W.Z. Haddad (eds.), *Christian-Muslim Encounters*, (Gainesville: 1995), 406.

[24] *Ibid.*

But dialogue must not concede to Muslims what Christians ought not to concede. It is one thing for secularists to hold that Christianity and Islam are merely types of belief that are not to be regarded as true in any ultimate sense. It is quite wrong for committed Christians to follow the same reasoning. Cragg criticised Hans Küng for stepping beyond the bounds of authentic dialogue by conceding truth to the Qur'ān that it does not contain. The German theologian stated in a speech he had made in Iran in 1985 that the Qur'ān was "an effective word of the all-forgiving and merciful God for believing Muslims".[25] Cragg protests that Küng has misread the Qur'ān as being effectively a word of divine forgiveness when it is not.

> "The Qur'ān plainly disavows the principle concerning forgiveness which Christians believe is enshrined in the love that bears away and only so doing bears it away - the love and the principle being together present, respectively and divinely in the cross of Jesus. That cross, however, the Qur'ān strongly denies ... Further the Qur'ān repeatedly excludes the redemptive principle by its reiteration that no burden-bearer bears any burden but his own. If that is as it would seem to be then is truth **for** here consonant with truth **of** as to the cross? Perhaps the question cannot be answered."[26]

Despite the "perhaps" it is clear that Cragg does not think that a Christian ought to confess that divine forgiveness is effective on Qur'ānic terms, since divine forgiveness can only be effective through the cross. Cragg's doubt about the effectiveness of divine forgiveness in Islam colours all of his writing. However, Küng believes that salvation is available to Muslims as Muslims, and that divine forgiveness does not need to be restricted to the cross as Christians have tended to think.[27] Richard Jones' summary of Cragg's view of Islam as a way of salvation is apt.

> "Cragg takes a doubtful view of Islam as a way of salvation. Convinced that God is rightly understood only in Trinitarian terms, Cragg has to conclude that doctrinal elements in Islam tend to block Muslims from full saving knowledge of God. Convinced that humanity requires more than a mere reminder of its vocation Cragg remains constrained to proffer to Muslims additional dimensions of salvation not contemplated in the usual pattern of their response to God."[28]

In other words, Cragg is unwilling to accept that the Qur'ān reveals an adequate way of finding forgiveness with God. Muslims are ultimately in

---

[25] H. Küng, in *The Christian Century* (Chicago, 9 October, 1985). Cited by Cragg in *To Meet and to Greet* (London: 1992), 42.

[26] *Ibid.*

[27] See chapter nine for Küng's Christology.

[28] R.J. Jones, "Wilfred Cantwell Smith and Kenneth Cragg on Islam as a Way of Salvation", *IBMR* 16 (1992), 105-109, 109.

need of the revelation of God in Christ as the means of forgiveness. Dialogue then, for Christians, is the opportunity to make clear the conviction that God was in Christ reconciling the world to himself. Other ways of reconciliation are not true ways, and it is the task of Christians to clarify this in dialogue with Muslims. This explains Cragg's questioning of the transcendence of God in Islam, as exemplified in his dialogue with al-Farūqī, and why he complained that the latter had failed to answer the questions. Cragg's approach is to interrogate the coherence of transcendence without immanence, since without the Incarnation there can be no relationship between humans and God.

Jesus and the Muslim

Cragg wrote *Jesus and the Muslim* in 1985 to meet an unfulfilled need "to have the New Testament seriously read and studied in the Islamic world."[29] He notes that Muslims have yet to master the technical skills required for such a task and he is concerned that the "temperamental" skills needed are not in abundant evidence. Before embarking on a presentation of the life of Jesus, he casts a glance at the methods of his predecessors. He will not follow the tradition of reading Christian meanings into the Qur'ān that contradict the teaching of the Qur'ān as a whole. He cites, as an example, the reading of *sūras* 3:45 and 4:171, where Jesus is given the title "a word from him", in the light of the Prologue to John's gospel. This superimposition of the Johannine "Word" on the meaning of the Qur'ān is illegitimate. "It would be against the insistent themes of the Qur'ān to read this New Testament dimension into the Kalimah of the Surahs about Jesus."[30]

A better way is to enable the Muslim reader to discover the historical Jesus, but this raises the problem of the veracity of the gospels. Has the Muslim reader not heard of doubts among Christian scholars concerning the historical value of Matthew, Mark and Luke? Do these gospel writers not express their own convictions, or the convictions of groups they represent? So how much of the historical Jesus can be recovered by gospel archaeology? Cragg adopts a moderately critical stance in terms of gospel scholarship. On "the one hand there is no place here for infallibility," but on the other hand he acknowledges that "church situations fold back into the telling of the history of Jesus."[31] The middle way is to accept that all history is composed of what happened as well as the meaning of what happened. In other words the perspective of the gospel writers cannot be separated from

[29] K. Cragg, *Jesus and the Muslim* (London: 1985), preface xiv.
[30] *Ibid.*, 32.
[31] *Ibid.*, 85f.

the events they report. This should occasion no alarm, for all history is written from a particular point of view.

The Historical Jesus

Cragg takes the Muslim into the encounter with the historical Jesus by way of the kingdom that Jesus proclaimed, which is only apparently about an objective reality belonging to God. The heart of Jesus' message about the kingdom is a message about himself. "Jesus' message of the kingdom is not about something external to himself of which he merely tells. It is something he announces as operative through him."[32] Cragg recognises that this concept of "truth-through-personality" is very difficult for a Muslim to accept. "This New Testament awareness of truth in Jesus and not simply from him, of the word that he is rather than the words that he brings" is radically different from the concept of prophethood in Islam, "with its strong sense of wahy, or revelation-inspiration, as a language bestowal."[33]

The kingdom is demonstrated in Jesus' actions, which Cragg confines to acts of healing and compassion. The nature miracles seem to cause him difficulty. He expresses puzzlement at the decision of Jesus to condemn the fig tree [Mark 11:12-14; 20f]. This is no doubt due to Cragg's definition of Kingdom actions as, "the occasions of healing and compassion...All have to do with genuine suffering, emergency and need."[34] It is evident in such actions that Jesus reveals how he is at the centre of the kingdom, but acts of power for their own sake would not accomplish such a goal. Kingdom actions "are quite unlike the stories which occur in apocryphal writing about purely fortuitous 'miracles' such as the making of clay birds that flew."[35] He does not discuss the possible reaction that the dismissal of this miracle attested by the Qur'ān might have on a Muslim reader. This is very disturbing, given his insistence on taking the Qur'ānic account of Jesus seriously. In general, if the nature miracles in the gospels are not historical, then can the historical accuracy of the other miracles be trusted? Might they not also be products of enthusiastic faith?

Cragg is more concerned to get to the heart of Jesus' ministry, than to engage in a defence of the historicity of the miracle stories of the gospels. The heart of Jesus' life and work is 'suffering'. Echoing the thinking of *The Call of the Minaret*, he sees the verse "the Son of Man must suffer" [Mark 8:31] as the secret to all that motivated Jesus, whose determination to face the hostility of religious vested interests is the outward expression of this inner commitment.

---

32 *Ibid.*, 129.
33 *Ibid.*, 129f.
34 *Ibid.*, 141.
35 *Ibid.*

"Messiah may not abnegate or adjust his message to evade its hostile reception. On the contrary, in the Gospels, Jesus deliberately and strongly seeks out Jerusalem, the citadel and shrine of the forces and prejudices which disown him."[36]

We know how Jesus intended to face suffering from the way he spoke about the future in language borrowed from Isaiah 53. In his early work Cragg simply took it for granted that gospel scholarship could be relied on to support this view. So he wrote in *Sandals at the Mosque*, "Somehow the fact of suffering as integral to Messiahship had to be worked into the scheme of things, for minds to which the two concepts were unthinkable together."[37] By 1985 Cragg is aware that Jesus' predictions of his suffering are ascribed to the evangelists by many New Testament scholars, but argues that the gospel writers were not as creative as such scholars suppose.

"Words and haunting imagery from Isaiah 53 can be detected in the language of Jesus in anticipating the Cross ... It is of course, possible to attribute the alignment of the Gospel narrative and prophetic precedent to the evangelists, as somehow, the precedents determined the story. But could they, as it were, be self-fulfilling without a living self - the self of Jesus - to fulfil them? ...The role of the evangelists was responsive, not original."[38]

The last sentence is a big claim. If Cragg does not rely on infallibility, and admits that the recounting of Jesus is done by the early church, then it is but a small step to accept that the evangelists represented the attitude and concerns of the church of their time. Cragg does in fact acknowledge scholarly distinctions between parables as Jesus may have delivered them and the versions of the evangelists.

"The parable in Luke 16:1-12 has 'footnotes' from verses 8 to 12, on the part of the evangelist ... Readers have need of care to discern, if they can, the ways in which the present text has been formulated from its springs in Jesus via the oral reporting and the editing within church situations."[39]

This leaves the question open whether it is not Mark who structures his gospel around the three pronouncements of Jesus about his death. The dividing line between response and originality is then much less clear.[40]

---

[36] *Ibid.*, 151.

[37] K. Cragg, *Sandals at the Mosque*, 93.

[38] K. Cragg, *Jesus and the Muslim,* 156.

[39] *Ibid.*, 87f.

[40] It is now a common assumption in mainstream British scholarship that Jesus' reference to Isaiah 53 is the work of the early church. See for instance, M. Hooker, *The Gospel of Mark* (London: 1991), 248-251; and W.R. Telford, *Mark* (Sheffield: 1995), 134. Cragg could have appealed to an earlier generation of scholars who supported his view. See, for example, the staunch defence of Jesus' intention to die

The comment by Christopher Lamb on Cragg's handling of New Testament scholarship is disturbingly accurate; "Some have thought that his attitude to Biblical criticism seems to be to ignore its alleged results while defending its legitimacy of method."[41] Cragg responded to this criticism in his 1995 *The Lively Credentials of God*. To side with the reductionist critic is to end up with the impossible notion that the church invented Jesus. It takes more faith to be a sceptic than a conservative.

> "The case is strong for the view that the Gospels represent an event faith, a faith-event, a literature that deserves to be trusted if perceptively received as such. We have always to ask what kind of 'event' must Jesus and his 'Christhood' have been to have had this reporting ... To discount the documents as self-generating, self-deluded, or self-opinionated would be the ultimate credulity."[42]

Nevertheless, Cragg seems to be disinterested in the painstaking work of gospel scholarship, brushing aside the tensions between different gospel portraits. To ask for faith in the faith of the gospel writers is actually another form of infallibility. Cragg does not himself always trust in the judgment of the writers of the gospels, so it is difficult to know on what basis their presentation of Jesus is to be accepted or criticised. In the end it is not easy for Cragg to take a Muslim to the Jesus of history when he is unsure of how to secure the actual history of Jesus.

Jesus in the Qur'ān

Cragg is not averse to being original in his interpretation of the Qur'ān when he links *sūra* 5:113 to the last supper. In *sūra* 5:113 Jesus prays, "Lord, send a table from heaven to us that will be a celebratory feast for us, for all of us from first to last, a sign from you". Cragg picks out the table, the festival for the disciples, and the sign, as fitting into "the occasion of 'this last supper' in Jerusalem ...There is nothing unfitting in the Qur'ānic Jesus presiding at this mā'idah of communion with his disciples and of solace to their hearts."[43] But this begs the question of the content of the last supper. There is no indication in *sūra* 5:113, that Jesus intends the festival to celebrate his impending death. Indeed the only death that comes into

---

as a ransom for the people in terms taken from Isaiah 53 made by J. Jeremias, *New Testament Theology* vol.1 (London: 1971), 288-299.

[41] C.A. Lamb, *The Call to Retrieval: Kenneth Cragg's Christian Vocation to Islam* (London: 1997), 70.

[42] K. Cragg, *The Lively Credentials of God* (London: 1995), 171f.

[43] K. Cragg, *Jesus and the Muslim*, 158. Cragg had first put forward this interpretation in an article published in *The Muslim World* in 1959 under the psuedonym `Abd al-Tafāhum. Cragg was editor of the journal during his tenure at Hartford Seminary. See `Abd al-Tafāhum, "The Qur'ān and the Holy Communion", *MW* 49 (1959), 239-248.

view is that awaiting the unbelievers when God agrees to send the table. "God said: I will certainly send a table to you but whoever among you fails to believe afterwards, I will certainly punish more severely than any other member of the human race." The Qur'ānic context of the table is that of a miraculous sign that authenticates the sending of Jesus in the eyes of his disciples, but this type of authentication, as seen in the sign of the bird/birds made from clay, is not congenial to Cragg. It is, nevertheless, what the Qur'ān appears to be presenting, so the claim that the Qur'ān speaks of "the body and blood of the Lord" is open to the objection that Cragg makes about Johannine superimposition on the Qur'ānic "a word from him". Both readings do not take the overall message of the Qur'ān seriously in interpreting specific texts.

A similar issue of marrying the Qur'ān with the gospels arises in Cragg's interpretation of *sūra* 3:55, "O Jesus, I am causing you to die and I will exalt you to myself". This pronouncement of the death of Jesus, is linked by Cragg with Mark 10:33, "the Son of Man must suffer". Cragg argues on the basis of this connection, that the Qur'ān can be read to support Jesus' "will for" crucifixion.[44] However, only non-Muslims have interpreted *mutawaffi-ka* as "cause to die". Muslim interpretation has favoured "cause to sleep" or "cause to wait until the right time for death by natural causes, not at the hands of men".[45] Cragg does not enter into dialogue with such Muslim interpretation in order to justify his own Christian reading of the Qur'ān, but in a book addressed to Muslims this omission is less than helpful to his case.

Cragg is critical of Christians who have tried to interpret *sūra* 4:157-9 as supporting the crucifixion of Jesus. He does not think much of the argument that while the Qur'ān states that the Jews "certainly did not kill Jesus", the passage leaves room for the Romans to carry the blame. "If the context of 4:157-9 intended to substitute 'the Romans' it would surely have to say 'it was not they, the Jews, who killed him; it was the Romans' ...We cannot escape the negation of the crucifixion by confusion as to the agent."[46] For all Cragg's attempts to link the Qur'ān and the death of Christ, he finally admits that the Qur'ānic teaching about the death of Jesus by crucifixion is

---

[44] *Jesus and the Muslim,* 167, 169.

[45] See chapter one. Cragg's translation of *mutawaffi-ka* has not been accepted by any Muslim to date. Yūsuf `Alī translates "O Jesus, I will take thee to myself and raise thee to myself". A.H.M. Zahniser points out that only Christian interpreters have read the verb *tawaffā* in *sūras* 3:55 and 5:117 as 'causing to die'. "The meaning of 3:55 could be as adequately served by assuming that God completed Jesus' earthly mission without actual death as it would be assuming that he caused him to die." [A.H.M. Zahniser, "The Forms of *Tawaffā* in the Qur'ān: A Contribution to Christian-Muslim Dialogue", *MW* 79 (1989), 14-24, 23.]

[46] *Jesus and the Muslim*, 170.

that it was prevented by God. The Jews wanted him killed, Jesus was willing to go through with it, but God was against it happening. This is the great disappointment of the message of the Qur'ān and subsequent Islamic tradition. "Christianity lives by the confession of Jesus, veritably crucified and risen; Islam lives in the conviction that Jesus did not really die but was mysteriously received up into heaven."[47]

With such a yawning chasm between the Christian and the Muslim what is to be done? Cragg suggests an answer that differs from that given in *The Call of the Minaret*, where he thought that the best approach was not to argue, but to witness. Now there is room for argument. When Muslims object to the necessity of the cross as the only means of finding God's forgiveness, they do so "out of their confidence in divine competence, that his forgiveness of us is effortless and majestic."[48] Cragg suggests that this confidence is misplaced because it overlooks that forgiveness can only be effective in relationships. In other words there has to be a cost for God to forgive.

> "[Muslim] confidence in divine mercy is sound. But on reflection it surely melts away. It is clear that the redemptive action in Christ is truly the pattern of God's competence. Mercy, like justice and all else in God of which human experience is cognisant, is relational."[49]

Cragg knows what the Muslim reaction is likely to be; that it is quite wrong to insist that God must pay a price in order to forgive, and that it is rather the other way round. Cragg then uses the argument of not limiting God by granting him freedom, which may actually impose restrictions on him; in this case to limit the demonstration of his will and power to defeat evil utterly and completely. "Those who question the necessity of the Cross on the ground that forgiveness is effortless with God may be forbidding Him the will and power the Cross can measure."[50] More seriously, the refusal of Muslims to embrace the cross as God's act is a fundamental denial of the truths they hold dear. "Adamantly to exclude the Cross of Jesus from the wisdom of God is not truly to believe Allāhu Akbar. It is, rather, to withhold from His greatness what may well be its greatest measure and sign."[51] This kind of language is certainly not likely to sustain a quiet conversation in the courtyard of the mosque. Al-Farūqī's warning to Cragg about his language being suitable to the majesty of God ought to be heeded by Cragg here, since the very idea that Muslims should be denying God's greatness by denying an event that God has repudiated is monstrous.

---

47 *Ibid.*, 176.
48 *Ibid.*, 180.
49 *Ibid.*
50 *Ibid.*
51 *Ibid.*, 181.

Perhaps the counsel to avoid argument and simply witness, given in *The Call of the Minaret*, would maintain the conversation more effectively.

The Incarnation

Cragg begins his treatment of the Incarnation by studying the language of Sonship in the gospels. He suggests that Christians adopt non-physical terminology such as "filiality" to avoid misunderstanding, but although he is concerned that filiality is "a sadly abstract term for that warm communion with God we have traced in Jesus' ministry", he cannot think of a more appropriate term.[52] In *The Call of the Minaret* he outlined two problems that Muslims have with the Incarnation, but now he raises five questions Muslims ask about the Incarnation. Firstly, Does Christian faith not 'compromise God'? Does the Christian not 'violate divine transcendence'? The Christian may reply that the Muslim is actually the one who compromises God by denying the Incarnation. Such a denial "might indicate a Creator no longer vitally concerned with man."[53]

Secondly, "Should we not minimise God from the sort of human criteria that are in mind here?" Divine sovereignty must mean freedom from constraint from the human side, assumes the Muslim. The Christian should call this view of sovereignty "moral unaccountability on the part of God", and ought to press the Muslim to admit "we do no justice to that unutterable transcendence if we plead it to negate what is given in revelation."[54]

Thirdly, "Have we not put God under necessity?" Christians seem to imply some external constraint on God and so deny his sovereignty. But these constraints that seem to be external to God are actually internal to him. "The constraints of justice and love are within His own nature. His being characterised by them is His entire freedom." Indeed the Christian ought to turn the tables on the Muslim by arguing that it is the Muslim who puts constraints on God by insisting that, "He must be understood as arbitrary and despotic, or that He must be denied the liberty for the kind of loving initiative which Christians identify in Christ."[55]

Fourthly, this understanding of Christ as God Incarnate is tantamount to the greatest sin of all, associating with God what should not be associated with Him. Are Christians not deifying Christ? The answer is not too difficult, because the "Qur'ān is in fact rejecting adoptionism which Christians also repudiate." This is evident from *sūra* 17:111, "Say, Praise to God, who took not up a son" repeated in *sūras* 19:35,92 and 25:2. The verb 'take up' is used in *sūra* 2:54 of the Jews who "took to themselves" a calf

---

[52] *Ibid.*, 197.
[53] *Ibid.*, 198f.
[54] *Ibid.*, 199f.
[55] *Ibid.*, 200.

as a deity. Thus Christians can simply point out that Incarnation is about coming down (*tanāzūl*) not taking up (*ittikhādh*). "Deification in *ittikhādh* is all human and chronically misguided, in *tanāzūl* the initiative is all God's and blessedly compassionate." There is therefore no association, of what does not belong to God, in the Incarnation. Muslims can perhaps understand the Incarnation on the model of the Qur'ān itself. Muslims came to believe in the uncreatedness of the Qur'ān as Christians came to believe in the uncreatedness of Christ. Just as Muslims cannot fully explain the connection between the earthly Qur'ān in their hands and the heavenly Qur'ān that is believed to have descended, so Christians should not be judged for not being able to fully explain the connection between the historical Jesus and the pre-existent Christ.[56]

Fifthly, is Divine Unity not "at risk in this faith about Jesus as the Incarnate Word?" The Christian can turn to the Johannine expression 'the only begotten' in John 1:18 to find an answer. The Incarnation of God in Christ was not partial but complete. Since all of God is Incarnate there can be no division in God as a result of Incarnation. Seen this way the Incarnation upholds the unity of God.

> "The definitive, heavenly commissioned, incarnation of the pattern, in a once-for-all disclosure of its nature and its cost, could not be other than as singular as God is. It is seldom realised how close in this way is the Christian doctrine of 'the Word made flesh' to the Islamic passion for the divine unity."[57]

Cragg's five answers to Muslim questions do not use an analogy developed in two other pieces of writing; that Muḫammad is a clue to the Incarnation. In a 1974 essay he put forward the suggestion that the prophethood of Muḫammad must entail an association between God and humanity. "It is surely clear from the Qur'ān that Muḫammad's prophethood, far from being a cypher or a vacuity of mind and person, is a profound association of personal involvement and divine authorization."[58] This daring application of association language to Muḫammad's relationship with God flies in the face of Islamic sentiment, but Cragg draws back from pressing the metaphor. Instead he widens association to include all divine-human relationships.

> "Every instance of human charisma in divine employ, every coinciding of historical event with heavenly intent, contains in its own measure, this mystery of the eternal and temporal at rendezvous. To believe in the incarnation is not to exclusify that mystery. For it is relatively present in

[56] *Ibid.*, 203-5.

[57] *Ibid.*, 206.

[58] K. Cragg, "Islam and Incarnation", in J. Hick (ed.), *Truth and Dialogue,* (London: 1974), 134.

creation and without it this could not be the sort of world in which the incarnation could happen."[59]

In his *Muhammad and the Christian* of 1984, Cragg again leans on prophecy as a means of understanding Jesus. Prophecy is a pointer to what Incarnation signifies. Muhammad is actually a kind of John the Baptist, preparing the way for Jesus. Just as John was the last of the prophets and was superseded by the Messiah, so Muhammad, the final prophet according to Islam, must make way for the one who is more than a prophet.

> "Jesus, according to the Gospels used the words, Yea, I say unto you and more than a prophet, [Mt 11:9] in respect of the forerunner, John the Baptist, the Yahyā of the Qur'ān ... One prophet more than another, in range, in honour, or in impact - this is a view with which Islam is familiar enough. Indeed Muhammad's finality clinches it. Yet something more than prophethood itself - how can this be? It is this more upon which the whole New Testament proceeds - the more of Messianic action to redeem - the more of God's loving engagement with the sequel to rejected education of the world, the more of a divine expression of the Word, hitherto only spoken, but now in flesh and personality, in suffering and salvation."[60]

Thus the Incarnation can be seen in part in the prophets that God sent but only fully in Christ himself.

An Evaluation of Cragg's Christology

Cragg attempts to build his Christology on the historical records contained in the synoptic gospels. This marks him out from ninth century apologists as a twentieth century European Christian who is unwilling to base Christology on church tradition. He never appeals to credal formulations in his dialogical work in the way that ninth century writers did. Whereas ninth century Christology took Johannine Incarnational language as the basis for dialogue with Muslims, Cragg begins with Jesus the preacher of the kingdom, and the doer of compassionate deeds for those in need. Cragg is representative of a movement away from doing Christology from 'above' to 'below', away from the Incarnation of the eternal Son, to the human Jesus who is recognised as being in a unique relationship with God.[61]

---

[59] *Ibid.*

[60] K. Cragg, *Muhammad and the Christian* (London: 1984), 126f.

[61] For this shift see, for example, the nineteenth century English theologian R.C. Moberly who argued in an influential set of essays by Anglican theologians that the creeds "must wholly rest upon the history of our Lord Jesus Christ". [R.C. Moberly, *Lux Mundi* (1890), 243]. Twentieth century theology largely accepted Moberly's

While aware of radical criticism of the gospels Cragg is not inclined to shift from his early conviction that, from the beginning of his ministry, Jesus set his face to Jerusalem to die for recalcitrant humanity. There can be no guarantee of Divine forgiveness without the obedient self-offering of Christ, therefore, the redemption gained by Jesus is not a theory imposed on the Galilean carpenter by the early church but an outworking of his own decision. What the disciples came to see in him was not a product of their imagination but recognition of his divine character.[62] It is this realisation that Muslims need to arrive at too, so Cragg applies his energy to bring about a Muslim awakening to the 'real' Jesus, obscured by the Qur'ān and centuries of tradition.

Cragg's attempt to read new Christian meanings into the text of the Qur'ān to encourage Muslims to see Christ in a fresh way repeats previously established Christian readings as well as giving a completely new one. For example, Cragg agrees with Patriarch Timothy's opinion that the Qur'ān teaches that Christ died before being raised to heaven, when he translates *sūra* 3:55 as "O Jesus, I am causing you to die and I will exalt you to myself".[63] The novel reading is finding the Eucharist in *sūra* 5:113. The legitimacy of Christian readings is ultimately decided by whether they make sense to Muslims as possible interpretations. There has been little enthusiasm among Muslims for the Christian reading of *sūra* 3:55 so it seems highly unlikely that Cragg's discovery of the Last Supper in *sūra* 5:113 will fare any better. Nevertheless, Cragg believes that the able Christian communicator must look for interpretative keys in the language of Muslims, but is not ultimately concerned to remain within the meaning framework of that language. The goal is rather to persuade Muslims to move into a new conceptual arena.

Cragg shares with Pfander an Evangelical theology of forgiveness only through the cross. It is significant how much space is occupied by this idea

---

dictum, so that at the end of the century a leading German systematic theologian, Wolfhart Pannenberg, begins his chapter on "The Deity of Christ" with a detailed study of the historical Jesus. For Pannenberg it is essential that "we first begin to see the uniqueness of Jesus as a man". [W. Pannenberg, *Systematic Theology* vol.2 (Edinburgh: 1994), 326].

62 This places Cragg at the very conservative end of the scholarly spectrum. Even Howard Marshall, who has written extensively on the historical Jesus from a conservative position, is unable to affirm that Jesus intended to die for others from the outset of his ministry. According to Marshall, "Jesus must have reckoned with the possibility of his own violent death … The path of faithfulness to God carried the risk of persecution and even death as part of the divinely ordained way for the righteous in an evil world." [I.H. Marshall, *I Believe in the Historical Jesus* (London: 1977), 231]. Note the accidental nature of the cross in Marshall's account in contrast to Cragg's idea that Jesus intended to die from the beginning of his ministry.

63 For Timothy's argument see chapter two.

in their writing. Cragg, like Pfander, believes that Islam is an inadequate way of salvation, that Muslims can only find peace with God through faith in the dying saviour, and that the love generated by that salvation compels him to proclaim Christ to the Muslim world. The whole point of the life and ministry of Jesus is his self-giving sacrificial death to release humans from guilt before God. In other words, the Incarnation is dependent on the act of redemption. Lūqā, on the other hand, has more in common with ninth century writers who see the Incarnation as primarily a means of revelation. We see what God is like in the life of Christ. Certainly, Cragg appeals to the Incarnation as an act of condescension on God's part. Jesus reveals a God who suffers human weakness. He embodies God's kingdom as a rule of love.

However, Cragg gives scant attention to the union of divinity and humanity in Christ with which ninth century apologists were preoccupied. When he does deal with this central issue he makes a comparison between Muslim belief in the eternity of the Qur'ān and Christian faith in the eternity of the Incarnate Word. Here Cragg makes a rare appeal to an analogy from Islamic tradition, which puts him in touch with John of Damascus' argument about the eternity of God's speech.[64] Cragg believes in the union of divine and human natures, but the centre of his Christology is the love of God expressed in the self-giving of Jesus. He prefers to talk of 'God's loving engagement with the world' or 'a Divine expression of the Word in personality' rather than a union of two natures. This form of language might be understood in an Islamic sense as showing Jesus to be particularly open to the compassion of God and to his speech, but not as God become human. The following chapter will explore this possibility more fully in the work of Hans Küng and John Hick. Cragg does not want to be read in this way even though his writing continually depends on poetic ambiguity, since, for him, all of God is found in the Incarnate Christ.

In the final analysis, the Christology in *Jesus and the Muslim* is not essentially different from that found in *The Call of the Minaret* thirty years earlier. There is in Christ a revelation of God in person that is and will be unique. Muslims need to come into an awareness of that unique personal revelation because Islam has obscured the true nature of the historical Jesus and has limited the freedom of God to restrict himself to the human dimensions Jesus of Nazareth. The utter self-giving of God in love for humans can only fully be seen in the suffering of the Incarnate Christ on behalf of others. That is why revelation by prophetic pronouncement is always secondary to revelation by Incarnation, since speech may tell of love but cannot perform it. However, in the context of Muslim response to this Christology, Cragg has neither made much room for scholarly issues

[64] For John of Damascus' argument see chapter two:16.

concerning the facts of the life of Jesus nor for the challenge laid down by al-Farūqī concerning the freedom of God to limit himself.

Chapter Nine

The Christologies of John Hick and Hans Küng in Dialogue with Muslims

Kenneth Cragg's engagement with Islam arose from early exposure to the Muslim world of the Middle East, enabling him to develop a thorough understanding of the Islamic challenge to Christology. However, among European theologians his experience is rare. John Hick and Hans Küng are more typical of the recent interaction of Western theology and Islam. Both men were established theological writers before attempting to communicate with Muslims, and their Christological views were already developed for a Western context. The fact that they turned their attention to a global context for theology demonstrates a shift in the self-understanding of some Western Christian leaders away from simply doing theology in the traditionally Christian world of Europe and North America, to thinking about the Christian faith in non-Christian contexts.

In Hick's case the presence of Muslims in the United Kingdom urged him to rethink a theology worked out in training for the Presbyterian ministry in England and subsequent lecturing in theological faculties of North American and British universities. For Küng, a career as a theological lecturer in the University of Tübingen in Germany intersected with Islam through visits to the Muslim world in which he attempted to build bridges between Christianity and Islam. Both men were also concerned to relate Christian thought to other major religious traditions and attempted to dialogue with Hindus and Buddhists as well as with Muslims. Neither is an expert in Islamic thought, having no first hand knowledge of Arabic to read original Islamic texts, and the published dialogues they led were conducted in English with Muslim scholars familiar to Western university teaching. Hick and Küng are representative of a new reality in Christian thought, which is likely to be increasingly relevant in the Twenty-first century, as Christian theologians will continue to feel the need to address an Islamic context when articulating Christology.

John Hick's Christology

John Hick (b. 1922) has come relatively late to communicating a view of Jesus to Muslims. Having taught the Philosophy of Religion in the USA since the 1950's it was not until he occupied the H.G. Wood chair of

Theology at Birmingham University in 1967 that he began to dialogue with Muslims. His new awareness of other faiths was to bring about a 'Copernican revolution' in his thinking about Christ, which was a shift from Christocentrism to Theocentrism. An exposition of this shift comes at the beginning of a series of papers given at a trialogue of Christians, Muslims and Jews in September 1981, convened and chaired by Hick himself.[1]

From Christocentrism to Theocentrism

According to his own testimony at the trialogue, Hick at one time held that the Incarnation, Trinity and atonement were divinely revealed truths, but that he gradually came to accept that these concepts were better understood as products of human thinking. While he once thought that these doctrines were "straightforward reports of fact" he now concluded that they were "of the nature of theories."[2] This shift of perception involved the realisation that "theological formulations are always both fallible and culture-relative."[3] In his own theological pilgrimage there were two major causes for this paradigm shift, firstly, the results of scholarly research in the gospels, and secondly, the realisation that a religiously plural world required a new approach to doctrinal truth.

In dealing with the first cause of this 'Copernican' revolution, Hick became increasingly impressed with the work of gospel scholars who separated the historical Jesus from the Christ of the early church's faith. According to such scholars, the Jesus of history did not teach the Church's doctrines of Incarnation, atonement and Trinity. As an illustration of gospel scholarship he analyses Jesus' model prayer, pointing out that few scholars question the authenticity of this prayer as Jesus' own. The prayer suggests that a direct unmediated relationship with God is possible, and does not suggest the more developed theology of the Apostolic period.

> "The prayer includes no reference to the great theological themes ... of divine incarnation in the person of Jesus Christ or of atonement for the sins of mankind by his death on the cross or of God as a Trinity of Father, Son and Holy Spirit. It is indeed an extraordinary and thought-provoking fact that these traditional doctrines play no part at all in Jesus' own summary of his message to mankind. Jesus thought of God in purely monotheistic and unitarian terms."[4]

---

[1] See J. Hick, "A Recent Development within Christian Monotheism", in D. Kerr and D. Cohn-Sherbok (eds.), *Christians, Muslims and Jews,* (Birmingham: 1982), 1-19.

[2] *Ibid.,* 1.

[3] *Ibid.,* 2.

[4] *Ibid.,* 6.

The implications of gospel scholarship for Christian theology are obvious to Hick. Jesus must be seen as a man exceptionally conscious of God's presence, but not as God become human. Some theologians had already reached this conclusion but had nevertheless held that Jesus had a unique relationship to God.

The second cause of the 'Copernican' revolution was the dawning admission that Jesus was not unique in his capacity to relate truth about God. Hick came to see that other great religious figures, including Muhammad, were just as 'God conscious' as Jesus was.

> "If we see in the life of Christ a supreme instance of that fusion of divine grace and creaturely freedom that occurs in all authentic human response and obedience to God, then … there is now no difficulty, in principle, in acknowledging that the paradox of grace was also exemplified in the prophet Muhammad, and indeed in all other true servants of God."[5]

It follows firstly, that Islam is just as valuable as Christianity as a model for true spiritual experience, and secondly, that it is no longer right for Christians to regard religions such as Islam as "preliminary or defective, or inferior."[6] Rather they must see other religions in terms of complementarity rather than superiority. As a result, Christians and Muslims "can each see, in the best elements of the other tradition, convincing evidence that it too embodies an authentic awareness of and response to God, Allah - to whom be praise."[7] Hick then asks whether Muslims could accept divine Incarnation "in the sense of interactions of divine grace or inspiration with free human response, not only in the life of Jesus but in the lives of all true Messengers of God?"[8]

Of the five Muslims involved in the trialogue only Hasan Askari related to Christology in his paper, but he did not refer to Hick's views. Askari, a leading Indian Muslim scholar teaching in Birmingham at the time, understands the Qur'ānic picture of Jesus to be about his servanthood. The polemic of the Qur'ān against the language of sonship is not really about Jesus being "actually begotten."[9] In a much more profound sense the Qur'ān attacks sonship as a "metaphorical mode of stating the God-Man relationship." The Qur'ān offers a "no risk" concept of servanthood in exchange for the "ambiguous" idea of sonship, which ensures that God is never brought "to the level of creation" or "creation to the level of God."[10] Askari was not commenting directly on Hick's paper but on Christology in

[5] *Ibid.*, 14.

[6] *Ibid.*

[7] *Ibid.*, 19.

[8] *Ibid.*

[9] H. Askari, "The Qur'ānic Conception of Risala", in *Christians, Muslims and Jews*, 131.

[10] *Ibid.*

general, and it would be intriguing to see what he made of Hick's presentation. The difference between this conference and the Cragg/al-Farūqī meeting was the absence of published interaction between the participants. They read papers but did not talk to each other in the published proceedings.

Hick's equation of Jesus and Muhammad as men of 'grace' is a striking development for Christology, since it entails a re-reading of the New Testament portrait of Christ on which the whole tradition of the church has been based. By separating out the human Jesus from any of the New Testament ascription of divinity to him, it is in principle possible to align him with other religious leaders such as Muhammad. Nevertheless, the admission that not only Muhammad but also "other true servants of God" exemplify God's grace in an equivalent way is hardly likely to commend his view to Muslims. Cragg's comparison of the prophethood of Jesus and Muhammad is much more in tune with Muslim thought, because prophethood suggests being sent to declare God's word, and Muslims believe that Jesus was faithful to that calling. However, Hick's emphasis on the experience of God shown in the lives of Jesus and Muhammad along with all other servants of God does not relate so accurately to Islamic categories of receiving God's word. Muslims make a distinction between those who do right as true servants of God and those who have received God's instructions about how to do right. Therefore God's 'grace' may be given in very large measure to many humans, but God's 'word' is given only to a select number who are known by name in the Qur'ān.

Hick's Christology is the end product of a gradual acceptance of the normative value of the historical Jesus, so that what can be shown to be plausible historically is true. At one time he held the Incarnation, the atonement and the Trinity to be true, but no longer does because it is not clear that the historical Jesus believed in them. Certainly Hick is in tune with mainstream gospel scholarship in his assessment of the historical Jesus in a way that Cragg is not.[11] In other words, Hick has adopted the logical conclusion of gospel scholarship that Christology as we know it is basically a product of faith in Jesus rather than a faithful following of the actual teaching of Jesus. The latter yields results not too far removed from the

[11] Hick accepts the common conviction among scholars that Jesus did not apply the idea of ransom to his own death, but that it was read into his death by the early church. As far as the Incarnation is concerned, J.D.G. Dunn represents a majority of New Testament scholars in his view that the Incarnation is a late development in the faith of the early church found partially in Paul's letters, but fully only in the letters attributed to Paul such as Colossians, and in the Johannine writings. See J.D.G. Dunn, *Christology in the Making* (London: 1980). This reading of the gospels includes the assumption that Jesus could not have believed in the Trinity as proclaimed by him in Matthew 28:19.

teaching of Muhammad and other remarkable religious characters. He challenges fellow Christians, who continue to hold to the truth of the Incarnation and atonement on the basis that God revealed them to be true to the Apostles and the Councils of the Church, to step back in time to the actual teaching of Jesus on which a new common understanding of Christ can be arrived at by people of various faiths.

Muzammil Siddiqi Responds to Hick's Christology

In 1985, Hick organised another trialogue in California, after moving to Claremont Graduate School of Theology. Hick's paper was essentially a re-run of the one given in Birmingham in 1981, but this time his presentation on the Incarnation was given a reply by a Muslim, Muzammil H. Siddiqi, Imam and Director of the Islamic Society of Orange County in California, and Professor of Islamic Studies at California State University.[12] Siddiqi has two problems with Hick's enthusiasm for pluralism. Firstly, Hick does not make room for revelation, and secondly, Hick thinks different belief systems are equally valid. Siddiqi deals with the first problem by asking Hick, "Are all religions human responses to God or did God also take any initiative in revealing Himself self-disclosing, speaking, commanding the human beings?"[13] He attempts an answer on Hick's behalf. "Hick, probably, would say that either God never took such initiative, or, for the good cause of peace and pluralism, let us not emphasise this."[14] It is disappointing that Hick did not actually publish a reply in the collection of papers, but the fact that forty-five Jews, Christians and Muslims took part shows the limitations of genuine dialogue in such a huge gathering. Perhaps Hick would reply that revelation can never be separated from the God-consciousness of humans, and must be understood from within human experience. It is not surprising to find Siddiqi complaining that Hick's position is unsatisfactory, since it has been an article of faith virtually unchallenged from within Islam that Muhammad's conscious mind was totally separate from the wording of the Qur'ān. For Muslims the religious experience of Muhammad is secondary to his receiving the word of God, but Hick plays down the distinction between them.

Siddiqi approaches the second problem of the equivalent value Hick finds in the major religious traditions, by noting that Hick has only one criterion for 'value' and that is the effectiveness of different types of religious experience in bringing about salvation. He asks Hick, "How can

---

[12] See M.H. Siddiqi, "A Muslim Response to John Hick: Trinity and Incarnation in the light of Religious Pluralism", in J. Hick and E.S. Meltzer (eds.), *Three Faiths-One God: A Jewish, Christian, Muslim Encounter*, (London: 1989), 211-213.

[13] *Ibid.*, 211.

[14] *Ibid.*

or does one know that none of them is a more efficacious context of salvation than the other?"[15] He asks too, "What is salvation?" Neither of these questions is answered by Siddiqi. If Hick had responded he may well have argued that a variety of religious traditions have produced saints who equally show the marks of God's grace. Both Islam and Christianity have given the world people of outstanding spiritual and moral character, therefore both traditions are equally valid as a means of full human development, which, according to Hick, is the essence of salvation.

Siddiqi does approve of Hick's Christology, but does not spell out exactly what he admires. "I like John Hick's discussion on Christology. John knows quite well that his book The Myth of God Incarnate is very well received by Muslims. The Christology proposed by John Hick can serve as a good subject for dialogue between Muslims and Christians."[16] *The Myth of God Incarnate* was a collection of essays published in 1977 by John Hick and six British theologians and subsequently translated into Arabic. The essays put forward the view that the Incarnation as understood in the Apostolic and Patristic periods should not need to govern modern Christology. Use of the word 'myth' in the title led some to understand that the 'truth' was not to be found in theology, but only in history. One Muslim reviewer welcomed the book as "a rational, godsent lightening ... to explode an agelong blunder in Christian thought."[17] Siddiqi does not explain his approval of Hick's position, but he probably has in mind Hick's perception of Jesus as being only human and not divine. Hick's Jesus can largely be recognised by Muslims, but differences may still remain, especially about the historicity of the crucifixion.

The Myth of Jesus' Crucifixion?

In his *Metaphor of God Incarnate* of 1993, Hick recognises only one instance of direct disagreement between the Qur'ān and the gospels, the Qur'ānic denial of the crucifixion. Hick accepts the historicity of the crucifixion, which he includes in a very brief list of facts known about Jesus.

> "Scholars have listed such generally agreed points as that Jesus was a Galilean Jew, son of a woman called Mary; that he was baptized by John the Baptist; that he preached and healed and exorcised; that he called disciples and spoke of there being twelve; that he largely confined his activity to Israel; that he was crucified outside Jerusalem by the Roman

---

[15] *Ibid.*, 212.

[16] *Ibid.*, 213.

[17] See A.S. Sharafuddin, *About the Myth of God Incarnate – An Impartial Survey of its Main Topics* (Jeddah: 1978), 1.

authorities; and that after his death his followers continued an identifiable movement."[18]

None of these facts would cause any difficulties for Muslims except the crucifixion. Later in the book Hick raises the issue of this refusal on the part of Muslims, but does not believe that 'facts' are after all decisive in delivering well developed spiritual and moral human beings.

> "I suggest that differences of historical judgment, although having their own proper importance, do not prevent the different traditions from being effective, and so far as we can tell, more or less equally effective, contexts of salvation. Evidently, then, it is not necessary for salvation that we should have correct historical information."[19]

In other words, the crucifixion is not a myth in the sense that the atonement is. Though Jesus did not die for others to save them from the results of their sin, he certainly did die on a cross. But even this truth can be set aside in dialogue with Muslims, if it helps Christians and Muslims to work together to promote 'salvation'. Hick seems to believe that Muslims and Christians will continue to see salvation differently, but that in reality there are no fundamental differences in the final product of these two traditions. His task is to help Christians especially to come to accept this.

An Evaluation of Hick's Christology

It is hardly surprising that Hick should be criticised by more traditional Christians for his severe reductionism. In a response to such criticism in his 1995 *The Rainbow of Faiths*, Hick defends his scepticism about much of the material in the gospels. The book is written in the form of dialogues between Hick and a philosopher Phil and a theologian Grace. Grace challenges Hick's assumption that Jesus did not imply his divinity according to the gospels, even if he did not teach it explicitly. Did Jesus not assume divine authority in abrogating the Jewish Law and in forgiving sins? Hick replies,

> "I argue that it is possible to see an implicit claim to deity here. But on the other hand it is equally possible to see the material quite differently ... A strong stream of contemporary New Testament research today holds that he did not in fact abrogate the Law ... and in pronouncing forgiveness for sins Jesus was, out of his vivid awareness of God's mercy, declaring God's forgiveness ... not presuming himself to be God."[20]

---

[18] J. Hick, *The Metaphor of God Incarnate* (London: 1993), 18.
[19] *Ibid.*, 145.
[20] J. Hick, *The Rainbow of Faiths* (London: 1995), 96

Hick acknowledges that possible interpretations arise out of pre-suppositions.

> "It must be said that these are questions which the New Testament scholars will probably debate among themselves until the end of time. And I think you will notice that their interpretations are invariably correlated with their wider theological positions. If you want biblical confirmation for a conservative position, you can find it, and if you want biblical confirmation for a more liberal position you can find that. We all use the Bible selectively in the light of our theological outlook."[21]

Hick's pre-supposition is getting along with people of other faiths, and belief in the divinity of Jesus simply gets in the way of harmony. Grace asks whether the Incarnation should not simply be accepted as a mystery, and Hick replies, "that might be acceptable if the literally understood doctrine did not have literal implications which are so damaging to our relationship with the people of other faiths."[22]

In other words, the divinity of Jesus proclaimed within the New Testament by John and Paul has to be set aside for pragmatic reasons. But the very pragmatism at work in relation to those of other faiths fails to take account of the fact that the Christian tradition has been indelibly shaped by John and Paul. What Hick says of polemical dialogue later in *The Rainbow of Faiths* could well be turned against his own kind of theologising.

> "A Christian tries to persuade a Muslim that the Prophet Muhammad's experience of hearing the words of the Qur'ān came from his own conscious mind rather than being dictated by Gabriel on behalf of God, but this kind of polemical dialogue is usually fruitless except in producing alienation and enmity."[23]

It does not take much imagination to see that Hick is doing exactly the same within the Christian tradition. Hick tries to persuade traditional Christians that the Apostolic and Patristic faith in Christ as human and divine is not founded on fact and therefore is not true. But Hick's dialogue with other Christians may be fruitless except in producing alienation and

---

[21] *Ibid.*

[22] *Ibid.*, 99. Hick shares the sentiments of Indian theologian Stanley Samartha, the first director of the Dialogue Programme of the World Council of Churches in the 1970's, who argues that "elevating Jesus to the status of God or limiting Christ to Jesus of Nazareth are both temptations to be avoided … A Theocentric Christology avoids these dangers and becomes more helpful in establishing new relationships with neighbours of other faiths." [S.J. Samartha, "The Cross and the Rainbow: Christ in a Multireligious Culture", in J. Hick and L. Swidler (eds.) *The Myth of Christian Uniqueness: Towards a Pluralistic Theology of Religions,* (New York: 1987), 69-88, 80)

[23] J. Hick, *The Rainbow of Faiths*, 121.

enmity, since these Christians hold that their faith in Christ is the logical outcome of tendencies in the life and teaching of the historical Jesus. This is the position of the Catholic theologian, Hans Küng, who comes somewhere between Cragg and Hick in his Christology in dialogue with Muslims. Hick used to hold the Incarnational Christology of Cragg. What is striking about Hick is the rationale behind his Copernican Revolution. Moving from Christocentrism to Theocentrism has been done as a result of contact with believers of other faiths. The Incarnation is an obstacle to good relations with Muslims and Jews, so a pragmatic attitude must entail dropping such a conceptualisation.

In the desire to make himself a good neighbour, Hick has not really considered two consequences of his friendly overtures. The first has to do with those believers of other faiths he wants to get along with. They have concepts of what is appropriate to hold as true. In the case of Muslims, everything that the Qur'ān says is true. The fact that Hick is unwilling to endorse this conviction in its entirety puts him at odds with a fifth of the world's population. In what sense then does Hick love his Muslim neighbour, when he cannot affirm this essential item in Islam? Mahmut Aydin provides an answer in his insightful review of Hick's Christology. This Turkish analyst of contemporary Christian dialogue with Muslims suggests that Hick may want "Muslims to understand metaphorically the uncreatedness of the Qur'ān and the finality of the Prophet Muḫammad". In the end, "this demand of Hick could increase the anxieties of the dialogue partners" who "may think that if they enter into dialogue with each other, they may lose their beliefs".[24]

The second consequence concerns Hick's ability to represent the Christian third of the world's population. He acknowledges that Christians who have seen a split between the Jesus of history and the Christ of faith have usually been content to accept the value of the latter.[25] He thinks that faith in the Incarnation is a barrier to good relations with Muslims, but Christians who believe that Jesus is divine are just as capable of loving Muslims as Christians who do not. The condemnation of the vast majority of Christians to an inevitable conflict with Muslims because of their faith in the Incarnation and atonement seems premature. Pluralist and traditionalist Christians are equally capable of being good neighbours to people of other faiths, because although they see Jesus differently, they are able to love Muslims despite such differences. Love for Muslims is not dependent on theology alone.

---

[24] M. Aydin, *Modern Western Christian Theological Understandings of Muslims Since the Second Vatican Council* (Washington, D.C.: 2002), 212.

[25] See the responses to Hick's Theocentric Christology from theologians who uphold the Incarnation as true in *Christian Uniqueness Reconsidered,* (ed.) G. D'Costa, (New York: 1990).

Hans Küng's Christology

Hans Küng (b. 1928) has been a professor of theology at the University of Tübingen in Germany since 1960. He was an active participant in the proceedings of Vatican II in the early 1960's, and has promoted the new understanding of the Catholic Church concerning people of other faiths that emerged from the Council. In 1985 he published *Christianity and World Religions* without having engaged in much encounter with Muslims. But the book opened the path to engagement with Muslims outside Germany.[26]

Christianity and World Religions

In the section of his *Christianity and World Religions* concerned with Christianity and Islam, Küng believes it is vital to begin with the portrait of Jesus given in the Qur'ān in conversation with Muslims. The fundamental issue for Christians is that,

> "The Qur'ān should be interpreted from the standpoint of the Qur'ān not from that of the New Testament or the Council of Nicaea. For the Qur'ān Jesus is a prophet; a great prophet, like Abraham, Noah, and Moses - but nothing more. And just as in the New Testament John the Baptist is Jesus' precursor, so in the Qur'ān Jesus is the precursor - and highly encouraging example - for Muhammad."[27]

This does not mean that Küng is content to stay with the Jesus of the Qur'ān, since he believes it is essential to challenge Muslims to accept the historical Jesus of the gospels who is not fully shown in the Qur'ān.

> "The portrait of Jesus in the Qur'ān is all too one-dimensional, ill-defined, and devoid of substance - apart from the features on monotheism, the call for conversion in view of the judgment to come, and a few miracle stories. The historical Jesus was quite different. Despite what the Qur'ān says, he did not uphold the Law. Rather he opposed every kind of legalism with his radical love and for this reason was executed. But this is precisely what the Qur'ān, flying in the face of history, will not admit."[28]

The gospels reveal Jesus to have been a man who promoted "not his own person, role, or dignity, but God's kingdom, God's name, God's will, which man is to fulfil through service to his fellow men and women."[29] Jesus' life

---

[26] See the foreword to the second edition of *Christianity and World Religions* (New York: 1993), xii.

[27] H. Küng, *Christianity and World Religions* (New York: 1993), 110.

[28] *Ibid.*, 111.

[29] *Ibid.*, 116.

and ministry were marked by his relationship to God, which shows a "oneness with God as his Father."[30] This portrait of Jesus would not be impossible for a Muslim to integrate with the Qur'ānic account, but Jesus also claimed to act on God's behalf.

> "His claims went beyond those of a prophet, in that he assumed God's authority (especially with respect to the Law and the forgiveness of sins). He not only talked about forgiving sin, about challenging every hallowed tradition and rule, about tearing down all the boundaries separating clean and unclean, just and unjust - he did all these things. No wonder he was accused of blaspheming God, condemned and executed."[31]

The historical Jesus made himself out to be more than a prophet by assuming God's authority to forgive in a way not seen before in the Jewish tradition. He did not simply pronounce that God had forgiven a sinner, but rather forgave the man himself on God's behalf. It was recognition of this action that prompted the disciples to see Jesus' relationship with God in a unique light. However, it was only after the encounter of the disciples with the risen Jesus that they began to call him Son of God. "The crucified Jesus was made God's son through his resurrection and exaltation."[32] This means that the concept of sonship was for the early church "not a relationship of parentage, but an appointment ... not a physical divine sonship as Islam always assumed and rightly rejected but God's choosing Jesus and granting him full authority."[33] The picture is of shared authority between the Father and his appointed Son. If Christians could rest content with this picture of adoption then Muslims surely could find no difficulty with the Father and Son imagery. What then should Christians do with the concept of identity of being between God and Jesus that is expressed in the historic creeds? This development of faith in Christ arose from the Apostolic conviction that "God's word and will took on human form in Jesus."[34] Therefore the church today should believe that there was "a unity of knowledge, will, action, and revelation between God and Jesus."[35]

But Muslims would still find difficulty with this Christian view of Jesus. Talk of unity between God and Jesus is suspect because it seems to raise the human Jesus to a position of equality with God. Küng asks what separates Christians from Muslims, and decides that the revelation of God "in Jesus Christ" marks off Christians from Muslims, who "recognise Jesus as one of the prophets, but no more."[36] Küng believes that he can persuade

---

[30] *Ibid.*, 117.
[31] *Ibid.*
[32] *Ibid.*, 118.
[33] *Ibid.*
[34] *Ibid.*, 119.
[35] *Ibid.*
[36] *Ibid.*, 120f.

Muslims to take on board three aspects of the Jesus of the gospels. Firstly, the preaching and practice of Jesus relativizes the oppressive nature of Islamic law. Man has been set free, not from law, but from legalism. Secondly, Jesus' life, death and new life give us a new and deeper understanding of God as one who loves and has compassion for humanity. Thirdly, Jesus' death offers us a fresh source of meaning, however meaningless our suffering and failure may appear to be.[37] This version of the historical Jesus is rather different from Cragg's or Hick's. There is virtually no place for Cragg's Jesus who comes to die for others out of love for them, but Küng's Jesus opposes the law and forgives sin, both of which are rejected by Hick as false interpretations.[38]

Dialogue with Hossein Nasr

Küng was asked to engage in dialogue at Harvard University in 1984 with a leading Muslim scholar, Seyyed Hossein Nasr of George Washington University. The Iranian Hossein Nasr had an extensive knowledge of Christian thought, and was accustomed to the style of discourse found in contemporary Christian theology. Küng's presentation was in fact a condensed version of the chapter from *Christianity and World Religions*, which is analysed above. Nasr's response to Küng's Christology begins with Küng's criticism of the Qur'ānic portrait of Jesus. "To suggest that the Qur'ān had the wrong Christology makes absolutely impossible any

---

[37] *Ibid.*, 128.

[38] Küng reflects a tradition in German theology that pictures Jesus replacing dependence on law keeping with faith in himself. For example, Walter Kaiser describes Jesus' authoritative teaching as being not so much against, but above that of Moses, and that he called his disciples to have faith in him. [W. Kasper, *Jesus the Christ* (Tunbridge Wells: 1976), 102f.] That Jesus forgave sin in his own right has been a standard interpretation in much German gospel scholarship. Gerd Theissen and Annette Merz sum up Jesus' charisma in a way that continues to support Küng's position. "He implicitly attributed to himself a special nearness to God. He endorsed his words by putting an 'amen' in front of them as though he had received them from God. His antitheses deliberately transcended the Torah without contradicting it. He reactivated the traditional metaphor of father in a way which indicated a special relationship to God. He promised the forgiveness of sins which as a rule was hoped for from God himself." [G. Theissen and A. Merz, *The Historical Jesus* (London: 1998), 560.] By way of contrast, Hick's view that Jesus did not set himself above the Torah by asking for faith in himself reflects a particular strand of Anglo-Saxon theology. For instance, Ed Sanders thinks it is "virtually certain" that Jesus "did not explicitly oppose the law, particularly not laws relating to Sabbath and food." He insists that it is "incredible" to hold that Jesus "was one of the rare Jews of his day who believed in love, mercy, grace, repentance and the forgiveness of sin." [E.P. Sanders, *Jesus and Judaism* (London: 1985), 326.]

dialogue with Islam … It must always be remembered that for Muslims the Qur'ān, the whole Qur'ān and not only parts of it, is the word of God."[39]

In other words, there is little use Küng suggesting that improvements need to be made in the Qur'ānic picture. He must begin to dialogue on the basis that the Qur'ān is the word of God that is not misguided in its portrait of Jesus. But how then is dialogue possible when the gospel account of Jesus is different? Nasr has a way through by suggesting that truth can be seen in apparently contradictory ways.

> "In the future if there is to be a serious Islamic-Christian dialogue on the question of Christology it will have to deal with this issue of whether modern epistemology and modern philosophy allow, in fact, a single reality to be seen in two different ways without causing what appears to the modern mind as logical contradiction."[40]

He illustrates his point by looking at the apparent contradiction between the Qur'ān and the gospels over the crucifixion of Jesus. "I will stick my neck out as a Muslim and say that when the Qur'ān states that the Christ was not crucified that does not necessarily mean that God did not want another segment of humanity to see this very reality in a different way."[41] He seems to mean that God may have revealed two ways of seeing the same event. While the two ways cancel each other out on the level of human reasoning, we humans should always remember that God's thoughts are higher than ours. We cannot penetrate his thinking. We only receive revelation. But does this not imply that the gospel version of Jesus' death is revelation from God just as much as the Qur'ānic denial? Nasr puts the answer into a transcendent mode. "It must be realised that neither the Islamic nor the Christian view exhausts the possibilities of the 'Christic' reality in another universe as willed by God."[42]

At the end of Nasr's response Küng had the opportunity to reply to Nasr's criticisms. Küng was not prepared to accept the suspension of judgement for some 'Christic' reality beyond this world that might synthesise the thesis and antithesis of Islam and Christianity. "Let us say that the Gospels are wrong, and that the whole New Testament is wrong, that Jesus has not really been crucified. To say this from a source which comes from the seventh century is for an historically thinking man, I think, personally impossible."[43]

Given the opportunity to reply again to Küng, Nasr returned to the historicity of the crucifixion.

---

[39] S.H. Nasr, "Response to Hans Küng", *MW* 77 (1987), 96-105, 100.
[40] *Ibid.*
[41] *Ibid.*, 101.
[42] *Ibid.*
[43] H. Küng, "Reply to Hossein Nasr", *MW*, 121.

> "Whether he was crucified and died or whether, as the Muslims traditionally believe, God put someone else in his place and he was taken up to heaven, is not going to be either proven or disproven by historical texts of the period, because it is not the kind of phenomenon which can be exhausted by historical description ...Christ was in a sense too good to be crucified - to be killed. So no historical argument is going to destroy the truth, as you called it, of Islam by showing another version of sacred history."[44]

Truth then cannot be killed since the word of God lasts forever. History is not the judge of truth. Even if Jesus did die on the cross, the significance of that event would still need to be drawn out. For Islam, the significance is that God is always victorious. Men may try to do away with truth but God will be the ultimate winner of the argument.

Nasr repeated this double view of truth in a paper published in 1995, in which he identified seven outstanding problems for Islamic-Christian Dialogue.

1. Islam rejects the Incarnation since the Absolute cannot enter into the domain of relativity. Only a symbolic Incarnation is possible.
2. Islam claims finality in the current period of human history. Jesus himself predicted the role of the Paraclete who Muslims identify with the Prophet.
3. The Qur'ān is God's word. Few Christians have accepted this. But most Muslims see the Bible as abrogated or altered.
4. Christians have limited the spread of Qur'ānic Arabic in the last century and a half.
5. Islamic law is not only a set of principles but also a set of legal codifications. Christians should not try to undermine this truth.
6. Christianity and Islam have two contradictory accounts of the end of Jesus' life.
7. The assumption of modernism and post-modernism that religion must inevitably be relegated to the private domain conflicts with the Islamic conviction that the whole of life is governed by the word of God.[45]

The sixth point is of particular relevance to the debate with Küng. He basically reiterates his earlier view that God may have revealed two different perspectives on the death of Jesus.

> "Was Christ crucified or was he taken alive to Heaven and not crucified as asserted by Islam? Here one faces what seems to be an insurmountable

---

[44] S.H. Nasr, "Reply to Hans Küng", *MW,* 128.

[45] S.H. Nasr, "Comments on a Few Theological Issues in the Islamic-Christian Dialogue", in Y.Y. Haddad and W.Z. Haddad (eds.), *Christian-Muslim Encounters,* (Gainesville: 1995), 458-465.

> obstacle. One could say that a major cosmic event at the end of the earthly life of Christ could in fact be 'seen' and 'known' in more than one way, and that it is God's will that Christianity should be given to 'see' that end in one way and Islam in another."[46]

Nasr seems here to be comfortable with the notion that Islam is only one version of truth, but in other areas of dispute between Islam and Christianity he is unwilling to adopt a double theory of revelation. The other six issues mentioned by him all touch on the finality of the Qur'ān as the truth given by God. In none of these six issues is he prepared to allow the validity of alternative sources of truth that would contradict revelation as Islam understands it. So the concession to Christians over their insistence on the crucifixion of Christ is not granted in other areas of dispute.

An Evaluation of Küng's Christology

In his 1995 one volume survey of theology entitled *Christianity: The Religious Situation of Our Time*, Küng reflects on the options for Christology in the light of world religions. He engages in dialogue with advocates of Theocentric Christology, agreeing that the historical Jesus must be the basis for Christology, but holding that Christians are identified by their faith in Jesus alongside their faith in God. In relation to Muslims in particular, Christians should begin with, but cannot limit their view to, the portrait of Jesus found in the Qur'ān, because they are convinced that God has revealed himself and has offered redemption to humanity through Jesus.

The challenge of a Theocentric Christology is met by stressing that the New Testament as a whole regards Jesus as central to revelation and salvation. Küng repeats the differences between the historical Jesus and the faith of the early church from *Christianity and World Religions*, and re-affirms his commitment to the validity of the latter. Therefore the church cannot abandon faith in Jesus for a faith in God which could be defined more in terms of Jewish and Muslim forms of faith. Christians should continue to exercise faith in Christ as their way of believing in God.

> "It can be argued that the one God of Abraham himself constitutes the centre of the New Testament, its theocentricity. But the 'new' element in the New Testament is precisely the fact that this one God is never seen alone, but always together with the one who proclaimed him 'anew'... So while faith in the one God is unchanged, the centre of faith is defined afresh: Jesus' name stands for the kingdom of God, the coming of which he preached. Faith in God becomes specifically christological."[47]

---

46 *Ibid.*, 464.

47 H. Küng, *Christianity: The Religious Situation of Our Time* (London: 1995), 58.

Küng seems to hold that God's rule has to be understood with reference to Jesus, though it is not clear to what extent Jesus represents God, or shares in God's rule. However, he thinks that the New Testament vision of participation by Jesus in that rule is still important today. If this conjunction of God and Christ in the attitude of the early church is the benchmark for Christian self-understanding, then Christians will clash with people of other faiths. Küng is aware of the need for sensitivity in relating to those whose faith in God excludes honouring Jesus in this way. Hick's complaint that equating Jesus with God means a failure of love for Muslims is taken seriously by Küng. The remedy is to step into the place where Muslims feel comfortable, and to see Jesus from their point of view, before making suggestions as to how a Christian view of Jesus enhances a Muslim one. The practical outcome of this approach for Christians entails dropping the language of the Nicene Creed in favour of New Testament expressions of Christology. Muslims cannot understand, let alone accept, theology built on Greek philosophical concepts. Therefore, thinking of Christology in terms of an ontological union between God and Jesus is not a useful way of doing theology in the world of today. "The divine element in Jesus was emphasized so strongly and so exclusively at Nicaea that all the human characteristics of Jesus receded into the background."[48] A functional, rather than ontological, unity between Jesus and God is the only conceptualisation that is appropriate now.[49]

Küng does not really address the problems inherent in relating to the Jesus of the Qur'ān in this book, but he does believe that Christology can commence from the Qur'ān before ending up in the New Testament. As long as Christians set aside the convictions of the creeds, there can be a genuine conversation with Muslims about Jesus.

> "Down to the present day Islam, which accepts Jesus completely as prophet and even Messiah but rejects Hellenistic Christology, has not

---

[48] *Ibid.*, 195.

[49] The view that ontological categories are no longer useful for Christology is shared by many contemporary theologians. Oscar Cullmann held that the New Testament writers did not conceive of Christ's relationship to God in terms of a unity of being, but in terms of a unity of thought and action. [O. Cullmann, *The Christology of the New Testament* (London: 1959).] Many modern theologians have bypassed the ontological Christology based on Nicaea and Chalcedon in favour of a functional Christology based on the New Testament. For example, John Macquarrie thinks the Chalcedonian depiction of human and divine natures is too static. Nowadays if we "move away from the static understanding of nature (physis) as a fixed essence, to the dynamic or progressive understanding of physis as 'emergence' or 'coming into being', then the notion of the two natures 'concurring' in the person of Christ becomes intelligible." [J. Macquarrie, *Jesus Christ in Modern Thought* (London: 1990), 385.]

> been able to understand that here we have a historical person and a personal human life. So isn't it necessary to begin to understand Jesus Christ again 'from below' and to attach as much importance to his humanity as the Qur'ān does, going on from there, to understand how in turn God's wisdom has taken human form?"[50]

The answer to this question of how the conjuction between God and Jesus should be expressed in the light of the Qur'ān is not given by Küng. After a lengthy exposition of Patristic Christology, which he concludes is no longer adequate, Küng provides a summary creed that has little to do with the Jesus of the Qur'ān. "The 'heart' of Christian faith is not a theological theory but belief that God the Father works in a revealing, redeeming and liberating way in us through his Son Jesus Christ in the Spirit."[51] But such a statement of faith is quite unacceptable to Muslims, since God cannot need Jesus to do anything for or in us. Rather Jesus must remain one of the sent ones who called others to offer acceptable worship to God. The borderline which may never be crossed is the Qur'ānic conviction that each individual is responsible for his or her own destiny. Küng, however, does not discuss such a Muslim reaction. There is no serious consideration in this context of the provocative nature of the words "revealing, redeeming and liberating." While it is true that Muslims can think of Jesus revealing God's will as God's messenger, he cannot be thought of as actually rescuing anybody from bondage. The only way that redemptive language can work is to apply it to the intellect so that he could be said to summon people from ignorance.

But if Muslims respond that they are not redeemed from ignorance by Jesus but by the word that he brings, that of course is not his but God's only. So Jesus does not redeem but offers the way for others to redeem themselves. The same strictures apply to the idea of liberation. Jesus is a means by which people liberate themselves. In the light of his view that Islam provides salvation without a specifically Christian understanding of Jesus, do Muslims really need Jesus the way Christians need him? Küng made himself famous in Roman Catholic circles for his 1964 address in Bombay in which he expounded the new view of Vatican II that, "God's saving will also embraces those who acknowledge the Creator and among them especially the Muslims, who profess the faith of Abraham and together with us adore the one God, the Merciful One, who will judge men on the Last Day."[52] Küng put forward the idea that Christianity is the 'extraordinary' way of salvation and the other religions are 'ordinary' ways. In 1994 he re-affirmed his belief in these two ways of salvation.

---

[50] *Ibid.*

[51] H. Küng, *Christianity: The Religious Situation of Our Time*, 305.

[52] See "The Constitution of the Church", article 16, in *Documents of the Second Vatican Council*, (ed.) W.M. Abbott, (New York: 1965). Cited by Küng in *Christianity and World Religions* (1993), foreword xi.

> "For me as a Christian - to speak quite plainly here - Jesus Christ is and remains the way, the truth and the life (that is as it were my internal perspective), but (and this is at the same time my external perspective) I cannot avoid noting that 'the way, the truth, and the life' is for believing Jews the Torah, for Muslims the Qur'ān and for other religions someone or something else."[53]

But then the question arises, why worry about communicating a Christian view of Jesus to Muslims if there is no need for them to depart from a Qur'ānic basis of faith? Perhaps Küng should be content to explain a Christian view in dialogue without challenging the Islamic view of the crucifixion as he has done. Why should the Qur'ān stand accused of flying in the face of history? If the Qur'ān is an adequate vehicle for salvation then history hardly counts, and if Muslims can find God through Islam then they do not need to be told that their means of salvation is somehow less than adequate.[54] Küng might reply that the Qur'ānic portrait of Jesus is not adequate but that God is able to reveal truth, redeem sinners, and liberate oppressed humans through the Qur'ān despite the denial of the crucifixion. Perhaps he would say that the New Testament is a more complete account of revelation, redemption and liberation, and that the point of communicating the Christ of the Bible is to offer that fuller version of salvation to Muslims.

Küng, Hick and Cragg on Christology in Dialogue with Muslims

These three theologians share the common late twentieth century theological conviction that the Christological formulations of Nicaea and Chalcedon are no longer useful for Christology since they emphasise being rather than doing, static nature rather than active commitment.[55] Cragg can speak for all three when he says,

> "We return from Chalcedon to Gethsemane and to a Christology of action as sufficing for a Christology of nature … It is interesting to note that the Creeds and Chalcedonian Christology had ... no required theology of atonement. Content with the fact of the Cross they left the preaching of it to the Holy Spirit in the mind of the Church. It might have been well to

---

[53] H. Küng, "World Peace – World Religions –World Ethic", in the special volume of *Concilium* entitled *Islam: A Challenge for Christianity* (1994), 127-139, 136.

[54] Mahmut Aydin seems so relieved to be told by Küng that Islam is a means of salvation that he fails to defend the authenticity of the Qur'ānic account of history. See his exposition of Küng's Christology in his *Modern Western Christian Theological Understandings of Muslims*, 225-234.

[55] For a helpful study of the Christology of Küng and Hick among other recent theologians see S. Cowdell, *Is Jesus Unique?* (New York: 1996).

> have done the same with the incarnation had not Gnosticism and other perils needed refutation for there to be any authentic redemption at all."[56]

Hick and Küng hold that Hellenistic Christology is a barrier to talking about Christ to people who do not value Greek patterns of thought, and that New Testament Christology can best be read in Semitic categories of action rather than in Hellenistic categories of being, though Johannine Christology may be a fusion of the two. A return to a more Semitic reading of the New Testament may help Christians to dialogue with Muslims, though Hick's presentation is more rigorously 'semitic' than Küng's.

Cragg's Christology is about the self-giving of Jesus to reconcile humanity to God. This picture is dependent on the truth that Jesus alone among human beings is God in human flesh. Only the self-giving of God expressed in Christ redeems others from alienation to God. Cragg puts his efforts in dialogue with Muslims into persuading them that the Qur'ān allows for God to interact with his creation to make Incarnation possible. The God of traditional Islamic interpretation is too small, and the 'greatness' of God has to make room for the greatest act of all, that God was in Christ reconciling the world to himself. But this Incarnational Christology depends on the very ontological Nicene thought patterns that Cragg wishes to move away from, which only shows the difficulty of separating ontological and functional categories in Christology.

Küng's Christology focuses on the life of Jesus rather than his atoning death. Indeed, Küng hardly mentions the atonement at all in dialogue with Muslims, preferring to emphasise that Jesus of Nazareth represented God in his teaching and actions. This is seen especially in his authority to forgive sin directly and in his promulgation of an ethic of self-denial. He believes that Muslims can benefit from adopting this Jesus, who transcends the one they already know from the Qur'ān. The knowledge of God's forgiveness and the life of self-denial need to become part of Islamic life. The cross of Christ can then become a symbol of forgiveness and self-giving rather than a symbol of God-forsakenness and human weakness.

Hick's Christology differs radically from those of Cragg and Küng. The real Jesus did not represent God in a unique way. He was a Jew who especially advocated love for God and neighbour in the spirit of the best of Jewish tradition. But this is also the burden of the great religious ones in human civilisation, therefore it is the task of Christians in dialogue to help others concentrate on the best in their traditions. Muslims are just as capable of loving God and neighbour as Christians, since the Qur'ān emphasises these virtues. Dialogue ought to enable Christians and Muslims to work together to promote a common cause. Therefore it should be possible for Christians to overlook the denial of the crucifixion of Jesus in

[56] K. Cragg, *The Lively Credentials of God* (London: 1995), 140f.

the Qur'ān, seeing that this historical detail is not essential to bringing about love for God and neighbour. Cragg's Incarnational Christology gets in the way of a meeting of minds, and Küng's Jesus who uniquely represents God is not much better because he excludes any other humans from representing God in the same way. Hick is much closer to an Islamic way of seeing Jesus than Küng or Cragg, but he speaks for a much smaller number of Christians than they do. Nevertheless, the appropriation of New Testament scholarly debate on the historical Jesus by all three shows the importance of the 'real' Jesus to twentieth century theology. In the context of dialogue with Muslims, all three have drawn attention to material in the Qur'ān that supports the 'real' Jesus of the gospels.

In the final analysis, Cragg, Küng and Hick have not developed Christology on the basis of the Qur'ān, but rather have attempted to present a view of Christ already formed before interaction with the new context of Islamic ideas. They would probably hold a similar Christology even if put in another context of belief. However, their encounter with the Christ of Muslim faith has led them to draw various connections between Islamic perceptions and Christian ones. Cragg is more skilled at this task than Küng or Hick, and offers fresh ways for Muslims to see Christ by attempting to combine Islamic thought with mainstream Christian doctrine. This attempt on the part of Christians to suggest new insights to Muslims about their own traditions is taken probably as far as it may go by a dramatic version of the life of Christ based on the four gospels that was produced in 1987 for Muslim Arabs. The following chapter will examine this novel juxtaposition of Qur'ānic and gospel details that present Christ in Islamic idiom but with essentially Christian content. *Sīra al-Masīẖ* represents the culmination of earlier attempts to fuse the Qur'ānic and gospel portraits by Pfander, Lūqā and Cragg.[57]

[57] See the following chapter for a detailed critique of *Sīra al-Masīẖ* (Larnaca: 1987).

Chapter Ten

The Portrait of Christ in *Sīra al-Masīh̲*

A new Arabic harmonisation of the four gospels appeared in 1987, which presented the life of Christ using Islamic terminology and Qur'ānic style. The story of Jesus is divided into thirty chapters each headed by "in the name of God the merciful and compassionate one", combining material from all four gospels into one biographical account. It is written in rhyme with verse endings borrowed from the Qur'ān, and throughout the story, key words and phrases from the Qur'ān appear that are not found in standard translations of the gospels. This work takes the Qur'ān more actively into the telling of the life of Christ than any of the apologetic writing surveyed so far, though the eighth century Anonymous Apology and the presentation of Christ by Kenneth Cragg offer the closest parallels in terms of using Islamic thought forms.[1] In other words, this life of Christ is the most notable Christian attempt in the history of Christian-Muslim relations to view Christ from both Muslim and Christian perspectives.

The production of the work began in 1977 with the collaboration of several Christians from Orthodox, Catholic and Protestant backgrounds, under the leadership of a Christian Palestinian poet and an American Protestant missionary. Their working method was based on the belief that the Qur'ān could furnish words and ideas for a Christian life of Christ.

> "We believe it is time to consider the possibility that the Qur'ān is itself a prophetic witness to the unity of God, both in the face of the 7th Century Arabian idolatry and of the modern materialistic world in which we live. It is also a significant, albeit incomplete, witness to God's Messiah."[2]

This admission represents a fundamental paradigm shift for both the American Evangelical David Owen and for the Middle Eastern Christians involved in the writing of *The Life of Christ*. The idea that the Qur'ān is a prophetic word from God opens up fresh possibilities for the use of the Qur'ān in Christian writing. Although David Owen, the editor in chief of *The Life of Christ*, believed that it faithfully translated the original Greek of the gospels into Arabic, perhaps it should be seen as an exercise in indigenous theology for Arabs from a Muslim background, since Qur'ānic

---

[1] See chapter two for *The Anonymous Apology* and chapter eight for Cragg.

[2] D. Owen, "Project Sunrise: Principles, Description and Terminology", *Seedbed* 2 (1987), 52.

language is used in the translation in an unprecedented way.[3] For example, the use of the Qur'ānic name *`Īsā* for Jesus in *The Life of Christ* is a startling innovation for Christian Arabic writing, where the ancient Syriac *Yasu`a* is normally found. The kind of Christology implied by this use of Qur'ānic terminology will be studied in this chapter.

The Life of *`Īsā*

The use of the Qur'ānic name *`Īsā* for Jesus in *Sīra al-Masīh* separates the work from available gospel translations in Arabic which all use *Yasu`a*, the Syriac title for Jesus used by Christians before and after the arrival of Islam in the Middle East. Preference for the Syriac name for Jesus in Arabic Bible translation can be seen in the Smith-Van Dyke version of 1866, Today's Arabic Version of 1978, and The Living Arabic Bible of 1988, as well as in the colloquial Moroccan New Testament of 1932 and the Algerian-Tunisian New Testament of 1965. However, Bible translators in other parts of the Muslim world have not hesitated to use the Qur'ānic name. For example, the Urdu and Turkish New Testaments have *`Īsā*.

The depth of feeling on the adoption of *`Īsā* in Arabic translation is illustrated by a debate between R.D. Bernard and John Mansour, both Evangelical missionaries in the Arab world. Bernard objected to the use of *`Īsā* in *Sīra al-Masīh* because it is "not his God-given name", which means God saves. *`Īsā* has no meaning.[4] Mansour, on the other hand, supports the use of *`Īsā* by making the point that the Hebrew root underlying *Yasu`a* does not occur in Arabic. A proper equivalent for 'God saves' would be *Yahweh yunajji*, not *Yasu`a*.[5]

The use of *`Īsā* in *Sīra al-Masīh* is not totally unprecedented in Christian writing in Arabic. *Amazing Events in Palestine* (*`ajābu mā hadatha fī-filastīn*) was published in Lebanon in 1974, and presents the birth and childhood of Jesus with illustrations that include Mary being visited by an angel as she sits under a date palm. This Qur'ānic version of the birth story

[3] Owen argued that *The Life of Christ* was a dynamically equivalent translation of the four gospels following the translation principles of the United Bible Societies. According to E. Nida, the first proponent of dynamic equivalence, translation should enable an audience to receive the communication of Scripture as closely as possible to the intention of the original authors. [E.A. Nida, *Bible Translating* (London: 1961).] Owen believed that "contextualised Bible translation for the Muslim Arab world primarily calls for the use of Islamic theological terminology coupled with a high level of literary Arabic. The goal is a dynamically equivalent presentation of Scripture for the Muslim Arab readers of today." [D. Owen, "Project Sunrise", 51]

[4] R.D. Bernard, "You shall call his name Jesus", *Seedbed* 7 (1992), 35.

[5] J. Mansour, "A Rose by Any Other Name", *Seedbed* 8 (1993), 27.

is certainly unusual in a Christian publication. The Qur'ānic names *Yahyā* and *`Īsā* are used for John the Baptist and Jesus.[6]

The fact that *Sīra al-Masīh* uses *`Īsā* rather than *Yasu`a* sends a signal to the Muslim reader that *`Īsā* of the Qur'ān is the subject of the story. That this new Christian portrait does not ignore a Muslim understanding of Jesus is confirmed by the way *`Īsā* seldom calls God 'father'.

How *`Īsā* Speaks about God

The characteristic name for God used by Jesus in the gospels is 'Father', but in *Sīra al-Masīh* he normally simply refers to 'God'. For instance, the Lord's Prayer in *Smith-Van Dyke*, *TAV*, and *LAB* opens with *abāna*, 'our Father', whereas *Sīra al-Masīh* has *allāhumma*, 'O God'. According to Owen, *allāh* is a better dynamic equivalent of the Greek word *pater* than *ab* for a Muslim reader, since *ab* probably conveys a biological link between Jesus and God. "To avoid crude, anthropomorphic misinterpretations by Muslim readers, the Father-Son metaphor is retained only where the context itself explains its significance."[7]

Only nine times does *`Īsā* call God 'father' in *Sīra*; twice *abān* (chapter 24:18, and 18:42), twice *allāh al-abāwī* (8:28, and 12:21), twice *abī* (6:10, and 16:62), twice *yā abātī* (28:5, and 6), and once *yā abāta* (29:39). The first four references relate to how the disciples should think of God as a caring father who provides good things for them and are not so controversial for a Muslim reader. *`Īsā* calls God *abī* 'my father' when he says that his father is always at work and that he is working too, and when he tells his audience about what he has seen in his father's presence. He prays *yā abātī* 'O my father' when he asks for the cup of suffering to be taken from him in the garden of Gethsemane, and *yā abāta* 'O father' when he commits his spirit into his father's hands on the cross.[8]

Therefore only five references to God as father of *`Īsā* may possibly convey a biological connection between them. Compared with the sum of the references to God as the Father of Jesus in the conventional translations of the four gospels, *Sīra* has virtually removed the problem posed by a more exact rendering of the Greek *pater*. However, the radical ascription of Fatherhood to God by the historical Jesus is scarcely heard by the Muslim.

---

[6] See *`Ajābu mā hadatha fī filastīn* (Beirut: 1974).

[7] D. Owen, 56. For a detailed study of the Lord's Prayer in *Sīra al-Masīh* see M. Beaumont, "The Lord's Prayer in Smith-Van Dyke and Sīrat al-Masīh", *Seedbed* 5 (1990), 52-4.

[8] The equivalent gospel contexts for *abān* are Matthew 23:9, and Luke 11:13; for *allāh al-abāwīy* Matthew 7:11 and 10:29; for *Abīy* John 5:17 and 8:38; for *ya abāti* Matthew 26:39; and for *ya abāta* Luke 23:46.

That price has been thought worth paying in order to circumvent a false understanding of Christ on the part of the modern Muslim.[9]

`Īsā is not 'Son of God' or 'Son of Man'

Another striking feature of *Sīra* is the absence of the titles 'Son of God' and 'Son of Man' found regularly in existing translations. *`Īsā* is called *ibn* 'son' only three times in chapters 1:16, 16:59, and 23:37.

1. Chapter 1:16 recounts the message of the angel Gabriel to Mary from Luke 1:31f. "A boy will be given to you whose name is Jesus, exalted in this world and the next (*wajīhan fi-l-dunya wa-l-akhirati*), and he is to be called Son of the Most High". 'Son of the Most High' is found in *Smith Van-Dyke* and *LAV*, although *TAV* has 'Son of the Most High God'. The use of the Qur'ānic phrase, "*wajīhan fi-l-dunya wa-l-akhirati*", is a surprise since it does not translate the Greek but adds a description of *`Īsā* from *sūra* 3:45 of the Qur'ān, where Gabriel announces the birth of Jesus to Mary; "*al-Masīh̲u `Īsā ibnu maryama wajīhan fi-l-dunya wa-l-akhirati*" (the Messiah, Jesus, son of Mary, exalted in this world and the next). *Sīra* has re-interpreted the Lukan account by replacing 'son' with 'boy' possibly to show that the child was a normal human being. The Qur'ānic exaltation of *`Īsā* enables *Sīra* to link his normal human beginning to the later astonishing achievement of his life and ministry. It appears that the exaltation begins in this world before ascending to the place where God dwells, since the Qur'ānic phrase lends itself to this interpretation. However, *Sīra* does represent *`Īsā* claiming a pre-existent state, as can be seen in section 10.4 of this chapter. So there is a tension between the Qur'ānic and gospel accounts that is not resolved in *Sīra*, leading to possible confusion on the part of the Muslim reader.

2. Chapter16:59f, a rendering of John 8:34-36 which contrasts the role of servants in a household with that of the son, is virtually identical to *Smith Van-Dyke*. The Johannine connection between the son of the house and the heavenly Father is kept in *Sīra* at 16:62; "If the son sets you free you will be free ... I speak of what I have seen in the presence of God my Father". *`Īsā* is claiming to be a member of the family rather than a slave; "Whoever sins is a slave to sin. A slave does not always belong in the house but a son does." *`Īsā* has family rights that by implication others do not have. Whether he is adopted or born into the family is not clear in the dialogue. This ambiguity might be the reason for the inclusion of 'son' terminology

---

[9] The naming of God as 'father' by Jesus is accepted as authentic by the vast majority of gospel scholars, and thus it can be argued that *Sīra* is not so much a translation as a dramatisation in Islamic thought forms.

here, since all other Johannine examples of 'father-son' vocabulary are transformed into 'God-I' language in *Sīra*.

3. The third retention of 'son' language comes at 23:37 in the course of a story about the son of the vineyard owner being sent to retrieve the vineyard from rebellious tenants. This story provides indirect evidence for *`Īsā's* view of his own status, but does not amount to the use of 'son' language by *`Īsā* of himself. *Sīra* then has been exceptionally sparing with 'son' terminology. Furthermore, Jesus' favourite title for himself in the synoptic gospels, 'Son of Man' is totally absent from the portrait. Owen argues that 'Son of Man' does not communicate what Jesus intended, but rather is often understood to "imply that Jesus is not God". Therefore 'Son of Man' is nearly always rendered as 'I'.[10] Owen reflects the opinion of Geza Vermes, the Aramaic scholar, who argues that the expression 'Son of Man' is really no more than a term for 'I'. "In Galilean Aramaic, ie. the language of Jesus and his first followers, Son of Man was at least occasionally employed as a circumlocution."[11] Jesus also speaks of a future coming of the Son of Man in the synoptic gospels, but Vermes believes that these sayings are inauthentic. Morna Hooker agrees with Vermes that Jesus used 'Son of Man' to refer to himself, but thinks that he applied the eschatalogical Son of Man idea of Daniel 7 to himself too. "Jesus used the phrase not because he was claiming to be the messianic Son of man, but because he accepted for himself the role of obedient faith which the term evokes."[12] Whether Jesus proclaimed himself as the future Son of Man is a matter of continued debate. Tom Wright holds that Jesus may have used Son of Man for "someone in my position" in Mt 8:20 and 11:19, but the vast majority of uses relate to a future role, and that there is no need to view these as inauthentic.[13]

Sīra avoids this discussion by rendering the future son of man as *al-Mahdī*. This is not a Qur'ānic title, but is found in some of the *Ḫadīth* concerning the end times, where *al-Mahdī* is the one who God sends to establish justice among humanity.[14] For example, *Sīra* 25:48 renders Matthew 25:31, where Jesus speaks of the coming of the Son of Man to sit on a throne for judgment, as "the day is approaching; the hour of the *Mahdī's* glorious return with row upon row of angels; then he will sit on his throne." However, the fact that *al-Mahdī* sits on a throne to rule seems to

---

[10] D. Owen, "Project Sunrise", 56.

[11] G. Vermes, *Jesus The Jew* (London: 1983), 168. Maurice Casey supports the view that Son of Man "was a normal term for man which an Aramaic speaker might use to speak indirectly of himself." [M. Casey, "Idiom and Translation: Some aspects of the Son of Man Problem", *NTS* 41 (1995), 164-182, 169.

[12] M. Hooker, *Mark* (London: 1991), 93.

[13] N.T. Wright, *Jesus and the Victory of God* (London: 1996), 517f.

[14] See the article "*Al-Mahdī*", in *EI,* vol. 5 (Leiden; 1986), 1,231f.

challenge an Islamic conviction that only God sits on a throne to rule humanity. In the Qur'ān only God himself sits on a throne. His rule is bound up with his identity that must not be challenged by human pretenders. *Sūra* 23:117 links his throne with his uniqueness. *La illāha illah-wa rabbu al-`arshi al-karīmi* (There is no God but he, Lord of the noble throne). So when Jesus claims to have a throne, which is linked to God alone more than twenty times in the Qur'ān, an immediate challenge is mounted to the unity of God. Nevertheless *Sīra* directs attention to a coming *al-Mahdī* who represents God in the future judgement of humanity. *Al-Mahdī* does not rule in place of God but perhaps can be understood to rule the earth on God's behalf.

This use of *al-Mahdī* for the future Son of Man is based on the theory that *al-Mahdī* is identical to *`Īsā*, which is not undisputed in Muslim scholarship. The *Hadīth* collections of Bukhārī and Muslim do not mention a coming *al-Mahdī*. According to these collections *`Īsā* will return. However, Abū Dawūd, al-Tirmidhi, al-Nasā'i and the *Musnād* of Ibn Hanbal all record traditions concerning a coming al-Mahdī. Even before the collection of the *Hadīth*, two schools of thought appeared that continue to recent times in Sunni Islam. The first of these was represented by al-Hasan al-Basrī (d. 728) who maintained that *`Īsā* was identical to *al-Mahdī*, but his contemporary Muhammad b. Sirin (d. 728) held that *al-Mahdī* would make an appearance before *`Īsā*, and that the latter would pray behind him.[15] In the light of this analysis, the use of *al-Mahdī* as a dynamically equivalent expression for the future Son of Man may be justified on the grounds of the identification of *al-Mahdī* with *`Īsā* among some Muslim readers.

The virtual disappearance of 'the Son' from this life of *`Īsā* changes the impression of *`Īsā* considerably, since the removal of an expression that Jesus gave to himself, 'the Son of Man', means that the Muslim reader of *Sīra* is unable to hear the strangeness of this name. The fact that scholars are divided about the correct interpretation of the phrase shows how enigmatic the name is. Following one theory about the meaning of 'Son of Man', *Sīra* opts for the use of the personal pronoun 'I' as an equivalent. Owen's explanation for the adoption of this view appeals to an Aramaic substructure to the extant gospels in Greek.

> "Jesus was a Semite, and the original language of Jesus' teachings was a combination of Aramaic and Hebrew. To communicate to other Semitic peoples we may at times have to go behind the language of the Greek New Testament to its Aramaic-Hebrew origins in exegeting certain passages for our readers."[16]

---

[15] *Ibid.*

[16] D. Owen, "Project Sunrise", 52.

However, this argument can be used to support the retention of the Aramaic *bar nasha* (son of man) in Arabic. If *bar nasha* really was a circumlocation for 'I' then it is surely very significant that the four gospel writers chose not to translate 'Son of Man' as 'I' when they produced their Greek versions. Either the gospel writers did not know what 'Son of Man' meant or they felt that it was untransferable. In other words, none of them felt it appropriate to remove the ambiguity inherent in that Aramaic name. On this basis the grounds for using *ibn al-insān* (Son of Man) would be very strong in any translation into Arabic. This is the attitude of the *TAV* and *LAV*, but *Sīra* charts a different course in communication, developing a portrait of Jesus that fits him into the Muslim thought world without paying too much attention to strict standards of translation.

`Īsā with Allāh from Eternity

The greatest challenge for *Sīra* is the handling of material from the fourth gospel, for it is the gospel of John that explicitly proclaims a unifying bond between the Father and the Son. The Father-Son language common in John is replaced by *allāh-ana* (God-I). For instance, John 14:10 "I am in the Father and the Father is in me" becomes "I am with God and God is with me" (*inni ma`a allāhi wa-inna allāha ma`ī*) at *Sīra* 27:7. Then there is John's claim at the outset of his gospel that "the Word was God", which *Sīra* omits. Nevertheless, Thomas' confession "my Lord and my God" (*mawlaya wa illāhī*) is faithfully reproduced in the final chapter of *Sīra*. Could it be that this discovery of Thomas after the death and resurrection of Jesus is a model of how a Muslim reader might come to see Jesus? While a Muslim may have difficulties with ascribing divinity to Jesus, so did Jesus' first followers. Just as they came to see Jesus as united with God in such a way that Jesus ought to be worshipped, so perhaps *Sīra* can lead a Muslim along the same path. There is perhaps also a connection between Thomas' confession at the end of the story and the announcement of the angel Gabriel at the beginning, where *`Īsā* is announced as "son of the Most High". Jesus' story begins and ends on the same note of divine identity. He is worthy of worship at his birth by shepherds and astrologers just as he is due adoration by his disciples. Between these two events is the whole life of Jesus that acts as evidence for their validity. *Sīra* has therefore retained from Johannine language only Thomas' ascription of divinity to Jesus. Thus only once is any identity of being acknowledged between Jesus and God from the stock of instances from the Fourth gospel.

Despite this, *Sīra* has an emphasis on the eternity of *`Īsā* that more than matches claims in the Fourth gospel that Jesus has come from the presence of the Father. The 'word' of John 1:1 is actually named as *`Īsā* in the Prologue to *Sīra*; "*innama `Īsā kalimatu allāhi min al-azali tamathala la-na* *basharan*" (Jesus, word of God from eternity appeared among us as human). The connecting of *`Īsā* with the eternal Word is daring, since John keeps a distinction between the Word existing in eternity and the Word entering time, and the Word is named after the enfleshment but not before. *Sīra* presents the pre-existence of Jesus in a way that John does not. While *Sīra* removes John's portrait of the Son as metaphysically united with the Father there is an emphasis on a relationship between *`Īsā* and Allāh that existed in eternity outside of time.

This poses a challenge to the Muslim reader to think through the status of *al-kalima*. If God cast his word into Mary at the moment of Jesus' conception, then is his word not before time? Does Jesus not uniquely possess that word among humans? Can Jesus be thought of as possessing God's word in his conscious mind, rather than merely proclaiming it? *`Īsā* speaks in *Sīra* of having been with God before being sent by him. The pronouncement of Jesus about his relationship to Abraham from John 8:39-59 is found in *Sīra* 16:62; "I am telling you what I have seen in God my Father's presence". Not only is this one of *Sīra*'s rare uses of 'Father' on the lips of *`Īsā* but it is also an indication that *`Īsā* claims to have a relationship with God based on sight. It is not just a question of hearing from God but more being in a fellowship of persons who are in close proximity, not merely a visionary state but the outcome of a pre-temporal relationship between *`Īsā* and God. This is confirmed at the end of the passage at 16:87, where *`Īsā* claims to be the eternal Word who is before Abraham; "*Anā hūwa kalimatu al-azali wa qabla Ibrāhīm*". The addition of *al-kalima* to *anā* makes the link between *`Īsā* and the descent of the Word clear. While John leaves behind the concept of the Word in his prologue, *Sīra* re-introduces it here. Whereas John describes Jesus as the Word, Jesus never uses the title 'Word' of himself in the gospel, but in *Sīra `Īsā* does.

Perhaps it is better to challenge Muslims over the pre-existence of *`Īsā* rather than unity of being between Allāh and *`Īsā*, since the Qur'ān does not criticise Christians for their belief in Jesus' pre-existence, but for undermining the unity of God by their attitude to Jesus. In playing down a unity of being between Jesus and God, *Sīra* is defusing the Muslim reader's natural response to a Christian presentation of the life of Jesus. In emphasising the eternal relationship between Jesus and God, *Sīra* is encouraging the Muslim reader to think about Jesus from an unfamiliar angle.

`Īsā Seeks for Faith in Himself

Another feature of John's gospel is the way that Jesus calls for faith in himself, and *Sīra* follows this pattern. John asks his readers to exercise faith in Jesus and this too is repeated in *Sīra*. An example of the latter comes at *Sīra* 4:19; "God offered up the Messiah out of love for humanity so that all who believe in him would not be lost but would have eternal life." Apart from the replacement of 'only son' with 'the Messiah' the demand for faith is the same in *Sīra* as in John 3:16. An example of *`Īsā* asking for faith in himself can be found in 13:25; "*yuridu allāhu an yu'minu bi-ya*" (God wants you to believe in me). There are seven other places in *Sīra* where faith in *`Īsā* is sought; 4:28; 13:30, 33, 48; 16:22, 51; 21:10; 24:54; and 28:1.

How would a Muslim reader react to this portrait of Christ seeking faith in himself? The *`Īsā* of the Qur'ān says very little about faith, and when he speaks he asks for faith in God, but not faith in himself. He does however command his followers to obey him in *sūra* 3:49. Could this be seen as a parallel to the *`Īsā* of *Sīra* commanding trust in himself? It might well do, since a Muslim is familiar with the fact that both Jesus and Muhammad had followers who were expected to obey them. Faith in Jesus then becomes obedience to his commands.

`Īsā Forgives Sin

Sīra 5:45-50 follows Luke's version of the healing of the paralytic from Luke 5:17-26, deviating only slightly. "*`Īsā* said to the man, 'your sins are forgiven'. The religious leaders reacted to his pronouncement saying, 'Only God forgives sin. Who is this who utters blasphemy?' Perceiving their thoughts he said, 'So that you may know that I have authority to forgive sin, I say to this man, get up and carry your mat and go home'. The man went out praising God." There is no toning down here of the offence of *`Īsā* pronouncing what only God can do. The reaction of the religious leaders in the story may well be that of the Muslim reader. Here, then, is a claim by *`Īsā* to a divine prerogative. He is claiming to act as God does, by his own authority.

Luke records two more stories of sinners being pronounced forgiven by Jesus. Luke 7:36-50 concerns a woman who was known to have lived an immoral life anointing Jesus' feet. *Sīra* has a version of this story at 9:24-34. Verses 30-34 contain the pronouncement of forgiveness. "*`Īsā* said to Simon, 'God has forgiven whatever sins she committed in the past". "*`Īsā* said to the woman, 'God has forgiven you'". For the Muslim reader there is no mistaking the challenge of a declaration that such a woman has already been forgiven by God. So the reaction of those present in the story, "Who is this that forgives sins?" becomes a reaction shared by a Muslim reader. The third story recorded by Luke at 19:1-10, which contains a pronouncement of forgiveness, also reappears in *Sīra* 22:51-55. This is the account of Zacchaeus the hated tax-collector who surprisingly offers to pay back what he has stolen from the townspeople of Jericho after an encounter with Jesus. "*`Īsā* said to Zacchaeus, 'Today you have been saved along with your household, you son of Abraham'". *Sīra* emphasises the personal nature of Zacchaeus' salvation.

The impact of these pronouncements of forgiveness is the authority that *`Īsā* claims to exercise,[17] which is bound to challenge a Muslim reader. If the accent of forgiveness in Islamic tradition is eschatological, if forgiveness is finally only fully realised on the day of judgement, then this already realised forgiveness granted by *`Īsā* can only strike a Muslim reader as presumption at worst or exaggeration at best. Thus the gulf between the *`Īsā* of *Sīra* and the expectations of the Muslim reader is unbridgeable within Islamic presuppositions. *Sīra* has not avoided the difficulties inherent in presenting *`Īsā* as one who acts as God.

`Īsā Predicts His Death by Crucifixion

While *Sīra* plays down some of the Johannine expressions of the unity of Jesus and God, there is no similar attempt to reduce the tension of the cross. In *Sīra*, *`Īsā* predicts his own death no less than eight times at 4:18; 14:37; 15:27; 17:38; 22:13; 24:47; 26:1 and 28:8.[18] On five of these occasions, *`Īsā* predicts that he will be crucified, whereas in the gospels Jesus mentions crucifixion only once. *Sīra* 15:27 adds a prediction of the crucifixion to the otherwise identical passage in Mark 9:31. *Sīra* 17:38 has *`Īsā* claiming "no-one can kill me or crucify me of his own accord", which contrasts with Jesus in John 10:17 who says "no-one takes my life from me". In *Sīra* 24:47 *`Īsā* offers to his hearers, "the day I am lifted up on the cross I will draw all people to myself ", which may be compared with John 12:32f, "when I am lifted up from the earth I will draw all people to myself." The final prediction in *Sīra* 28:8 also adds the crucifixion to the original account. "The time appointed by your Lord has come. The corrupt of the earth will kill him; they will crucify him." Mark 14:41 reads, "the

---

[17] Mainstream gospel scholars accept the historicity of Jesus' offer of forgiveness as part of his message of the kingdom. For example, N.T. Wright notes that "the point about Jesus' welcome to sinners was that he was declaring, on his own authority, that anyone who trusted in him and his kingdom-announcement was within the kingdom." [N.T. Wright, *Jesus and the Victory of God,* 517f.)

[18] Equivalent gospel contexts are Jn 3:14f; Mk 8:31; Mk 9:31; Jn 10:11-16; Mk 10:33f; Jn 12:47; Mt 26:2; and Mk 14:41.

hour has come for the Son of Man to be put into the hands of sinners." Twice *Sīra* offers a direct response to the denial of the crucifixion in the Qur'ān at *Sūra* 4:157, "They did not kill him, they did not crucify him", by having *`Īsā* use the two verbs 'kill' and 'crucify' in a positive sense at 17:38 and 28:8. The *`Īsā* of *Sīra* offers a different way of understanding the Qur'ān than most Muslims would be prepared to accept.

The overall impression of the eight predictions by *`Īsā* of his impending death is likely to be far reaching on the Muslim reader. Far from painting a Qur'ānic portrait of God's messenger rescued from the murderous Jews, *Sīra* drives home the New Testament centrality of the cross. The way the predictions are spread out over the thirty chapters makes the impact constant and regular. *Sīra*, by not merging the death predictions of the four gospels into a narrow band of two or three predictions, has heightened the drama of the cross. *`Īsā* speaks of ransoming others by his death. Since *`Īsā* offers his life not just as a martyr to the cause of God's will, but also as a means of enabling spiritual life to arise in those who have faith in him, then the *`Īsā* of *Sīra* is further distanced from the *`Īsā* of the Qur'ān who comes to instruct but not to redeem.

`Īsā Offers His Life to Redeem Others

There are four references in *Sīra* to the saving power of *`Īsā's* death. In chapter 13:40 he pronounces, "this bread is my body which I give as a ransom (*fidā`*) for all people". 13:42 adds, "unless you eat my flesh and drink my blood you will be among the lost." John 6: 51 and 53 read, "the bread I give is my body which I offer for the life of the world ... If you do not eat the flesh of the Son of Man or drink his blood you will not have life." John does not record the last supper though this discourse probably refers to it.[19] *Sīra* 22:45 reads, "I have not come to get people to serve me but to be a saving ransom for many of you", which follows Mt 20:28 closely. Lastly, *Sīra* 26:10f records the last supper with the ending, "this is my blood with which you gain access to intercession (*al-shafā`a*) if you hold onto the promise of the Merciful One (*al-rahmān*)", which replaces "this is my blood...for the forgiveness of sins" in Mt 26:27. *Al-shafā`a* (advocacy, or intercession) appears thirteen times in the Qur'ān. The context is most often the day of judgement, on which there will be nobody to intercede for unbelievers. *Sūra* 19:87 of the Qur'ān, *La yamlikuna al-shafā`ata illā man ittakhadha `inda al-rahmāni `ahdan* (They do not gain

[19] See, for example, D.M. Smith, "that an author could write 6:52-58 with no thought of the Lord's Supper is difficult to believe, given the pervasiveness of the sacrament at an early date." [D.M. Smith, *The Theology of the Gospel of John* (Cambridge: 1995), 158.]

access to intercession unless they hold onto the promise of the Merciful One), provides a close parallel. *`Īsā* in *Sīra* offers to be the intercessor between people and God of which the Qur'ān speaks. *Sīra*, therefore, presents *`Īsā* using this Qur'ānic language to show that he is the content of the covenant with *al-rahmān*. To receive his body and blood by faith is to enact that covenant. By participating in this covenant, salvation from *jahannam* (Qur'ān, *Sūra* 19:87) is guaranteed. Thus what the Qur'ān announces about escape from judgement *`Īsā* fulfils.

This is an incredibly daring application of Qur'ānic language to *`Īsā*. Access to salvation comes by cleaving to him in the way that Christians have always done, by feeding on his body and blood. God's promise of salvation is mediated by *`Īsā*, so he is the intercessor that Muslims ought to turn towards. What is proclaimed in the Qur'ān is found in the one who lays down his life for all. By now the Muslim reader may have reached the end of his patience. But he may also have come to understand what is vital to Christian faith. Now he may be able to see why the Eucharist is so central to Orthodox and Catholic worship, and why for most Protestants faith in the redeeming work of Christ is of first importance.

Evaluation

The Christology of *Sīra* is firmly based on the accumulated portraits of the four gospels. The *`Īsā* of *Sīra* is clearly recognisable to a Christian familiar with the New Testament. The birth of *`Īsā* is basically the account in Matthew and Luke, with details derived from *Sūra* 19 of the Qur'ān. The teaching of *`Īsā* is co-extensive with all four gospels, with little from the fourth gospel omitted. His healing work and his raising the dead are fully documented. The Qur'ān has, of course, little to add to his teaching, but it is significant that the miracle of the making of birds from clay is not found in *Sīra*. To the Muslim reader this signals that *Sīra* is unwilling to acknowledge the veracity of a story about *`Īsā* found in the Qur'ān. In terms of Qur'ānic material about *`Īsā*, then, *Sīra* adds what does not contradict the gospel portraits. That *`Īsā* should be "exalted in this world and the next" fits with the way the gospel writers portray him; that *`Īsā* should, as a minor, transform clay into birds, does not, because his ministry commenced in adulthood. For the same reason *`Īsā* cannot speak as an infant of his future work as he does in *Sūra* 19 of the Qur'ān. In other words *Sīra* does not attempt to build a new portrait of *`Īsā* on the foundations of the Qur'ān. Rather the opposite is the case, since the four gospels determine what is an acceptable picture of Jesus. Only those aspects of the Qur'ān that merge with the gospels can be used.

What is significant about *Sīra*'s Christology is the way the four gospels are adapted for a Muslim readership. While the Qur'ān is not the foundation of the portrait, it does have an influence on the way *`Īsā* is actually presented. Attention paid to what the Qur'ān denies about *`Īsā* makes *Sīra* the most penetrating attempt so far by Christians to retell the story of Jesus in a way that might commend itself to Muslims. This is most obvious in the rewriting of the Father-Son language. The great tradition of Christian apologetics to Muslims has, as we have documented, attempted to explain the Father-Son language. *Sīra*, goes beyond this impasse by virtually removing the metaphor. The alleged biological bond between Jesus and God, which is keenly felt by Muslims to be at the back of Christian belief, can quietly be laid aside. This Christian document scarcely allows the allegation to surface. Where Father-Son language is used, the context shows that the relationship is a spiritual one. While an argument may be made for more Father-Son language to be retained, there can be no reasonable doubt that *Sīra* has succeeded in removing a psychological obstacle in the mind of the Muslim reader. If apologists have always insisted that the relationship between Father and Son is only spiritual and never physical, then *Sīra* has removed the need to make the argument. This is a considerable gain.

Another gain for *Sīra* is the careful handling of the Johannine language identifying Jesus as God. The simple removal of "the Word was God" from the story enables Jesus' claim to be "one with the Father" to become a unity of thought or will. This has far reaching consequences for the Muslim reader. Since Jesus is not actually identified with God in *Sīra*, a Muslim reader is enabled to experience him in a familiar monotheistic framework. With the removal of explicit references to Jesus' identity of being with God, it becomes possible for a Muslim to be in the same position as a Jew in Jesus' own time. The question for both Jew and Muslim is "How does this Jesus relate to the one true God?"

Sīra makes the point particularly strongly that *`Īsā* volunteers to die according to the will of God. His death is no accident but is right at the centre of what he is trying to achieve in his life of service. The servant of God dies because it is where his service inexorably leads. But this service of God is also service of his fellow human beings. What God wills for *`Īsā* is no less than a vicarious death that redeems others from bondage. Why God wills the death of *`Īsā* is not answered in *Sīra*, though it may remain a question in the Muslim reader's mind. If others are enslaved, then *`Īsā* knows his task is to release them by dying on their behalf. The death of *`Īsā* becomes a focus of faith for his followers, and this is not the result of their own perception of him after the event, but quite clearly the teaching of *`Īsā* himself. To remember his death is enjoined on his disciples by the master. Here *Sīra* shows affinities with Pfander and Cragg in their emphasis on the atonement in the presentation of Jesus. It is as a result of his perfect obedience that Jesus' life has value for us. It is the release from sin that his death effects in us. In the end the cross is central to the Christology of *Sīra*.

Therefore, it is consistent with this centrality that *Sīra* should be willing to play down Incarnational language such as "only begotten" but at the same time be willing to present *`Īsā* repeatedly predicting his coming death. Thus it is no surprise that Johannine language about the death of Christ is retained where most Incarnational Johannine language is not.

In summary, this retelling of the story of Christ is a fresh and original attempt to attract Muslim readers to an essentially Christian narrative. By taking seriously the challenge concerning the sonship of Christ emanating from the Qur'ān, *Sīra* may enable Muslims to see the Christian claims about Christ from a new angle. This is an important advance in Christian-Muslim dialogue on Christ and may be the opening for other Christian initiatives in the future. Conversely, the Qur'ānic denial of the crucifixion is dealt with in *Sīra* not by displacement but by counterclaim. Whereas Christ hardly calls himself God's son, he repeats the prediction of his impending crucifixion more frequently in *Sīra* than in the gospels. Perhaps this risk is too great, since the Muslim reader is far more likely to be offended by the repetition than he would by a more veiled account of the death of Christ.

Chapter Eleven

The Christologies of Kenneth Cragg, John Hick, Hans Küng and *Sīra al-Masīh̲*, and Muslim Response

The two questions asked of the ninth century apologists in chapter six may be profitably posed to their twentieth century equivalents. Firstly, what developments in Christology can be observed as a result of engagement with the Islamic context? Secondly, what impact did these presentations of Christology have on Muslims? The answer to the first question in the ninth century apologetics was little development in content but a considerable effort to defend established Christology in terms that Muslims might find acceptable. The answer now is similar. Cragg, Hick and Küng do not alter their Christologies to any extent in the Islamic context, but they do attempt to defend their established views in ways that might be understood by Muslims. *Sīra al-Masīh̲*, however, is more an original appoach to Christology from within an Islamic context, rather than an already established view applied to it. The answer to the second question can be found in the dialogue partners of the three modern apologists. Only Hick's Christology is enthusiastically received for his acceptance of Islamic premises for the interpretation of Christ's significance.

The Christology of Kenneth Cragg

Cragg presents to Muslims the Incarnation and atonement as essentially true for them as much as for Christians. From *The Call of the Minaret* to *Jesus and the Muslim* he believes that Muslims need to believe in the revelation of God in Christ rather than merely the speech of God in Christ's mouth. In his early work he speaks of a personal revelation in Jesus of Nazareth that goes way beyond the normal Islamic idea that God speaks but does not appear to humans. In his dialogue with al-Farūqī, Cragg puts forward the argument about personal revelation in Incarnation as essential for Muslims to accept.[1] The central point of *Jesus and the Muslim* is "truth through personality" though he acknowledges that the notion is difficult for Muslims to accept. Thirty years of apologetics by Cragg reveal how impenetrable the Islamic notion of revelation as speech alone actually remains.

[1] See chapter eight.

He presses Muslims to accept that personal revelation is the only means of divine identification with sinful humanity. By coming to deal with rebellious humans on their own ground God is seen to have put an end to their waywardness once and for all. But this focus on the atonement comes up against the fact that the death of Christ is denied by the Qur'ān. To Muslims who are raised on this distortion of the truth, Christians should proclaim that the cross is not the failure of God's prophet, but the door to victory over all that might defeat God's rule in the world he made. At the heart of personal revelation is the forgiveness of sin. If according to Islam God forgives without the cost of coming into relationship with sinful humans then that forgiveness is not nearly so profound as that which is offered through the death of the Incarnate Christ. The true greatness of God is not the maintenance of a transcendent detachment from sin but an engagement with sin by its defeat on the cross.[2]

In the end this is the Apostolic gospel applied to an Islamic thought world, and so is not a Christology built on Islamic conceptions. Even though Cragg understands fully the nature of Muslim attitudes to Christ and to the Christian claims about him he adopts an unhelpful polemical tone that never really changes through his long career. He finds Islam guilty of turning Jesus into a successful prophet who is a scarcely recognisable figure when compared with the Jesus of history.[3] But this very aggressive tone is bound to make Muslims question whether Cragg is really taking Islam as seriously as he claims, and whether he truly wants to dialogue with them on equal terms. In terms of the forgiveness of God, Muslims will doubtless continue to deny that God has restricted his freedom to the death of Christ as Cragg argues. For Cragg to place this historical necessity on God is to demean his greatness. Future dialogue would be better served by avoiding such direct assault on Islamic thought perhaps by arguing that God was under no necessity to forgive through the cross, but that he chose to show his compassion to humanity through the death of Christ.

Cragg's insistence that the historical Jesus intended to die for the salvation of humanity leaves him at odds with most Christian gospel scholars, and opens himself to the criticism that he speaks on behalf of traditional conservative Christians who ignore the findings of Biblical scholarship when he claims otherwise. He is an exponent of the Christology of the early church but is unwilling to accept that this is the case because he wants to maintain that theology is firmly embedded in history. The difficulty for Cragg's Christology in dialogue with Muslims is that the latter are able to distinguish between the historical Jesus and the faith of the early church by studying the Christian scholarship that Cragg ignores. Nevertheless, Cragg does speak for the vast majority of Christians who

---

[2] See chapter eight.

[3] See chapter eight.

uphold the Apostolic convictions of the Incarnation and atonement and they will continue to find inspiration from his determined efforts to persuade Muslims that God was in Christ reconciling humans to himself.

The Christology of John Hick

Hick's Christology once looked rather like Cragg's in that he held to the revealed status of the Incarnation and atonement until his adoption of Theocentrism. The shift in Hick's understanding of the role of Apostolic theology in Christology coincided with his encounter with people of other faiths in the late 1960's. Therefore his abandonment of the beliefs that God was in Christ ontologically and that God dealt with sin through the cross was not solely related to an awareness of Muslim conceptions of Christ, but was also caused by a wider interaction with Hindus, Sikhs and Buddhists. In terms of Islamic perceptions, Hick thinks that a functional rather than ontological relationship between Jesus and God is essential for common life. Being able to live together in harmony rather than in communal strife necessitates Christians seeing Jesus as a Spirit filled man who was exceptionally conscious of God, but not as a man who is the union of divine and human natures. This enables Muslims to agree with Christians that Jesus was among the greatest saints and enables Christians to agree with Muslims that Muḫammad was among the greatest prophets of God to humanity.[4] Hick's Christology is much more likely to be received warmly by Muslims than Cragg's since Jesus is aligned with other prophets in status, but at the same time is unlikely to be accepted by most Christians who view Christ as much more than a prophet.

As far as the death of Jesus of Nazareth is concerned, there is no historical doubt for Hick that it took place, but the function of that death in the faith of the New Testament church need not be upheld by the modern church. If the latter could set aside the notion of atonement through the cross so central to the Apostolic testimony then good relations with Muslims may follow. After all, the forgiveness of God for human sin can be received without the narrow focus of the death of the Incarnate Christ. Salvation in its broadest sense has been achieved by many humans who knew nothing of the saving effects of Christ's death. So at this point in human history, Christians need to give full acknowledgement to these facts, even though they may continue to value the New Testament faith and the developed theology of the church for internal worship and life. In other words, Hick recommends a generous attitude on the part of Christians to the life of God in Islamic tradition that gives equality to Islamic spirituality. The 'grace' of God has surely been at work in Muḫammad and a host of his

---

[4] See chapter nine.

followers down the centuries just as much as in Jesus and many of his followers. Ultimately Christ is an exemplar for others of a true spiritual life, and he will always have an outstanding role for Muslims as well as Christians.[5] This attitude to divine forgiveness is likely to appeal to Muslims as true to Islam, but is not going to be accepted by the majority of Christians who maintain a definite connection between the death of Christ and forgiveness for sin.

In the final analysis, by confining Christ to being an exemplar for the spiritual experience of others, Hick parts company with mainstream Christians who continue to uphold the Incarnation and atonement as true, and therefore he does not represent majority Christian opinion in dialogue with Muslims. Hick's pioneering Christology leaves him exposed on the fringes of Christianity with the result that he can only speak for a small number of like-minded theologians. Thus while providing an attractive portrait of Christ from a Muslim point of view, Hick may mislead Muslims into thinking that he is in the vanguard of a new approach to Christology that will become increasingly accepted by other Christians when this is unlikely to be the case.

The Christology of Hans Küng

Küng comes somewhere between Cragg and Hick in his estimation of Christ. He believes that the Incarnation was an Apostolic overlay on the much more modest claims of Jesus of Nazareth, who was proclaimed Son of God only after his death and resurrection. In fact this conviction of the early church did not initially involve an ontological identification between Jesus and God, but only a relationship of equal authority. If Christians could give up the more ontological identity between Father and Son found in later New Testament writing and in the creeds of the Patristic period, then relations with Muslims would improve dramatically. Everything gained by two centuries of gospel scholarship should be harnassed by Christians in their expession of Christology at the end of the twentieth century. Muslims then would have no serious quarrel with Christians about the language of Christ's sonship, since it would refer only to an adopted rather than an essential status. All the arguments concerning eternal sonship mounted by Christians in the past then become redundant, and Christians and Muslims are able to relate on equal terms about Jesus.[6] Certainly, Küng's desire to eliminate ontology from Christology is likely to find a warm response from Muslims, but his denial of the Apostolic faith in the essentially divine character of Christ distances him from most Christians.

---

[5] See chapter nine.

[6] See chapter nine.

Küng recognises that some details in the portrait of Christ in the gospels may yet cause conflict between Christians and Muslims. Jesus' criticism of the Jewish law implies a criticism of Islamic law, though Küng does not specify details of which parts of the latter come under scrutiny. He seems more concerned to promote Jesus' attack on organising spritual life around rule keeping, but concedes that this is a major difficulty for most Muslims who value such a form of community life. Another difficulty arises in the fact of the death of Jesus on the cross being annulled by the Qur'ān. Küng challenges modern Muslims to engage in historical criticism of their scriptures in the same way that Christians have done with the Bible, and so accept the historical fact of the cross. He encourages Muslims to follow the suggestion of M.M. Ayoub that the denial of the crucifixion in *Sūra* 4:157 can be understood as a denial of the death of God's 'word'.[7]

Küng's polemical approach to the interpretation of the Qur'ān is hardly likely to commend him to Muslims but he seems oblivious to this problem. Like Cragg he thinks history must win the argument over theology, though unlike Cragg he does not insist that God's forgiveness comes through the historical event of the death of Christ. Forgiveness may be granted by God to Muslims without the mediation of Christ's death as a sacrifice for sin, so the value of Christ's death lies rather in the expession of God's love in the self-giving of Jesus, and the assurance that God is involved in human suffering to bring new meaning and hope.[8]

Küng then rejects Cragg's insistence on the Incarnation and atonement as essential to Christology and to ongoing relations with Muslims. On the other hand, he disagrees with Hick's reading of Jesus' attitude to Jewish law, and to his setting aside of the death of Jesus. Both of these details from the gospels must be upheld by Christians as historical facts and cannot merely be regarded as interpretations of Jesus' life that are negotiable because Muslims do not approve. On the contrary, one of the tasks of genuine dialogue between Christians and Muslims is to get consensus on the facts of history, and Muslims have to be persuaded that this is essential to good relations between the two faith communities.

Like Hick, Küng has been interested in relationships between Christians and people of many different faiths rather than merely Christian relations with Muslims, so his Christology reflects this wider audience. His understanding of Christology in dialogue with Nasr does not differ in any important respect from that presented in his 1976 *On Being a Christian*, and his subsequent treatment of Christology in his 1995 *Christianity: The Religious Situation of Our Time* does not answer Muslim questions about Christian perceptions of Christ. Despite dialogue with Nasr, Küng does not make Islamic thought central to his construction of Christology, and this is

[7] For Ayoub's view see chapter one.

[8] See chapter nine.

bound to make his presentation of Christ seem to Muslims unconnected to their perceptions of him.

Küng's Christology departs from mainstream Catholic doctrine which continues to insist on the Incarnation and atonement as essential to faith in Christ, and therefore his ability to represent his own church community in dialogue with Muslims is put in question. Muslims who wish to understand Catholic faith in Christ cannot rely on Küng's Christology and this limits the impact of the dialogue between Nasr and Küng to a large extent.

The Christology of *Sīra al-Masīh̲*

The Christ of *Sīra al-Masīh̲* is certainly similar to the Christ of the gospels in many respects. He performs the same miracles, tells the same stories, makes similar authoritative pronouncements in God's name, and sets himself on a collision course with Jewish leaders that leads to his arrest and crucifixion. However, he speaks a different kind of language from that found in the gospels in some respects. He rarely calls God his Father and never refers to himself as Son of man. Instead of speaking of the future Son of man, he talks about *al-Mahdī* coming at the end of the age. His followers never call him Son of God as they often do in the gospels. *Sīra*'s Christ has no identity of being with God, although he does appear to have an eternal relationship with him. Therefore the eternal Christ has a status of equal authority to God that is expressed in his teaching and actions in God's name. There is a kind of Incarnation in view here; the eternal Word becomes human, but there is no mention of the eternal Son taking flesh. Without doubt *Sīra* has presented a form of Incarnation tailored to Muslim sensibilities over ideas of sonship. By virtually eliminating any talk of a father-son relationship between Jesus and God *Sīra* has accepted the force of Qur'ānic criticism of Christian thinking about Christ.[9] This imaginative reshaping of the gospel story avoids the need to advance an apologetic for traditional gospel language as Cragg and Küng have done.

Sīra has gone beyond anything seen in the history of Christian-Muslim dialogue. Cragg and Küng stand outside the Islamic world in their thinking, and do not hesitate to judge the Qur'ān as containing an erroneous portrait of Christ. *Sīra* is composed from within the Islamic world by Christians fully aware of the reality of life as a minority in an Islamic milieu. Only *Sīra* among modern presentations of Christ for Muslims has accepted the full responsibility of speaking about Christ in terms that Muslims may receive without instantly rejecting as unsound. Muslims may well find this portrait congenial to their perceptions of Christ in such a way that they are

[9] See chapter ten.

enabled to see the fuller life of Christ found in the gospels as completing the summary details in the Qur'ān.

Even though *Sīra* has overemphasised Christ's predictions of his crucifixion, the way that he speaks of his death inverts the Qur'ānic denial in *sūra* 4:157, "they did not kill him, they did not crucify him" to drive the point home that he was killed, he was crucified. The very telling of the story makes use of Islamic language to suggest to Muslim readers another interpretation of the denial of Christ's death. Instead of seeing *sūra* 4:157 as simply wrong in the way that Cragg and Küng have done, *Sīra* turns the negative statement into a positive one to offer Muslims a challenging new view of Christ's death. Once again *Sīra* shows the importance of engaging with Muslims from within an Islamic worldview rather than coming from outside as Cragg and Küng have done. Still, the denial of the crucifixion may not so easily be undone by *Sīra*'s transformation of negation to affirmation and the basic contradiction between gospel testimony and Qur'ānic counter claim remains a continuing problem for Christian-Muslim dialogue. In terms of answering the question about how Christology has developed as a result of engagement with the Islamic context, it is the case that *Sīra* has taken that context more completely into the presentation of Christ than Cragg, Küng or Hick have done.[10]

Nevertheless, *Sīra* has not replaced standard translations of the gospels in Arabic, and therefore has a limited role among Arabic speaking Christians. Whether such a contextual version of the gospels can become more widely accepted by Christians remains to be seen. In other words, Arab Muslims, who may be drawn to the Christ presented in *Sīra*, are still faced with the traditional portrait prized by Arab Christians as a whole with all the problems inherent in the established versions of the gospels that *Sīra* has attempted to overcome. Once again, creative theology in dialogue comes up against traditional modes of expressing faith held by the majority to be essential.

Muslim Responses to Christian Views of Christ in the Twentieth Century

The Truth about Christ Comes from the Qur'ān

The Muslim dialogue partners of Cragg and Küng, al-Farūqī and Nasr, both base their understanding of Christ on the Qur'ānic portrait. Al-Farūqī's discussion of the Incarnation depends on the assumption that the Qur'ān forbids the association of God with any aspect of the world he created. In other words, the Qur'ān prohibits the Christian notion of a descent of God

[10] See chapter ten.

to the earth to indwell a particular human being in Palestine. Thus any dialogue about Jesus of Nazareth has to be conducted on the basis of this Qur'ānic restriction. Cragg's challenge to al-Farūqī to make room for the possibility of Incarnation as part of God's freedom of action is met by the warning that God has revealed in the Qur'ān that certain divine actions are inconceivable as contradictory to the character of God. If God is transcendent then he cannot be immanent in the created world, the latter cancels the former. Christ then must be seen as human but not divine.[11]

Nasr objects to Küng's criticisms of the Qur'ān by asserting that for all Muslims without exception the whole of the Qur'ān is the word of God and not just certain parts of it. Therefore Küng's challenge to Muslims to reject the truth of *sūra* 4:157 and come to accept that Jesus was crucified is flatly turned down by Nasr on behalf of the worldwide Muslim community. No Muslim can state that a section of the Qur'ān is wrong in its claims, and Christians ought not to insist that Muslims do to the Qur'ān what Christians have done to the Bible. If Christians want to dialogue with Muslims then they will have to adhere to this principle, otherwise no serious conversation can take place.[12]

The approach of Cragg and Küng to the Qur'ān is not likely to be the best way forward for twenty-first century dialogue between Christians and Muslims, because any direct challenge to the authority of the Qur'ān simply frustrates genuine dialogue. If Muslims are completely united in their conviction that the whole of the Qur'ān is the unadulterated speech of God then Christians who attempt to dialogue with Muslims must accept that the starting point for dialogue is the acceptance of this Islamic premise. Even Hick fails to observe the principle when he asks Muslims to accept a variety of scriptures as equally revelatory, so that in the end the Qur'ān is on the same level as Hindu or Buddhist sacred texts. Thus while accepting its spiritual value, he does not accord the Qur'ān the status that Muslims do. A more fruitful approach to dialogue could arise if Christians were to develop concepts and arguments for their Christology from the teaching of the Qur'ān in the way that *Sīra* has done.

The Historical Jesus did not Teach His Equality with God in Terms of the Trinity or the Incarnation

Al-Farūqī is adept at using Christian gospel scholarship to confound traditional Christian readings of the teaching of Jesus. Thus the Trinitarian ideas in Mat 28:19 cannot be ascribed to Jesus but rather to the early church. The same applies, of course, to the Johannine emphasis on the eternal identity of the Word with God, and to the sayings of Jesus in the

---

[11] See chapter eight.
[12] See chapter nine.

fourth gospel claiming eternal equality between himself and his Father. Cragg seems unwilling to discuss the disparity between the heightened Incarnational and Trinitarian thought in the gospels and Jesus' own thought patterns, but it is clear that Muslims need to be treated to a more discriminating analysis of the gospels by Christians who dialogue on Christology.[13]

Siddiqi's approval of Hick's Christological ideas is related to Hick's ability to separate out the historical Jesus from the Christ of the early church's faith. Muslims seem happier to dialogue with Christians who accept the results of their own gospel scholars than with those who choose to ignore them. Hick's insistence that Jesus upheld Jewish law, only declared forgiveness on God's behalf and not on his own authority, and never presumed to be divine, is a good basis for dialogue with Muslims in the mind of Siddiqi.[14] Nevertheless, some explanation of the rise of Incarnational and Trinitarian thought needs to be given by Christians in dialogue, lest the whole history of the Christian faith be left unexplained to Muslims. If Sharafuddin could call the Incarnation "an agelong blunder in Christian thought"[15] it is obviously vital that Christians can give an appropriate apologetic for the faith of the early church.

Cragg does expound the message of Paul and John in *Jesus and the Muslim* but fails to adequately explain how their understanding of the Incarnation developed from the teaching of Jesus. His insistence on the awareness of the historical Jesus of his divinity on the one hand and his mission to die for the sins of humanity on the other means that for Cragg there is only a small step between Jesus' self revelation and the early church's faith in him. However, if Jesus did not teach his Incarnation or his atonement for sinful humanity then another account is required of how the Apostolic message arose. Küng explores this shift in *Christianity: The Religious Situation of Our Time* but not in the context of a Muslim readership. Therefore a major task of future dialogue must be the careful explanation of the development of New Testament faith in the Incarnation, atonement and Trinity, all of which are present in the very gospels that provide information about the historical Jesus. If the gospels are composed in the light of faith in the Incarnation, atonement and Trinity then presentations of Christ for Muslims should benefit from unfolding the reasons behind this process.

---

[13] See chapter eight.

[14] See chapter nine.

[15] *Ibid.* For a similar assessment of the Incarnation as a mistaken development in Christian thought see M 'Ata al-Rahīm, *Jesus-A Prophet of Islam* (London: 1977).

Nasr's Two Kinds of Revelation

The suggestion of Nasr that God may have intended to reveal the death of Christ to Christians and the non-crucifixion of Christ to Muslims is intriguing even if it is idiosyncratic. No doubt he adopted this scheme to make room for the historical fact of the cross while at the same time maintaining the veracity of the Qur'ānic denial of the fact. However, he failed to maintain the same double view of revealed truth in relation to other aspects of Qur'ānic dispute with the Bible. Thus Islamic law which is clearly given in the Qur'ān is non-negotiable as revelation from God, and Christians should not attempt to challenge the revealed character of that law in dialogue. Any dialogue on ethics must come up against the disparity between the ethics of Jesus and the Qur'ān, but Nasr is warning that Muslims are not ready to make concessions on revelation in this area, except perhaps to allow each community to follow their own understanding of right behaviour.[16] This discussion of Islamic law as the revealed will of God does have a bearing on the suggestion of some Christians that dialogue with Muslims should in future avoid theological ideas and concentrate on ethics. The conclusion to this book will examine this proposal in the light of Nasr's refusal to allow Christians to question the revelatory character of Qur'ānic ethics.

The Qur'ānic insistence that Jesus came with the same message as Abraham and Moses and that he confirmed the *Torah* brought to the Jews could be a basis for Christian-Muslim dialogue if Sanders and Hick are right about Jesus' attitude to Jewish law. If Jesus confirmed the law rather than definitively undermined it then he may appear to Muslims as a recognisable figure. Certainly, Hick hopes that the new view of Jesus as an upholder of the law will create a new climate for Christian-Muslim relations. Nevertheless, Küng's trenchant rejection of this interpretation of Jesus' teaching shows that debate on specific details of Christ's teaching may continue without consensus for some time to come. If Jesus wanted to replace law keeping with faith as the majority of gospel scholars believe then the Sanders-Hick school of interpretation may struggle to become representative of mainstream Christian thought.

As a result of this divide Muslims will doubtless be able to argue that the lack of consensus among gospel scholars demonstrates the inherent weakness of the gospels as authentic source material for the life of Christ. Traditional accusations of corruption of the pure *Injīl* brought by Jesus will continue to be fuelled by these disagreements between Christians over the actual teaching of Jesus.

---

[16] See chapter nine.

Conclusion

Developments in Christology are seen in the way Islamic concerns are addressed by the Christian apologists. Cragg has a more thorough understanding of Muslim thought than Küng or Hick and thinks the main issue for dialogue is an inadequate Muslim view of the transendence of God. If Muslims could accept that transendence includes immanence then the Incarnation would become intelligible for them. For Cragg, the development is not so much in Christology as in the doctrine of God. Küng and Hick leave behind an Incarnational Christology as no longer acceptable for modern Christians who want to dialogue with people of other faiths. Küng thinks that the early Apostolic belief that Jesus was adopted by God can be retained but that the later ideas of eternal sonship and ontological equality between Christ and God must be discarded. Christ reveals the authority of God in his teaching, the power of God in his healings, and the love of God in his death. He believes that this more semitic Christology will appeal to Muslims. Hick thinks that this portrait is still too far removed from the real Jesus who was only a human channel for God's authority, power and love. He claimed no unique divine qualities for himself. If Christians could jettison the whole Apostolic superstructure placed on Jesus then relations with people of other faiths would dramatically improve, and Christians would be able to accept other religious leaders, such as Muhammad, on equal terms with Christ. Küng and Hick do not address Islamic thought in isolation from other religious worldviews, though they believe that their Christologies foster dialogue with Muslims. *Sīra* presents Christ as an obedient servant of God who is able to teach with divine authority, perform mighty divine deeds, and die as a means of bringing God's forgiveness to wayward humans. There are hints of him having an eternal origin and equality of status with God, but these are not emphasised to allow Muslims to appreciate this Christian life of Christ without rejecting it outright. Here Muslim perceptions meet gospel scholarship to produce a contextualised life of Christ that makes a unique contribution to Christian/Muslim dialogue.

The response by the Muslim dialogue partners shows that any insistence on aspects of Christology that contradict the Qur'ānic account of Christ fails to convince. Cragg's reinterpretation of transcendence is unnacceptable to al-Farūqī because the Qur'ān does not support it. God cannot become human on any sane reading of the Qur'ān, and Christians ought not to give misleading Qur'ānic interpretations in dialogue with Muslims. Küng's accusation that the Qur'ān is wrong about the cross offends Nasr who points out that dialogue should be conducted on non-polemical principles. Hick's eirenic approach to Islamic ideas hides a more aggressive tone when Siddiqi challenges him to admit the truth of divine revelation. Hick's failure to acknowledge revelation on Islamic terms counts against his seemingly more Islamic account of Christ. *Sīra*'s attempt to turn the Qur'ānic denial of the crucifixion into a prediction of the cross would probably be regarded by Muslims as completely illegitimate.

On the other hand, Muslims do appreciate the Christian effort to reinterpret Christ in human terms. Nasr hails Küng and Siddiqi applauds Hick for taking Islamic convictions seriously in their presentations of Christ. Certainly their very human Jesus is more acceptable to Muslims as a starting point for dialogue than Cragg's Incarnate Christ, whose humanity is rather muted in the process of carrying out of his divine mission to redeem humanity. *Sīra*'s hidden Incarnate Christ could therefore be helpful in dialogue with Muslims, since Christ speaks and acts as one called by God to serve his people. While it is true that *Sīra*'s Christ sometimes suggests that he acts on the basis of a divine status, for the most part he is recognisably human to a Muslim reader. There is much then to be gained in dialogue on Christology by presenting the life of Christ in such a way that Muslims can meet the Christ of history before they are asked to consider the faith of the Church in him.

Chapter Twelve

Conclusion

Ninth and Twentieth Century Presentations of Christ for Muslims

This book has analysed Christian apologetic writing on Christ from the two most creative periods of Christian-Muslim relations. During the early decades of the ninth century, Christian theologians in the Middle East engaged in debate with Muslim intellectuals on the basis of a common language and shared ideas, which represented a significant development in Christian appreciation of Islam over earlier apologetic writing. Subsequent Christian presentations of Christology for Muslims over many centuries failed to match those of the ninth century for creativity and insight into Muslim categories of thought. Dialogue between Christians and Muslims in the last decades of the twentieth century produced another creative period of Christian apologetics. Some theologians saw the importance of presenting Christology in dialogue with Muslims and opened up fresh avenues of thinking about Christ in Islam and Christianity.

Ninth Century Defence of the Incarnation as Compatible with Islamic Thought

The characteristic of ninth century apologetics was the attempt to argue for the truth of the Incarnation on the basis of premises acceptable to Muslims. This effort was determined by the fact of Islamic political control in the Middle East that had two conequences for Christians. Firstly, since considerable numbers of nominal Christians were embracing Islam, Christian leaders felt the need to mount a credible intellectual defence of the truth of Christianity in order to stem the transfers out of their community. In addressing Christians, Abū Qurra, Abū Rā'iṯa and `Ammār were trying to demonstrate that Christianity was actually a more complete account of truth than that given in Islam. In other words, the revelation of God according to Islam was not so much untrue as incomplete. Therefore members of the churches could maintain their faith in Christ without sacrificing their intelligence. Secondly, since Christians were not free to directly criticise Islam in their writing, theologians had to use indirect ways to uphold Christian ideas when addressing Muslims. Thus they never at any time opposed the teaching of the Qur'ān as false, but rather based Christian truth on Qur'ānic teaching. This appeal to foundational truths in Islam allowed these apologists to argue that Christian truth was compatible with the teaching of Islam when rightly understood.

While eighth century apologists had made a beginning in defence of the Incarnation, the three early ninth century theologians surveyed took debate to higher levels of sophistication. For example, Patriarch Timothy's defence of the Incarnation in 781-2 was a careful explanation of the two natures-two hypostases Nestorian Christology, which did not attempt to argue for the divine becoming human in Christ on Islamic principles. `Ammār, the Nestorian theologian of the generation after Timothy, not only expounded Nestorian Christology to Muslims but also argued that the Incarnation was essential to the knowledge of God by human beings. Indirectly, `Ammār was criticising Islam for witholding that knowledge in the restriction of revelation to God's speech. Christianity, according to `Ammār offered a fuller and therefore truer account of revelation in the union of the divine and human natures of Christ. In this way, the ninth century theologian argued with Muslims on their terms rather than merely making intelligible to Muslims what Christians believed.

All three ninth century apologists attempted to argue for the immanence of God in time and space as a way of defending the truth of the Incarnation by joining in current Islamic debate about the relationship between God and the created world. So Abū Rā'iṯa quoted Muslim interpretation of the throne texts of the Qur'ān to argue that God's relationship with Jesus is akin to his relationship to his throne in that he is both in one place and in every place simultaneously. Since Muslims could envisage divine immanence alongside divine transcendence they could be led to see Christ as a focus for the immanence of the transcendent God. Al-Bāqillānī's rejection of the parallel between God sitting on a throne and indwelling a human body shows that the argument was taken seriously by Muslims after the early ninth century.

Another feature of the three ninth century apologists was their attempt to deal with Islamic denials of Christological convictions. Since the Qur'ān denied that God took a son, Abū Qurra usually and Abū Rā'iṭa and `Ammār always avoided the title 'Son of God' in favour of 'Word of God'. In addition, they spoke not of God taking a son, but of the Word taking a body, most probably to deflect Muslim attention away from the Qur'ānic text towards the genuine Christian understanding of Christ's divine status. If Muslims could comprehend that Christians actually accepted the denial that God took a son then they might be willing to consider the Christian conviction that the Incarnation meant the appropriation of a human body by the divine Word. Despite disagreement between the three apologists over the manner of the 'taking' they could unite on the basic fact that it happened. This indirect criticism of Islamic thought was consonant with their position as Christian subjects of Islamic rule, and serves as an example to modern Christians in dialogue with Muslims of the re-use of Qur'ānic language by Christians to aid communication in particularly sensitive areas.

The denial of the death of Christ was more challenging for the ninth century apologists, though `Ammār developed good illustrations from life to show the value of the self-giving of Christ for needy humans. However, none of the three were able to turn the text of the Qur'ān to good account in explaining the crucifixion that was so comprehensively denied there. The limits of dialogue appear to have been reached at this point despite the effort to harness Muslim perceptions of Christ on their part. The fact that modern apologists have not been able to improve on the performance of these ninth century writers in respect of the denial of the cross shows just how intractable this text of the Qur'ān remains.

Twentieth Century Presentation of the Historical Jesus as Supplementing the Qur'ānic Portrait of Christ

Whereas the ninth century apologists were concerned with defending a developed theology of Incarnation, their twentieth century counterparts were preoccupied with historical concerns underlying a developed theology. Since an emphasis on the facts of history was a characteristic of European theological writing in the nineteenth and twentieth centuries it is hardly surprising that modern Christians engaged in dialogue with Muslims about Christ should begin with his biography. Cragg, Küng, Hick and *Sīra* all shared the conviction that Muslims had partial knowledge of the historical Jesus in the Qur'ān that needed to be filled out by more detailed information found in the gospels. The assessment of the Qur'ānic contribution varied. Küng complained not only of the paucity but also the distortion of history in the Qur'ānic account of Jesus. Cragg too held the Qur'ān to be falsifying the historical fact of the crucifixion while at the same time symbolically alluding to the historical event of the last supper. While ninth century apologists had refrained from criticising the truth of the Qur'ān, these two twentieth century theologians did not hesitate to judge the Qur'ān to contain historical error. They reasoned that the Qur'ān should be subjected to historical scrutiny just as the gospels had been, in order to separate developed theology from historical fact. This was why the Qur'ān was commended by Cragg and Küng for mentioning the healing ministry of Jesus but reproved for denying his crucifixion.

While Cragg and Küng stressed the essential nature of history for faith, Hick abandoned his earlier agreement with this view for his later theory that faith can be divorced from history altogether. Thus Hick's criticism of the Qur'ān for failing to contain an accurate historical account of the death of Jesus was muted by his abandonment of the importance of history for faith. Muslims and Christians can agree to differ on the fact of the cross since salvation is found through religious experience rather than knowledge of history, and thus they should celebrate their common faith in God arrived at by different routes and leave aside evident differences over the historical Jesus. *Sīra*, on the other hand, turned the Qur'ānic denial text into an affirmation, so challenging Muslims to accept that the Qur'ān is wrong to deny what happened to Christ. In the end, all four twentieth century examples of apologetic writing held that the Qur'ān was wrong about the end of Jesus' life. The denial of the cross by Muslims remained an impenetrable wall for Christians engaged in dialogue.

Modern apologetics dealt with the denial of sonship in a variety of ways. Cragg talked of 'filiality' to avoid biological nuances and he argued that Christ's eternal status is akin to the eternal status of the Qur'ān in order to make a case for the Incarnation. In contrast, Küng and Hick argued that the Incarnation was redundant in contemporary Christology and should no longer be a cause of division between Christians and Muslims. Küng was prepared to retain the title of 'son'in the sense of Christ being adopted by God, but Hick decided that it was too great a barrier to dialogue to be kept in use. *Sīra* followed Hick for the most part except in a few situations where the title clearly had no biological reference. These responses to the denial of sonship demonstrate the search for genuine communication on the part of Christians in dialogue with Muslims. Perhaps the best solution was to avoid the idea as much as possible.

Nevertheless, the historical fact that Jesus called himself 'son of man' was largely ignored in these modern presentations. *Sīra*'s removal of the favourite title from Jesus' lips illustrates the sensitivity felt over the word 'son' appearing at all in a life of Christ. This wariness over 'son of man' contrasts strangely with the polemical defence of the cross in modern writing for Muslims. A case could be made for Christians to separate out two types of 'son' ascription, one by Jesus himself that did not assert equality with God, and 'son of God' applied to him by others to mean identity of status but not by Jesus himself. Küng pointed out that the claim of Jesus to a special relationship with God as his 'father' was raised to a higher level by the early church in the ascription of a divine status to Jesus, but he made little of the distinction in his dialogue with Nasr. In the final analysis, the presentation of the historical Jesus for Muslims stood in need of greater precision over the use of the title 'son' than was actually offered in the writing surveyed.

Types of Christology in Ninth and Twentieth Century Apologetics

The ninth century apologists shared a common Incarnational Christology even though they disagreed over the exact manner of the union of the divine with the human in Christ. In the twentieth century Cragg and *Sīra* also held to aspects of an Incarnational Christology. However, Küng and Hick believed that modern Christians could no longer think of a descent of the divine in Christ despite the long tradition of such a belief in the church. Küng suggested that the man Jesus was given divine status as a result of his ministry rather than prior to his birth as Christian tradition taught. Hick let go of divine entry concepts altogether, preferring to see Jesus as a man supremely at one spiritually with God.

Christ as Divine and Human: Five Versions of Incarnational Christology

The versions of the Incarnation by Abū Qurra, Abū Rā'iṯa, `Ammār, Cragg and *Sīra* can be classified as ontological or functional. The three ninth century writers believe in an ontological union of the divine and human in Christ, but the two twentieth century representatives hold to a more functional union of the divine and human. Among the three ontological Christologies, Abū Rā'iṯa represents the Word/flesh Alexandrian tradition, which took the divine to be the operative principle in Christ. In this Christology, the humanity of Christ is a passive receptacle for divine thought and action. At the other extreme, `Ammār represents the Word/human nature Antiochene tradition, which understood a union of two separate natures in Christ. In this Christology, the humanity of Christ is in active co-operation with the divine nature throughout the life of Christ, with the result that there is a genuine interplay between the human and divine minds in Christ in thought and action. Abū Qurra's adherence to the Chalcedonian definition is seen in his insistence that after the union of the Word with the human nature taken from Mary and perfected from corruption there was complete harmony between the two minds in Christ.

The two modern functional Christologies avoid the idea of a union of being in Christ. Cragg thinks that an ontological union neither is reflected in early New Testament Christology nor is adequate in modern times. He has no doubt however, that the descent of the divine is essential for a right understanding of the significance of Jesus of Nazareth. *Sīra* presents Jesus as claiming an eternal existence but not an ontological union with God. Here the Johannine unity of being is removed from Jesus' speech while the *logos* is named as Jesus existing from the beginning. Thus in *Sīra* Christ may not be ontologically united with God but he exists with God before entering time as a human being.

Abū Rā'iṯa's one nature Christology seems least likely to make sense to Muslims since he insists that Christ had only a divine mind. In other words, a Muslim would rightly understand him to believe that Jesus was not a human being in the normal sense, but God hidden in a human body. Jesus then appeared to be human but according to Abū Rā'iṯa was actually divine. In order to avoid this conclusion Abū Rā'iṯa borrowed the Islamic idea of divine attributes and applied it to Christ, with the result that Christ is the divine Word who has two attributes of divinity and humanity. This allows him to argue that the humanity of Christ is not totally obscured by his divinity as a Muslim may imagine. Christ did feel pain and did die in his human attribute, but the divine attribute was untouched by suffering. Still, this would be no solution for a Muslim who would be able to point out that in this scheme the Word does not feel pain or die, and so the mind of Christ remains aloof from all weakness and suffering. Christ then is simply not human. Ultimately, the Word/flesh tradition fails to allow for a truly human Christ and as such is an inadequate Christology.

`Ammār's two nature Christology surely would fare better with Muslims, since Christ is regarded by him as having a human mind as well as a human body, and thus is recognisable as a human being. In addition, `Ammār's Christ has real struggles in performing the will of God that suggest a dialectical relationship between his two natures. The human side of Christ is tested to the end of his life in order to show perfect obedience to God even though Christ has a divine side that presumably has no difficulty fulfilling God's commands. This ambivalence in Christ is a precursor of modern psychological understanding of competing drives in humans and makes `Ammār's Christ seem real to modern people. Muslims could see this Christ as human yet not understand the connection between his humanity and his divinity. They might think that the divinity of Christ either is incapable of enabling the humanity to do the will of God or is essentially cut off from the humanity when Christ suffers pain and death. Whichever way `Ammār puts the case they would probably conclude that the divinity is compromised by the humanity. Finally, the Word/human nature tradition gains on the human side of Christ but loses the importance of the divine in him. A better balance is needed in the dual characteristic of Christ's thinking and acting.

Abū Qurra's Chalcedonian version of the two natures Christology offers a stronger integration between the divine and human in Christ. For Abū Qurra, Christ's human mind is always in tune with his divine mind, so that there is no struggle in carrying out the will of God. There is no lifelong testing of the human mind but rather a harmonious co-operation in which the divine mind informs and influences the human one to think and act appropriately. Thus when the human nature feels pain and succumbs to death, the divine nature is still very much working in Christ to compensate for the suffering taking place in the human nature. Christ may suffer and die but Christ at the same time does not suffer or die, since the two minds experience different realities simultaneously without cancelling the other out. Muslims might be able to see their own view of God's messengers always thinking and acting in the will of God in this Christology. However, the co-operation between the divine and human minds in Christ would not fit into their conception of Jesus as one of those messengers. While they could accept a co-operation between the human mind of Christ and God's mind in terms of Christ receiving messages from God, they could not agree to the divine mind implanted in Christ as presented here. Nevertheless, of the three ninth century Christologies, Abū Qurra's is the most satisfactory, since his Christ is far more integrated in thought and action than `Ammār's dialectical Christ, and far more human than Abū Rā'iṯa's one dimensional Christ.

Cragg dismisses Chaledonian Christology as undynamic and static and so seeks for a more realistic way of combining the divine and human in Christ. He represents much twentieth century theology in wishing to move away from ontological to functional categories in Christology. But in order to achieve a more dynamic portrait of the Incarnation along the lines of the hymn to Christ in Philippians 2, he jettisons talk of divine and human natures in favour of divine presence. Thus God was present in Christ revealing himself through the teaching and actions of Jesus of Nazareth. Some were willing to acknowledge the presence of God in this remarkable man, but others refused to accept the evidence before them. Cragg believes it is important not to argue that Jesus' disciples invested him with divinity after his death, but to steadfastly hold that they recognised his divine power, authority and character while he lived with them. He was as much the eternal Lord of the cosmos before his resurrection and exaltation as he would be in the experience of the early church that worshipped him as such. For Cragg, the central point of Christology is the personal revelation of God in Christ, but this cannot be expressed in the ontological language of the ancient creeds. When we look at Christ we see God, and that should suffice for a modern creed. Muslims could certainly see a human being in Cragg's Christ, since there is no talk of a divine mind thinking and acting. However, they would probably fail to spot God in Christ's teaching and actions, since any Godly words and deeds they come across in the gospel accounts could simply be attributed to Jesus performing the will of God as prophets normally do. Therefore a functional Christology is capable of being interpreted by Muslims as a great man functioning in the will of God, but not as a great man functioning as God. Nevertheless, a Christology of divine presence bridges the gap bewteen the Apostle Paul and modern psychology in a way that makes better sense at the end of the twentieth century than the ontological Christology of John's gospel and the Patristic period.

Sīra's Christology also reflects the same modern unease about ontological categories in the removal of the Johannine claims that Jesus is one with the Father, and that the Word is God. There is no testimony to an identity of being between Jesus and God in this life of Christ, but Jesus does talk of existing before Abraham, and Jesus the Word certainly was with God at the beginning of the world. Therefore, Jesus pre-existed his human life in another spiritual state that predated creation. This is Incarnation of the Word of God without specifying the relationship between Jesus the divine Word and Jesus the human. *Sīra* has stripped away the ontological Christology found in the fourth gospel while retaining claims to an equality of status between Jesus and God made there. This in turn enhances Jesus' authority to forgive sin directly, rather than merely in God's name, taken from the synoptic gospels and repeated unchanged here. Jesus then functions as God in offering forgiveness because he existed with God in eternity. Muslims would relate to Christ in *Sīra* more easily than in the gospels themselves since the titles 'father' and 'son' are virtually absent and Jesus never claims an identity of being with God. The two main difficulties for Muslims are the pre-existence of Jesus and his redeeming death. *Sīra*'s functional Christology goes some way towards meeting the needs of modern Christians for a Christ who is credible as a human being but who also displays divine characteristics, but the decision to keep the eternity of the Word but not the identity between Christ and God from the fourth gospel will probably strike them as inconsistent and untenable.

Christ as a Man Appointed to Divine Status

The importance of Christology from below rather than from above is argued for by Küng and results in his seeing Jesus of Nazareth as elevated to a position of divine authority because of his committed obedience to God. Küng believes that the idea of the descent of the Word is a late development in the thinking of the early church and that modern Christology ought to go back to the more functional Christology of Paul and Luke for inspiration. Their Christ is appointed to a divine position and this elevation of Jesus to divine status should be the theme of modern Christology rather than the notion of a pre-existent Christ found in John and deutero-Pauline literature. This is Küng's way of doing Christology from below and might strike a cord with Muslims for the basic acceptance that Christ was just the same as any other human at the outset of his life. After all, the five versions of the Incarnation detailed above are inescapably determined by the non-Islamic notion that Jesus had a form of pre-existence. At least Küng inhabits the same world as Muslims in his insistence on beginning with the human Jesus. Whether they would welcome the appointment of Christ to a divine role is another matter. Certainly, those Muslims who believe that Muḫammad has a continuing role as advocate for human wrongdoing under God may not find this Christology so difficult to understand. Jesus, like Muḫammad, has been granted authority that normally is exercised by God. Küng, however, seems to believe that Christ reveals God in himself in a way that goes beyond the Muslim understanding of Muḫammad's role, and therefore his Christology transcends what Muslims would be comfortable with.

Modern Christians who share Küng's distaste for Incarnational Christology would probably agree with him in his basic approach, but Incarnationalists will question whether Christ could be appointed to divine status after a purely human beginning, and whether Luke and Paul really believe in an appointment Christology. If the hymn to Christ in Philippians 2 is pre-Pauline or even from Paul himself then the notion of a divine descent was there at the beginning of the early church and did not emerge in a subsequent period. If this is the case modern Christians have to accept that the early church believed from the first that Christ was the one who came down from God to raise humanity up. In other words, Küng's rejection of divine descent places his Christology outside mainstream Christian belief and therefore reduces his appointment Christology to a speculative proposal that lacks firm grounding in tradition.

Christ as a Man in Spiritual Identity with God

Hick's Christ is not divine at all and therefore looks more like the Qur'ānic Christ than any of the above versions. Hick holds that a spiritually aware Jesus is more acceptable for Muslims than a divine Christ, and that the need to find an accommodation with people of other faiths inevitably leads Christians to reshape their traditional beliefs to fit into a wider religious consciousness. In doing so he puts forward a reductionist scheme where the historical Jesus is merely a monotheistic Jew who was elevated to divine status by the church. His call to modern Christians to stop insisting on the universal Lordship of Christ in favour of an allegiance to the universal presence of the Real expressed in a rainbow of religious traditions is unlikely to be heeded by many of them. The vast majority of Christians will probably carry on believing in the Apostolic testimony to Christ that Hick has abandoned. Muslims will doubtless continue to welcome Hick's purely human Christ as a breath of fresh air from the Christian side, hoping that others will follow his lead. However, Christology in dialogue with Muslims should not depend on participants who are unrepresentative of a significant Christian constituency, so a Hickian approach to Jesus can only have a marginal value for Christian/Muslim dialogue.

Dialoguing with Muslims on the Incarnation

If neither Hick's purely human spiritual Christ nor Küng's Christ appointed to divine status adequately represents received tradition then some kind of Incarnational Christology is required. The two modern examples, Cragg and *Sīra*, show that none of the three ninth century Christologies can be used today without significant change. At the beginning of the twenty-first century, Christians do not tend to think of an ontological identity of being between Christ and God, and therefore the relationship between Christ and God has to be expressed in more functional categories. Cragg's notion of Christ as the personal revelation of God is part of the solution, but the descent of the divine still needs to be articulated within this framework.

Therefore, recognition of Christ's eternal pre-existence is essential within the concept of revelation in history. *Sīra*'s attempt to promote an eternal and temporal Christ is noteworthy, and provides a model for future dialogue that takes Muslim perceptions seriously.

Prospects for Dialogue on Christology

Future dialogue about Christ between Christians and Muslims will depend on the way the Qur'ānic denials of sonship and the crucifixion and the developed Islamic conviction that the Incarnation is impossible are dealt with. Perhaps the first of these issues is simpler to handle, but the historicity of the cross and the transcendence of God disallowing Incarnation are much more demanding. As a result of these seemingly unbridgable differences between Muslims and Christians some voices are calling for dialogue to avoid Christology and to concentrate on the ethical teaching of Jesus instead. However, the authority of Jesus' teaching depends on the assessment made of his status, and that takes dialogue back to the question of the revelation of God in Jesus, unless appeal is made solely to human reason.

Christ as 'Son'

There is substantial agreement among the Christian and Muslim writers surveyed that the title 'son' is metaphorical rather than literal. Christians commonly pointed out that God is 'father' to Christ his 'son' not in a biological manner, but in a way that is analogous to a human family relationship. Ayoub and Nasr accepted this symbolic understanding of Christ as son but called for greater clarity in the use of the image by Christians. One way to do this would be to talk of 'father' and 'son' as metaphors of identity between God and Jesus. This identity can firstly be interpreted through the discourse of the historical Jesus when he calls God 'my father' in intimate terms, suggesting a relationship akin to a familial one. Secondly, the faith of the early church in Christ may be explored through the way the title 'son of God' is applied to Jesus. For the first Christians the connection between God and Jesus was so unique that the latter could bring others into the family of God on the basis of that special relationship. Muslims might be open to such a relational interpretation, particularly those who see Muḫammad as having a similar role of advocacy for others before God. Therefore progress is possible in future dialogue on the Qur'ānic denials that God took a son, or that he begets, since Muslims and Christians alike can stand on the truth of these statements.

The Crucifixion of Christ

The gap between Christians and Muslims is as wide as ever over the fact of the crucifixion, so that there does not seem to be much room for future resolution of the Qur'ānic denial of the cross. Ayoub's suggestion that the denial be read in theological rather than historical terms holds some promise because of his acceptance of the fact of Jesus' death on the cross. Perhaps other Muslims will come to see that the Qur'ān denies the complete defeat of Christ rather than the event of the crucifixion. Certainly, Christians can agree with Ayoub that God's truth is not defeated by the death of Christ, and would probably be willing to affirm Ayoub's interpretation of the Qur'ān. Christians for their part may be able to add to Ayoub's reading the idea that the raising of Jesus to God that comes immediately after the denial of the crucifixion also proves that the death of Christ does not defeat his purpose. This is of course how Christians understand the raising of Christ from the dead. If Ayoub's acceptance of the death of Christ becomes popular among Muslims then they may be open to the Christian conviction of God's complete victory over evil expressed in the lifting up of Christ.

The Incarnation

The biggest gap between Christians and Muslims is the Christian belief in the indwelling of the divine in Christ. Unless Muslims develop a more dynamic concept of the transcendence of God they will not be able to agree with the Christian notion of a real divinity in Christ. Muslims for their part are pleased when Christians give up the idea of divine presence in Christ and presumably hope that more Christians will follow Hick's example. So this standoff between Muslims and Christians seems set to continue. Christians might take the initiative in trying to make sense of the Incarnation by following the example of the ninth century apologists in their appeal to anthropomorphic language in the Qur'ān. They might argue: if God acts in the created world then he is not so transcendent that he is separated from it; and if his action relates to a particular place and time then he is not simply outside space and time; and if he delegates decision making to humans then his transcendence is co-ordinated with history. Christians could perform a useful role as interrogators of an Islamic belief in transcendence that is in need of reform in the twenty-first century. Perhaps this is the period of history in which Muslims will begin to develop a view of God co-operating with human thought and decision rather than controlling it. Perhaps Muḫammad may come to be seen as co-operating with God in the production of the Qur'ān rather than being merely an empty mouthpiece. If such developments take place, then the idea of the indwelling of the divine in Christ will become more intelligible, if not more acceptable to Muslims.

The Ethics of Jesus

Since belief in the status of Christ causes dispute between Christians and Muslims it might seem simpler to avoid dialogue on his status and discuss his teaching instead. The leading American Catholic theologian on inter-faith dialogue, Paul Knitter, has proposed that debate about doctrine should give way to dialogue on behaviour. According to Knitter, belief in Christ is "primarily a matter of acting with and like Christ."[1] Christians should live out the kingdom of God that Jesus proclaimed as a "spirit-filled mystic and a social prophet."[2] Knitter has had more experience in dialogue with Hindus and Buddhists, but his call is echoed by Pierre Claverie, Catholic Bishop of Oran in Algeria. In a letter entitled 'Believing in Dialogue' he indicates five fruitful issues for Christian-Muslim dialogue: submission to God, secularism, democracy, the role of women, and the status of non-Muslims.[3] All five subjects relate to personal and social ethics, since submission to God, in Claverie's mind, has to do with behaviour rather than belief. Agreement on the ethics of Jesus may remain a challenge for Christians if the debate between Hick and Küng about Jesus' attitude to the Jewish law continues to divide interpreters of the gospels. Division among Muslims about the contemporary relevance of Qur'ānic law may well be a feature of twenty-first century Islam. If Claverie's topics are discussed, Muslims will probably be as divided over each of them as Christians over the teaching of Jesus, therefore, dialogue on the teaching of Jesus will be no more straightforward than dialogue on his status. The authority of his teaching will have to be faced when a clash between his teaching and Islamic tradition emerges. Whether Muslims will be prepared to grant him the authority to challenge Islamic norms is a difficult question to answer. It is because Christians believe in the divine status of Christ that they grant him the authority to instruct them, so in the end, dialogue on the teaching of Christ cannot avoid dialogue on Christology.

---

[1] P. Knitter, *Jesus and the Other Names: Christian Mission and Global Responsibility* (New York: 1996), 69.

[2] P. Knitter, *One Earth Many Religions: Multifaith Dialogue and Global Responsibility* (New York: 1995), 93.

[3] P. Claverie, *Lettres et Messages D'Algérie* (Paris: 1996), 66.

Final Words

There were different strategies in dialogue on Christology in the ninth and twentieth centuries. Some drew heavily on Christian tradition and attempted to commend received views of Christ in terms Muslims might understand if not accept. In the modern period, others developed fresh ways of perceiving Christ and offered their new insights to Muslims. Both ninth and twentieth century apologists took Islamic concerns seriously enough to challenge Muslims to rethink their perception of Christ, but there were no major breakthroughs over the denial of the cross or the divinity of Christ. In terms of future dialogue on Christ it may be possible to bypass these difficulties by discussing the ethics of Jesus. However, if Muslims question his authority to teach there will be a continuing need for creative Christology in dialogue with Muslims.

Bibliography

`Abd al-Tafāhum, 'The Qur'ān and the Holy Communion', *The Muslim World* 49 (1959), 239-248

Abrahamov, B., *Anthropomorphism and Interpretation of the Qur'ān in the Theology of Al-Qāsim ibn Ibrāhīm* (Leiden: E. J. Brill, 1996)

*`Ajāba ma hadatha fī filastīn* (Beirut: Matbū`āt Al-Sharq Al-Awsat, 1974)

Al-Akbar, 'al-Nāshi', *Kitāb al-Awsāt fī-l-Maqālāt* (ed. J. van Ess, Beirut: Dar al-Nashar, 1971)

`Alī, M., *The Holy Qur'ān: English Translation and Commentary* (Woking: Islamic Review Office, 1917)

`Alī, Y., *The Meaning of the Holy Qur'ān* (Lahore, 1934) (ninth edition, Beltsville: Amana Publications, 1998)

Arnaldez, R., *Jésus dans La Pensée Musulmane* (Paris: Desclée, 1988)

Al-Ash`arī, Abū-l-Hasan `Alī, *Kitāb Maqālāt al-Islāmiyyīn wa Ikhtilāf al-Musallīn* (ed. H. Ritter, Wiesbaden: 1963)

Askari, H., 'The Qur'ānic Conception of Risala', in *Christians, Muslims and Jews,* eds. Kerr, D., and D. Cohn-Sherbock, (Birmingham: Conference of Christians, Muslims and Jews, 1982), 124-134

Assfy, Z.H., *Islam and Christianity* (York: William Sessions, 1977)

Atiya, A.S., *A History of Eastern Christianity* (London: Methuen, 1968)

`Ata al-Rahīm, M., *Jesus – A Prophet of Islam* (London: Muslim Information Services, 1977)

Austin, R.W.J., *Ibn al`Arabī: The Bezels of Wisdom* (London: SPCK, 1980)

Aydin, M., *Modern Western Christian Theological Understandings of Muslims Since the Second Vatican Council* (Washington, D.C.: The Council for Research in Values and Philosophy, 2002)

Ayoub, M.M., 'Towards an Islamic Christology: an Image of Jesus in Early Shi`i Literature', *The Muslim World* 66 (1976), 163-188

__ 'Towards an Islamic Christology, II: The Death of Jesus, Reality or Delusion', *The Muslim World* 70 (1980), 91-121

__ 'Jesus the Son of God: A Study of the terms *Ibn* and *Walad* in the Qur'ān and *Tafsīr* Tradition' in Haddad, Y.Y. and W.Z. Haddad (eds.), *Christian-Muslim Encounters*, (Gainesville: University of Florida Press, 1995), 65-81

Bacha, C., *Les oeuvres arabes de Théodore Aboucara, Évêque d'Haran* (Beyrouth: 1904)

__ *Un Triate des Oeuvres Arabes de Théodore Abou-Kurra* (Paris: 1905)

Balic, S., 'The Image of Jesus in Contemporary Islamic Theology', in Schimmel, A., and A. Falaturi (eds.), *We Believe in One God*, (London: Burns and Oates, 1979), 1-8

Al-Bāqillānī, Abū-Bakr, *Kitāb al-Tamhīd* (ed. R.J., McCarthy, Beirut: Librairie Orientale, 1957)

Beaumont, I.M., 'The Lord's Prayer in Smith-Van Dyke and Sīrat al-Masīh', *Seebed* 5 (1990), 52-4

__ ''Ammār al-Basrī on the Incarnation', in D. Thomas (ed.), *Christians at the Heart of Islamic Rule,* (Leiden: Brill, 2003), 55-62

Bernard, R.D., 'You shall call his name Jesus', *Seedbed* 7 (1992), 34-39

Bettenson, H., *The Early Christian Fathers* (London: Oxford University Press, 1969)

__ *The Later Christian Fathers* (London: Oxford University Press, 1970)

Bidawid, R.J., *Les Lettres du Patriarche Nestorien Timothée I* (Rome: Studi e Testi, 187, 1956)

Blackwell's Dictionary of Eastern Christianity (Oxford: Blackwell, 1999)

Bultmann, R., *The Theology of the New Testament* (Vol. 1, London: SCM Press, 1951)

Campbell, W., *The Qur'ān and the Bible in the Light of History and Science* (Marseille: Media Services, 1986)

Casey, M., 'Idiom and Translation: Some Aspects of the Son of Man Problem', *New Testament Studies* 41 (1995), 164-182

Caspar, R., *Pour un regard Chrétien sur L'Islam* (Paris: Centurion, 1990)

Caspar, R., and J.M. Gaudeul, 'Textes de la Tradition Musulmane concernant le Tahrīf des Écritures', *Islamochristiana* 6 (1980), 61-104

Caspar, R., and a Group of Christians Living in Tunisia, *Trying to Answer Questions* (Rome: Pontificio Istituto di Studi arabi e Islamici, 1989)

Chabot, J-B., *Chronique de Michel le Syrien: Patriarche Jacobite d'Antioche,* 4 vols. (Paris: 1899-1910)

__ Anonymi Auctoris Chronicum ad A. C. 1234 Pertinens *Corpus Scriptorum Christianorum Orientalium* 109 (1937)

Charfi, A., 'Christianity in the Qur'ān Commentary of Tabarī', *Islamochristiana* 6 (1980), 105-148

Claverie, P., *Lettres et Messages d'Algérie* (Paris: Editions Karthala, 1996)

D'Costa, G., (ed.) *Christian Uniqueness Reconsidered* (New York: Orbis, 1990)

Cowdell, S., *Is Jesus Unique?* (New York: Paulist Press, 1996)

Cragg, K., *The Call of the Minaret* (New York: Oxford University Press, 1956)

__ *Sandals at the Mosque* (London: SCM Press, 1959)

__ 'Islam and Incarnation', in J. Hick (ed.), *Truth and Dialogue,* (London: Sheldon Press, 1974), 126-139

__ 'Legacies and Hopes in Muslim/Christian Theology', *Islamochristiana* 3 (1977), 1-10

__ *The Pen and the Faith: Eight Modern Muslim Writers and the Qur'ān* (London: George, Allen and Unwin, 1983)

__ *Muhammad and the Christian. A Question of Response* (London: Darton, Longman and Todd, 1984)

__ *Jesus and the Muslim. An Exploration* (London: George, Allen & Unwin, 1985)

__ *Christ and the Faiths* (London: SPCK, 1986)

__ *The Arab Christian* (London: Mowbray, 1992)

__ *To Meet and to Greet* (London: Epworth Press, 1992)

__ 'Prepositions and Salvation', *International Bulletin of Missionary Research* 17 (1993), 2f

__ 'Ismā'il al-Farūqī in the Field of Dialogue', in Haddad, Y.Y., and W.Z. Haddad, (eds.) *Christian-Muslim Encounters,* (Gainesville: University of Florida Press, 1995), 399-410

__ *The Lively Credentials of God* (London: Darton, Longman and Todd, 1995)

Cullmann, O., *The Christology of the New Testament* (London: SCM Press, 1959)

Dharamraj, G.E., and J.S. Dharamraj, *Christianity and Islam: A Missiological Encounter* (Delhi: ISPCK, 1998)

Dick, I., 'Deux écrits inédits de Théodore Abuqurra', *Le Muséon* 72 (1959), 53-67

Dodge, B., (ed. and trans.) *The Fihrist of al-Nadīm* (Vols. 1& 2, New York: Columbia University Press, 1970)

Dunn, J.D.G., *Christology in the Making* (London: SCM Press, 1980)

Elliott, J.K., *The Apocryphal New Testament* (Oxford: Clarendon Press, 1993)

The Encyclopaedia of Islam (vol. 5, Leiden: E.J. Brill, 1986)

Al-Farūqī, I., 'On the Nature of Islamic Da'wah', *The International Review of Mission* 65 (1976), 391-409

Ferré, A., 'La Vie de Jésus d'après les Annales de Ṯabarī', *Islamochristiana* 5 (1979), 7-29

__ 'L'historien al-Ya`qūbī et les Évangiles', *Islamochristiana* 3 (1977), 65-83

Gaudeul, J-M., *Encounters and Clashes* (Vols. 1&2, Rome: Pontificio Istituto di Studi arabi e Islamici, 1984)

Gibson, M.D., (ed.) *A Treatise on the Triune Nature of God* (London: Cambridge University Press, 1899)

Goddard, H., 'Modern Pakistani and Indian Muslim Perceptions of Christianity', *Islam and Christian-Muslim Relations* 5 (1994), 165-188

__ *Christians and Muslims* (Richmond: Curzon Press, 1995)

__ *Muslim Perceptions of Christianity* (London: Grey Seal, 1996)

__ *A History of Christian-Muslim Relations* (Edinburgh: Edinburgh University Press, 2000)

Graf, G., *Des Schriften des Jacobiten Ḫabīb ibn Hidmah Abū Rā'iṯah, Corpus Scriptorum Christianorum Orientalium* 130 and 131 (1951)

Griffith, S.H., 'Ḫabīb ibn Ḳhidmah Abū Rā'iṯah, a Christian *mutakallim* of the First Abbasid Century', *Oriens Christianus* 64 (1980), 161-201

__ '`Ammār al-Baṣrī's *Kitāb al-Burhān:* Christian *Kalām* in the First Abbasid Century', *Le Muséon* 96 (1983), 145-181

__ 'The Monks of Palestine and the Growth of Christian Literature in Arabic', *The Muslim World* 78 (1988), 1-28

__ 'Reflections on the Biography of Theodore Abū Qurrah', *Parole de L'Orient* 18 (1993), 143-170

__ '*Melkites, Jacobites* and the Christological Controversies in arabic in Third/Ninth-century Syria', in D. Thomas (ed.), *Syrian Christians Under Islam* (Leiden: Brill, 2001), 9-55

Grillmeier, A., *Christ in Christian Tradition* (Vol, 1, London: Mowbrays, 1975; Vol. 2:1, 1987; Vol, 2:2, 1995; Vol 2:4, 1996)

Grimm, H.J., (ed.) *Luther's Works* (Vol 31, Philadelphia, Fortress Press, 1957)

Guillaume, A., *The Life of Muhammad: a Translation of (ibn) Ishāq's "Sīrat Rasūl Allāh"* (London: Oxford University Press, 1955)

Haddad, R., *La Trinité divine chez les théologiens arabes 750-1050* (Paris: Beauchesne, 1985)

Hamid, A., *Islam and Christianity* (New York: Carlton Press, 1967)

Hayek, M., *Le Christ de L'Islam* (Paris: Editions de Seuil, 1959)

__ "Ammār al-Basrī: La Première Somme de Théologie Chrétienne en Langue Arabe, ou Deux Apologies du Christianisme', *Islamochristiana* 2 (1976), 69-133

__ *`Ammār al-Basrī: Apologie et Controverses* (Beirut: Dar el-Machreq, 1977)

Hick, J., 'A Recent Development within Christian Monotheism', in Kerr, D., and D. Cohn-Sherbock (eds.), *Christians, Muslims and Jews*, (Birmingham: Conference of Christians, Muslims and Jews, 1982), 1-19

__ *Problems of Religious Pluralism* (London: Macmillan, 1985)

__ 'Trinity and Incarnation in the Light of Religious Pluralism', in Hick, J., and E.S. Meltzer (eds.), *Three Faiths-One God: A Jewish, Christian, Muslim Encounter*, (Basingstoke: Macmillan, 1989), 197-210

__ *The Metaphor of God Incarnate* (London: SCM Press, 1993)

__ *The Rainbow of Faiths* (London, SCM Press, 1995)

Hitti, P.K., *History of the Arabs* (tenth edition, London: Macmillan, 1970)

Hooker, M., *The Gospel of Mark* (London: A. & C. Black, 1991)

Hopkins, J., *Nicholas of Cusa's De Pace Fidei and Cribratio Alkorani* (Minneapolis: Arthur J. Banning, 1994)

Hoyland, J.S., and S.N. Banarjee, *Commentary of Father Monserrate S. J. on his Journey to the Court of Akbar* (London: Oxford University Press, 1922)

Hoyland, R.G., *Seeing Islam as Others Saw It. Studies in Late Antiquity and Early Islam 13* (Princeton: The Darwin Press, 1997)

Hussein, M.K., *City of Wrong* (Amsterdam, N. V. Djambatan, 1959)

Husain, M.K., *The Hallowed Valley. A Muslim Philosophy of Religion* (Cairo: American University of Cairo Press, 1977)

Jackson, P., 'Jesuits at Akbar's court', *Salaam* 16 (1995), 100-113

Al-Jāhiz, Abū `Uthmān, 'Reply to the Christians' (ed.) I.S., Allouche, 'Un Traite de Polemique Chrétien-Musulmane au IX'e Siècle', *Hesperis* 26 (1939), 129-150

Jeremias, J., *New Testament Theology* (Vol 1, London: SCM Press, 1971)

Jones, R.J., 'Wilfred Cantwell Smith and Kenneth Cragg on Islam as a Way of Salvation', *International Bulletin of Missionary Research* 16 (1992), 105-110

Joseph, J., *The Nestorians and their Muslim Neighbors* (Princeton: Princeton University Press, 1961)

Kasper, W., *Jesus The Christ* (Tunbridge Wells: Burns and Oates, 1976)

Kateregga, B.D., and D.W. Shenk, *Islam and Christianity* (Grand Rapids: Eerdmans, 1981)

Keating, S.T., "Ḫabīb ibn Khidma Abū Rā'iṯa al-Takrītī's 'The Refutation of the Melkites concerning the Union [of the divinity and humanity in Christ] (III), in D. Thomas (ed.) *Christians at the Heart of Islamic Rule,* (Leiden: Brill, 2003), 39-53

Kerr, D., 'Christology in Muslim-Christian Dialogue', in Berkey, R.A., and S.A. Edwards (eds.), *Christology in Dialogue* (Cleveland: The Pilgrim Press, 1996), 201-220

Khalidi, T., *The Muslim Jesus* (Cambridge: Harvard University Press, 2001)

Knitter, P.F., *One Earth Many Religions: Multifaith Dialogue and Global Responsibility* (New York: Orbis, 1995)

__ *Jesus and the Other Names. Christian Mission and Global Responsibility* (New York: Orbis, 1996)

Küng, H., 'Dialogue with Hossein Nasr', *The Muslim World* 77 (1987), 80-95; 121-3

__ *Christianity and the World Religions* (London: Collins, 1987. Second Edition, New York: Orbis, 1993)

__ 'World Peace – World Religions – World Ethic', *Islam: A Challenge for Christianity, Concilium,* (1994), 127-139

__ *Christianity: The Religious Situation of Our Time* (London: SCM Press, 1995)

Lamb, C.A., *The Call to Retrieval: Kenneth Cragg's Christian Vocation to Islam* (London: Grey Seal, 1997)

Lawrence, C., *Jesus as Prophet in Christianity and Islam: A Model for Interfaith Dialogue* (Delhi: ISPCK, 1997)

Leirvik, O., *Images of Jesus Christ in Islam: Introduction, Survey of Research, Issues of Dialogue* (Uppsala: Swedish Institute of Missionary Research, 1999)

Lūqā, I., *Al-Masīḫiyya fī l-Islām* (Rikon: The Good Way, no date)

McAuliffe, J.D., *Qur'ānic Christians* (Cambridge: Cambridge University Press, 1991)

Macquarrie, J., *Jesus Christ in Modern Thought* (London: SCM Press, 1990)

Mansour, J., 'A Rose by Any Other Name: A Response to R. D. Bernard', *Seedbed* 8 (1993), 26-28

Marquet, Y., 'Les Ihwān al-Ṣafā et le Christianisme', *Islamochristiana* 8 (1982), 129-158

Marshall, I.H., *I Believe in the Historical Jesus* (London: Hodder & Stoughton, 1977)

De Matteo, I., 'Confutazione contro I Christiani dello Zaydati al-Qāsim b. Ibrāhīm', *Revista degli Studi Orientali* 9 (1921-2), 301-64

Merad, A., 'Revelation, Truth and Obedience', in Samartha, S.J., and J.B. Taylor (eds.) *Christian-Muslim Dialogue. Papers from Broumana,* (Geneva: WCC, 1972), 58-72

Michel, T., *Pour Comprendre le Christianisme: Un Chrétien présente sa foi aux Musulmans* (Milan: I.M.O. – Sac. Giampiero Alberti, 1992)

Mingana, A., 'The Apology of Timothy the Patriarch before the Caliph Mahdi', *Woodbrooke Studies* 2 (1928), 1-162

Moon, J.S., 'From Carey to Zwemer. Karl Pfander', *The Bulletin of Christian Institutes of Islamic Studies* 1 (1967), 46-57

Moucarry, C., *Faith to Faith: Christianity and Islam in dialogue* (Leicester: IVP, 2001)

Muslim-Christian Research Group, *The Challenge of the Scriptures. The Bible and the Qur'ān* (New York: Orbis, 1989)

Nasr, S.H., *Islamic Life and Thought* (London: George, Allen and Unwin, 1981)

__ 'Response to Hans Küng', *The Muslim World* 77 (1987), 96-105; 124-8

__ 'Comments on a Few Theological Issues in the Islamic-Christian Dialogue', in Haddad, Y.Y., and W.Z. Haddad, *Christian-Muslim Encounters,* (Gainesville: University of Florida Press, 1995), 458-465

__ 'Islamic-Christian Dialogue. Problems and Obstacles to be Pondered and Overcome', *The Muslim World* 88 (1998), 218-237

Nau, F., 'Un colloque du patriarche Jean avec L'émir des Agaréens et faits divers des années 712 à 716', *Journal Asiatique* 5 (1915), 225-79

Nazir-Ali, M., *Islam: A Christian Perspective* (Exeter: Paternoster Press, 1983)

__ *Frontiers in Muslim-Christian Encounter* (Oxford: Regnum, 1987)

Nida, E.A., *Bible Translating* (London: BFBS, 1961)

Owen, D., (ed.) *Sīra al-Masīh̲* (Larnaca: 1987)

__ 'Project Sunrise: Principles, Description and Terminology', *Seedbed* 2 (1987), 50-59

Pannenberg, W., *Systematic Theology* (Vol 2, Edinburgh: T. & T. Clark, 1994)

Parrinder, G., *Jesus in the Qur'ān* (London: Sheldon Press, 1965)

Paul D'Antioche, *Lettre aux Musulmans*, (ed.) P. Khoury, (Beyrouth: L'Institut de Lettres Orientales de Beyrouth, 1964)

Pfander, K.G., *Mīzān Al-H̲aqq* (Beirut: 1877)

Phipps, W.E., *Muh̲ammad and Jesus. A Comparison of the Prophets and Their Teachings* (London: SCM Press, 1996)

Powell, A.A., *Muslims & Missionaries in Pre-Mutiny India* (Richmond: Curzon Press, 1993)

Putnam, H., *L'Église et L'Islam sous Timothée I (780-823)* (Beirut: Dar el-Machreq, 1975)

Rahmatullāh, ibn Khalīl, *Iz̲hār al-H̲aqq* (Beirut: Dār al-Kutub al-`Ilmiya, 1993)

Räisänen, H., 'The Portrait of Jesus in the Qur'ān: Reflections of a Biblical Scholar', *The Muslim World* 70 (1980), 122-133

Al-Rāzī, Fakhr al-Dīn, *Al-Tafsīr al-Kabīr* (Beirut: 1978)

Rissanen, S., *Theological Encounter of Oriental Christians with Islam during Early Abbasid Rule* (Åbo: Åbo Akademi University Press, 1993)

Robinson, N., 'Fakr al-Dīn al-Rāzī and the Virginal Conception', *Islamochristiana* 14 (1988), 1-16

__ 'Creating Birds from Clay: A Miracle of Jesus in the Qur'ān and in Classical Muslim Exegesis', *The Muslim World* 79 (1989), 1-13

__ *Christ in Islam and Christianity. The Representation of Jesus in the Qur'ān and the Classical Muslim Commentaries* (Basingstoke: Macmillan, 1991)

Sahas, D.J., *John of Damascus on Islam* (Leiden: E.J. Brill, 1972)

Samartha, S.J., 'The Cross and the Rainbow: Christ in a Multireligious Culture', in Hick, J., and L. Swidler (eds.), *The Myth of Christian Uniqueness: Towards a Pluralistic Theology of Religions,* (New York: Orbis, 1987), 69-88

Samir, S.K., 'The Earliest Arab Apology for Christianity', in Samir, S.K., and J.S. Nielsen (eds.), *Christian Arabic Apologetics During the Abbasid Period (750-1258),* (Leiden: E.J. Brill, 1994), 57-114

Sanders, E.P., *Jesus and Judaism* (London: SCM Press, 1985)

Sargent, J., *Life and Letters of the Rev. Henry Martyn* (London: New edition, Seeley and Co., 1862)

Schirrmacher, C., 'The Agra Debates of 1854', *The Bulletin of the Henry Martyn Institute of Islamic Studies* 13 (1994), 74-84

Schumann, O., *Der Christus der Muslime* (Köln/Wien: Böhlau Verlag, 1988)

Sharafuddin, A.S., *About the Myth of God Incarnate – An Impartial Survey of its Main Topics* (Jeddah: 1978)

Siddiqi, A.H., (tr.) *Sahīh Muslim* (Lahore: Muhammad Ashraf, 1990)

Siddiqi, M.H., 'A Muslim Response to John Hick: Trinity and Incarnation in the light of Religious Pluralism', in Hick, J., and E.S. Meltzer *Three Faiths-One God: A Jewish, Christian, Muslim Encounter*, (Basingstoke: Macmillan, 1989), 211-13

Siddiqui, A., *Christian-Muslim Dialogue in the Twentieth Century* (Basingstoke: Macmillan, 1997)

__ (ed.) *Ismā'īl al-Farūqī. Islam and Other Faiths* (Leicester: The Islamic Foundation, 1998)

Smith, D.M., *The Theology of the Gospel of John* (Cambridge: Cambridge University Press, 1995)

D'Souza, A., 'Jesus in ibn Arabī's Fusūs al-Hikam', *Islamochristiana* 8 (1982), 185-200

Sperber, J., *Christians and Muslims* (Berlin: W de Gruyter, 2000)

Stevenson, J., *Creeds, Councils, and Controversies* (London: SPCK, 1966)

__ *A New Eusebius* (revised edition, London: SPCK, 1987)

Swanson, M.N., *Folly to the Hunafā'* (PhD Thesis, Rome: Pontificio Istituto di Studi arabi e Islamici, 1992)

__ 'Some Considerations for the Dating of *fī tatlīt allāh al-wāhid* (Sinai Ar.154) and *al-gāmi` wugūh al-īmān* (London, British Library op. 4950)', *Parole de L'Orient* 18 (1993), 118-141

__ 'The Cross of Christ in the Earliest Arabic Melkite Apologies', in Samir, S.K., and J. S. Nielsen (eds.), *Christian Arabic Apologetics During the Abbasid Period (750-1258)*, (Leiden: E.J. Brill, 1994), 115-145

__ 'Beyond Prooftexting: Approaches to the Qur'ān in some early Arabic Christian Apologies', *The Muslim World* 88 (1998), 297-319

Sweetman, J.W., *Islam and Christian Theology* (Vol 2:1, London: Lutterworth Press, 1955)

Al-Tabarī, Abū Ja`far, *Jāmi` al-Bayān fī Tafsīr al-Qur'ān* (Cairo: 1954)

Al-Tabarī, `Alī, 'Radd `alā al-nasārā', (eds.) Khalife, I-A., and W. Kutsch, *Mélanges de L'université Saint Joseph* 36 (1959), 113-48

Taylor, V, *The Life and Ministry of Jesus* (London: Macmillan, 1954)

Telford, W.R., *Mark* (Sheffield: Sheffield Academic Press, 1995)

Theissen, G. and A. Merz, *The Historical Jesus* (London: SCM Press, 1998)

Thomas, D., *Anti-Christian Polemic in Early Islam. Abū `Īsā al-Warrāq's "Against the Trinity"* (Cambridge: Cambridge University Press, 1992)

__ 'The Miracles of Jesus in Early Islamic Polemic', *Journal of Semitic Studies* 39 (1994), 221-243

__ 'The Bible in Early Muslim Anti-Christian Polemic', *Islam and Christian-Muslim Relations* 7 (1996), 29-38

__ '`Abū Mansūr al-Māturīdī on the Divinity of Jesus', *Islamochristiana* 23 (1997), 43-64

__ *Early Muslim Polemic against Christianity. Abū Īsā al-Warrāq's "Against the Incarnation"* (Cambridge: Cambridge University Press, 2002)

__ 'Early Muslim Responses to Christianity', in Thomas, D. (ed.), *Christians at the Heart of Islamic Rule,* (Leiden, Brill, 2003), 231-254

Thomas, D., and C. Amos, (eds.) *A Faithful Presence. Essays for Kenneth Cragg* (London: Melisende, 2003)

Troll, C.W., 'Sayyid Ahmad Khān on Matthew 5:17-20', *Islamochristiana* 3 (1977), 99-105

__ *Sayyid Ahmad Khān* (New Delhi: 1978)

__ 'Catholic Teachings on Interreligious Dialogue. Analysis of Some Recent Official Documents, with Special Reference to Christian-Muslim Relations', in Waardenburg, J., (ed.), *Muslim-Christian Perceptions of Dialogue Today. Experiences and Expectations*, (Leuven: Peeters, 2000), 233-275

Urvoy, D., 'Ramon Lull et L'Islam', *Islamochristiana* 7 (1981), 127-146

Vander Werff, L.L., *Christian Mission to Muslims* (South Pasadena: William Carey Library, 1977)

Vermes, G., *Jesus The Jew* (London: SCM Press, 1973)

Voorhis, J.W., 'The Discussion of a Christian and a Saracen', *The Moslem World* 25 (1935), 266-273

Watt, W.M., *Muslim-Christian Encounters. Perceptions and Misperceptions* (London: Routledge, 1991)

Wessels, A., *Images of Jesus. How Jesus is Perceived and Portrayed in Non-European Cultures* (Grand Rapids: Eerdmans, 1990)

__ *Arab and Christian? Christians in the Middle East* (Kampen: Kok Pharos Publishing House, 1995)

Wright, N.T., *Jesus and the Victory of God* (London: SPCK, 1996)

Zahniser, A.H.M., 'The Forms of tawaffā in the Qur'ān: A contribution to Christian-Muslim Dialogue', *The Muslim World* 79 (1989), 14-24

__ 'The Word of God and the Apostleship of `Īsā: a Narrative Analysis of Al-`Imrān (3): 33-62', *Journal of Semitic Studies* 36 (1991), 77-112

Zebiri, K., *Muslims and Christians Face to Face* (Oxford: Oneworld, 1997)

Glossary of Arabic Terminology

a<u>h</u>datha: to bring into being
akhadha: to take
aqānīm: hypostases (of the Trinity)
azalī: eternal
basharī: human
birr: righteousness
bunuwwa: sonship
dhāt: essence
<u>H</u>adīth: traditions of the Prophet Mu<u>h</u>ammad
<u>h</u>alla: to indwell
haykal: temple
<u>h</u>ulūl: indwelling (of the divine in the human)
injīl: the book revealed to Jesus according to the Qur'ān
insān: human being
ittakhadha: to take (to oneself)
jahannam: hell
jahiliyya: period of ignorance before the revelation of the Qur'ān
jasad: body
jawhar: substance, essence
kalima: word
khalaqa: to create
lāhūtī: divine
libās: clothing
mahall: dwelling place
Mahdī: one who will preceed the end times according to some of the traditions of the Prophet Mu<u>h</u>ammad
mawlūd: begotten
muta'annis: Incarnate
mutajassid: Incarnate
nafs: mind, being (the essential quality of being human)
nāsūtī: human
qunūm: hypostasis (of the Trinity or the Incarnate one)
sāra: to become
shafā`a: advocacy, intercession
shakhs: person, individual
shirk: association of another being with God
sifāt: attributes (of God)
sūra: chapter of the Qur'ān

taḫrīf: the corruption of Jewish (and Christian) Scripture
ta'annasa: to become Incarnate
ta'annus: Incarnation
tahāra: purity
tajassada: to become Incarnate
tajassud: Incarnation
ṭabī`a: nature
tanāzūl: descent, indwelling
torah: the book revealed to Moses according to the Qur'ān
walad: offspring
wilād: born
zamanī: temporal

General Index

REGNUM EDINBURGH 2010 SERIES
Series Listing

David A. Kerr, Kenneth R. Ross (eds.)
Edinburgh 2010
Mission Then and Now
2009 / 978-1-870345-73-6 / xiv + 343pp (paperback)
2009 / 978-1-870345-76-7 / xiv + 343pp (hardback)

No one can hope to fully understand the modern Christian missionary movement without engaging substantially with the World Missionary Conference, held at Edinburgh in 1910. As the centenary of the Conference approaches, the time is ripe to examine its meaning in light of the past century and the questions facing Christian witness today. This book is the first to systematically examine the eight Commissions which reported to Edinburgh 1910 and gave the conference much of its substance and enduring value. It will deepen and extend the reflection being stimulated by the upcoming centenary and will kindle the missionary imagination for 2010 and beyond.

Daryl M. Balia, Kirsteen Kim (eds.)
Edinburgh 2010
Witnessing to Christ Today
2010 / 978-1-870345-77-4 / xiv +301pp

This volume, the second in the Edinburgh 2010 series, includes reports of the nine main study groups working on different themes for the celebration of the centenary of the World Missionary Conference, Edinburgh 1910. Their collaborative work brings together perspectives that are as inclusive as possible of contemporary world Christianity and helps readers to grasp what it means in different contexts to be 'witnessing to Christ today'.

Claudia Währisch-Oblau, Fidon Mwombeki (eds.)
Mission Continues
Global Impulses for the 21st Century
2010 / 978-1-870345-82-8 / 271pp

In May 2009, 35 theologians from Asia, Africa and Europe met in Wuppertal, Germany, for a consultation on mission theology organized by the United Evangelical Mission: Communion of 35 Churches in Three Continents. The aim was to participate in the 100th anniversary of the Edinburgh conference through a study process and reflect on the challenges for mission in the 21st century. This book brings together these papers written by experienced practitioners from around the world.

Brian Woolnough and Wonsuk Ma (Eds)

Holistic Mission

God's plan for God's people 2010 / 978-1-870345-85-9

Holistic mission, or integral mission, implies God is concerned with the whole person, the whole community, body, mind and spirit. This book discusses the meaning of the holistic gospel, how it has developed, and implications for the the church. . It takes a global, eclectic approach, with 19 writers, all of whom have much experience in, and commitment to, holistic mission. It addresses critically and honestly one of the most exciting, and challenging, issues facing the church today. To be part of God's plan for God's people, the church must take holistic mission to the world.

Kirsteen Kim and Andrew Anderson (Eds)

Mission Today and Tomorrow

2011/978-1-870345-91-0

The centenary of the historic and influential World Missionary Conference held in Edinburgh 1910 presented a unique opportunity for the whole church worldwide to come together in celebration, reflection and recommitment to witnessing to Christ today. Edinburgh 2010 also engaged in serious study and reflection on the current state of world mission and the challenges facing all those who seek to witness Christ today. The results of this research was presented and debated within the context of Christian fellowship and worship at the conference in June 2010. This record of that conference is intended to give the background to that Call, to share the spirit of the conference, and to stimulate informed and focused participation in God's mission in Christ for the world's salvation.

Tormod Engelsviken, Erling Lundeby and Dagfinn Solheim (Eds)

The Church Going Glocal

Mission and Globalisation 2011/978-1-870345-93-4

This book provides thought-provoking and inspiring reading for all concerned with mission in the 21st century. I have been challenged by its contributors to re-think our Gospel ministries in our new local contexts marked by globalisation and migration. With its biblical foundation, its missiological reflection and interaction with contemporary society I warmly recommend this volume for study and pray that it will renew our passion for the Gospel and compassion for people.

REGNUM Studies in Global Christianity

(Previously GLOBAL THEOLOGICAL VOICES series)

Series Listing

David Emmanuuel Singh (ed.)
Jesus and the Cross
Reflections of Christians from Islamic Contexts
2008 / 978-1-870345-65-1 / x + 226pp

The Cross reminds us that the sins of the world are not borne through the exercise of power but through Jesus Christ's submission to the will of the Father. The papers in this volume are organised in three parts: scriptural, contextual and theological. The central question being addressed is: how do Christians living in contexts, where Islam is a majority or minority religion, experience, express or think of the Cross? This is, therefore, an exercise in listening. As the contexts from where these engagements arise are varied, the papers in drawing scriptural, contextual and theological reflections offer a cross-section of Christian thinking about Jesus and the Cross.

David Emmanuuel Singh (ed.)
Jesus and the Incarnation
Reflections of Christians from Islamic Contexts
2011/978-1-870345-90-3

In the dialogue of Christians with Muslims nothing is more fundamental than the Cross, the Incarnation and the Resurrection of Jesus. This book contains voices of Christians living in various 'Islamic contexts' and reflecting on the Incarnation of Jesus. The aim of these reflections is constructive and the hope is that the papers weaved around the notion of 'the Word' will not only promote dialogue among Christians on the roles of the Person and the Book, but, also, create a positive environment for their conversations with Muslim neighbours.

Sung-wook Hong
Naming God in Korea
The Case of Protestant Christianity
2008 / 978-1-870345-66-8 / xiv + 170pp

Since Christianity was introduced to Korea more than a century ago, one of the most controversial issue has been the Korean term for the Christian 'God'. This issue is not merely about naming the Christian God in Korean language, but it relates to the question of theological contextualization—the relationship between the gospel and culture—and the question of Korean Christian identity. This book examines the theological contextualization of the concept of 'God' in the contemporary Korean context and applies the translatability of Christianity to that context. It also demonstrates the nature of the gospel in relation to cultures, i.e., the universality of the gospel expressed in all human cultures.

Hubert van Beek (ed.)
Revisioning Christian Unity
The Global Christian Forum
2009 / 978-1-870345-74-3 / xx + 288pp

This book contains the records of the Global Christian Forum gathering held in Limuru near Nairobi, Kenya, on 6 – 9 November 2007 as well as the papers presented at that historic event. Also included are a summary of the Global Christian Forum process from its inception until the 2007 gathering and the reports of the evaluation of the process that was carried out in 2008.

Paul Hang-Sik Cho
Eschatology and Ecology
Experiences of the Korean Church
2010 / 978-1-870345-75-0/ 260pp (approx)

This book raises the question of why Korean people, and Korean Protestant Christians in particular, pay so little attention (in theory or practice) to ecological issues. The author argues that there is an important connection (or elective affinity) between this lack of attention and the other-worldly eschatology that is so dominant within Korean Protestant Christianity. Dispensational premillennialism, originally imported by American missionaries, resonated with traditional religious beliefs in Korea and soon came to dominate much of Korean Protestantism. This book argues that this, of all forms of millennialism, is the most damaging to ecological concerns.

Dietrich Werner, David Esterline, Namsoon Kang, Joshva Raja (eds.)
The Handbook of Theological Education in World Christianity
Theological Perspectives, Ecumenical Trends, Regional Surveys
2010 / 978-1-870345-80-4/ 759pp

This major reference work is the first ever comprehensive study of Theological Education in Christianity of its kind. With contributions from over 90 international scholars and church leaders, it aims to be easily accessible across denominational, cultural, educational, and geographic boundaries. The Handbook will aid international dialogue and networking among theological educators, institutions, and agencies. The major objectives of the text are (1) to provide introductory surveys on selected issues and themes in global theological education; (2) to provide regional surveys on key developments, achievements, and challenges in theological education; (3) to provide an overview of theological education for each of the major denominational / confessional traditions; and (4) to provide a reference section with an up-to-date list of the regional associations of theological institutions and other resources.

David Emmanuel Singh & Bernard C Farr (eds.)

Christianity and Education

Shaping of Christian Context in Thinking

2010 / 978-1-870345-81-1/ 244pp (approx)

Christianity and Education is a collection of papers published in *Transformation: An International Journal of Holistic Mission Studies* over a period of 15 years. It brings to life some of the papers that lay buried in shelves and in disparate volumes of *Transformation,* under a single volume for theological libraries, students and teachers. The articles here represent a spectrum of Christian thinking addressing issues of institutional development for theological education, theological studies in the context of global mission, contextually aware/informed education, and academies which deliver such education, methodologies and personal reflections.

J.Andrew Kirk

Civilisations in Conflict?

Islam, the West and Christian Faith 2011- 978-1-870345-71-2

Samuel Huntington's thesis, which argues that there appear to be aspects of Islam that could be on a collision course with the politics and values of Western societies, has provoked much controversy. The purpose of this study is to offer a particular response to Huntington's thesis by making a comparison between the origins of Islam and Christianity; the two religions that can be said to have shaped, in contrasting ways, the history of the Western world. The early history of each faith continues to have a profound impact on the way in which their respective followers have interpreted the relationship between faith and political life. The book draws significant, critical and creative conclusions from the analysis for contemporary intercultural understanding, and in particular for the debate about the justification of violence for political and religious ends.

REGNUM STUDIES IN MISSION
Series Listing

Kwame Bediako
Theology and Identity
The Impact of Culture upon Christian Thought
in the Second Century and in Modern Africa
1992 / 1-870345-10-X / xviii + 508pp

The author examines the question of Christian identity in the context of the Graeco–Roman culture of the early Roman Empire. He then addresses the modern African predicament of quests for identity and integration.

Christopher Sugden
Seeking the Asian Face of Jesus
The Practice and Theology of Christian Social Witness
in Indonesia and India 1974–1996
1997 / 1-870345-26-6 / xx + 496pp

This study focuses on contemporary holistic mission with the poor in India and Indonesia combined with the call to transformation of all life in Christ with micro-credit enterprise schemes. 'The literature on contextual theology now has a new standard to rise to' – Lamin Sanneh (Yale University, USA).

Hwa Yung
Mangoes or Bananas?
The Quest for an Authentic Asian Christian Theology
1997 / 1-870345-25-8 / xii + 274pp

Asian Christian thought remains largely captive to Greek dualism and Enlightenment rationalism because of the overwhelming dominance of Western culture. Authentic contextual Christian theologies will emerge within Asian Christianity with a dual recovery of confidence in culture and the gospel.

Keith E. Eitel
Paradigm Wars
The Southern Baptist International Mission Board Faces the Third Millennium
1999 / 1-870345-12-6 / x + 140pp

The International Mission Board of the Southern Baptist Convention is the largest denominational mission agency in North America. This volume chronicles the historic and contemporary forces that led to the IMB's recent extensive reorganization, providing the most comprehensive case study to date of a historic mission agency restructuring to continue its mission purpose into the twenty-first century more effectively.

Samuel Jayakumar

Dalit Consciousness and Christian Conversion

Historical Resources for a Contemporary Debate

1999 / 81-7214-497-0 / xxiv + 434pp

(Published jointly with ISPCK)

The main focus of this historical study is social change and transformation among the Dalit Christian communities in India. Historiography tests the evidence in the light of the conclusions of the modern Dalit liberation theologians.

Vinay Samuel and Christopher Sugden (eds.)

Mission as Transformation

A Theology of the Whole Gospel

1999 / 0870345133/ 522pp

This book brings together in one volume twenty five years of biblical reflection on mission practice with the poor from around the world. The approach of holistic mission, which integrates proclamation, evangelism, church planting and social transformation seamlessly as a whole, has been adopted since 1983 by most evangelical development agencies, most indigenous mission agencies and many Pentecostal churches. This volume helps anyone understand how evangelicals, struggling to unite evangelism and social action, found their way in the last twenty five years to the biblical view of mission in which God calls all human beings to love God and their neighbour; never creating a separation between the two.

Christopher Sugden

Gospel, Culture and Transformation

2000 / 1-870345-32-0 / viii + 152pp

A Reprint, with a New Introduction, of Part Two of Seeking the Asian Face of Jesus

Gospel, Culture and Transformation explores the practice of mission especially in relation to transforming cultures and communities. - 'Transformation is to enable God's vision of society to be actualised in all relationships: social, economic and spiritual, so that God's will may be reflected in human society and his love experienced by all communities, especially the poor.'

Bernhard Ott

Beyond Fragmentation: Integrating Mission and Theological Education

A Critical Assessment of some Recent Developments in Evangelical Theological Education

2001 / 1-870345-14-2 / xxviii + 382pp

Beyond Fragmentation is an enquiry into the development of Mission Studies in evangelical theological education in Germany and German-speaking Switzerland between 1960 and 1995. The author undertakes a detailed examination of the paradigm shifts which have taken place in recent years in both the theology of mission and the understanding of theological education.

Gideon Githiga

The Church as the Bulwark against Authoritarianism

Development of Church and State Relations in Kenya, with Particular Reference to the Years after Political Independence 1963-1992

2002 / 1-870345-38-x / xviii + 218pp

'All who care for love, peace and unity in Kenyan society will want to read this careful history by Bishop Githiga of how Kenyan Christians, drawing on the Bible, have sought to share the love of God, bring his peace and build up the unity of the nation, often in the face of great difficulties and opposition.' Canon Dr Chris Sugden, Oxford Centre for Mission Studies.

Myung Sung-Hoon, Hong Young-Gi (eds.)

Charis and Charisma

David Yonggi Cho and the Growth of Yoido Full Gospel Church

2003 / 1-870345-45-2 / xxii + 218pp

This book discusses the factors responsible for the growth of the world's largest church. It expounds the role of the Holy Spirit, the leadership, prayer, preaching, cell groups and creativity in promoting church growth. It focuses on God's grace (charis) and inspiring leadership (charisma) as the two essential factors and the book's purpose is to present a model for church growth worldwide.

Samuel Jayakumar

Mission Reader

Historical Models for Wholistic Mission in the Indian Context

2003 / 1-870345-42-8 / x + 250pp

(Published jointly with ISPCK)

This book is written from an evangelical point of view revalidating and reaffirming the Christian commitment to wholistic mission. The roots of the 'wholistic mission' combining 'evangelism and social concerns' are to be located in the history and tradition of Christian evangelism in the past; and the civilizing purpose of evangelism is compatible with modernity as an instrument in nation building.

Bob Robinson

Christians Meeting Hindus

An Analysis and Theological Critique of the Hindu-Christian Encounter in India

2004 / 1-870345-39-8 / xviii + 392pp

This book focuses on the Hindu-Christian encounter, especially the intentional meeting called dialogue, mainly during the last four decades of the twentieth century, and specifically in India itself.

Gene Early

Leadership Expectations

How Executive Expectations are Created and Used in a Non-Profit Setting

2005 / 1-870345-30-4 / xxiv + 276pp

The author creates an Expectation Enactment Analysis to study the role of the Chancellor of the University of the Nations-Kona, Hawaii. This study is grounded in the field of managerial work, jobs, and behaviour and draws on symbolic interactionism, role theory, role identity theory and enactment theory. The result is a conceptual framework for developing an understanding of managerial roles.

Tharcisse Gatwa

The Churches and Ethnic Ideology in the Rwandan Crises 1900-1994

2005 / 1-870345-24-X / approx 300pp

Since the early years of the twentieth century Christianity has become a new factor in Rwandan society. This book investigates the role Christian churches played in the formulation and development of the racial ideology that culminated in the 1994 genocide.

Julie Ma

Mission Possible

Biblical Strategies for Reaching the Lost

2005 / 1-870345-37-1 / xvi + 142pp

This is a missiology book for the church which liberates missiology from the specialists for the benefit of every believer. It also serves as a textbook that is simple and friendly, and yet solid in biblical interpretation. This book links the biblical teaching to the actual and contemporary missiological settings with examples, making the Bible come alive to the reader.

Allan Anderson, Edmond Tang (eds.)

Asian and Pentecostal

The Charismatic Face of Christianity in Asia

2005 / 1-870345-43-6 / xiv + 596pp

(Published jointly with APTS Press)

This book provides a thematic discussion and pioneering case studies on the history and development of Pentecostal and Charismatic churches in the countries of South Asia, South East Asia and East Asia.

I. Mark Beaumont
Christology in Dialogue with Muslims
A Critical Analysis of Christian Presentations of Christ for Muslims from the Ninth and Twentieth Centuries
2005 / 1-870345-46-0 / xxvi + 228pp

This book analyses Christian presentations of Christ for Muslims in the most creative periods of Christian-Muslim dialogue, the first half of the ninth century and the second half of the twentieth century. In these two periods, Christians made serious attempts to present their faith in Christ in terms that take into account Muslim perceptions of him, with a view to bridging the gap between Muslim and Christian convictions.

Thomas Czövek,
Three Seasons of Charismatic Leadership
A Literary-Critical and Theological Interpretation of the Narrative of Saul, David and Solomon
2006 / 978-1-870345484 / 272pp

This book investigates the charismatic leadership of Saul, David and Solomon. It suggests that charismatic leaders emerge in crisis situations in order to resolve the crisis by the charisma granted by God. Czovek argues that Saul proved himself as a charismatic leader as long as he acted resolutely and independently from his mentor Samuel. In the author's eyes, Saul's failure to establish himself as a charismatic leader is caused by his inability to step out from Samuel's shadow.

Jemima Atieno Oluoch
The Christian Political Theology of Dr. John Henry Okullu
2006 / 1-870345-51-7 / xx + 137pp

This book reconstructs the Christian political theology of Bishop John Henry Okullu, DD, through establishing what motivated him and the biblical basis for his socio-political activities. It also attempts to reconstruct the socio-political environment that nurtured Dr Okullu's prophetic ministry.

Richard Burgess
Nigeria's Christian Revolution
The Civil War Revival and Its Pentecostal Progeny (1967-2006)
2008 / 978-1-870345-63-7 / xxii + 347pp

This book describes the revival that occurred among the Igbo people of Eastern Nigeria and the new Pentecostal churches it generated, and documents the changes that have occurred as the movement has responded to global flows and local demands. As such, it explores the nature of revivalist and Pentecostal experience, but does so against the backdrop of local socio-political and economic developments, such as decolonisation and civil war, as well as broader processes, such as modernisation and globalisation.

David Emmanuel Singh & Bernard C Farr (eds.)

Christianity and Cultures

Shaping Christian Thinking in Context

2008 / 978-1-870345-69-9 / x + 260pp

This volume marks an important milestone, the 25th anniversary of the Oxford Centre for Mission Studies (OCMS). The papers here have been exclusively sourced from Transformation, a quarterly journal of OCMS, and seek to provide a tripartite view of Christianity's engagement with cultures by focusing on the question: how is Christian thinking being formed or reformed through its interaction with the varied contexts it encounters? The subject matters include different strands of theological-missiological thinking, socio-political engagements and forms of family relationships in interaction with the host cultures.

Tormod Engelsviken, Ernst Harbakk, Rolv Olsen, Thor Strandenæs (eds.)

Mission to the World

Communicating the Gospel in the 21st Century:

Essays in Honour of Knud Jørgensen

2008 / 978-1-870345-64-4 / 472pp

Knud Jørgensen is Director of Areopagos and Associate Professor of Missiology at MF Norwegian School of Theology. This book reflects on the main areas of Jørgensen's commitment to mission. At the same time it focuses on the main frontier of mission, the world, the content of mission, the Gospel, the fact that the Gospel has to be communicated, and the context of contemporary mission in the 21st century.

Al Tizon

Transformation after Lausanne

Radical Evangelical Mission in Global-Local Perspective

2008 / 978-1-870345-68-2 / xx + 281pp

After Lausanne '74, a worldwide network of radical evangelical mission theologians and practitioners use the notion of "Mission as Transformation" to integrate evangelism and social concern together, thus lifting theological voices from the Two Thirds World to places of prominence. This book documents the definitive gatherings, theological tensions, and social forces within and without evangelicalism that led up to Mission as Transformation. And it does so through a global-local grid that points the way toward greater holistic mission in the 21st century.

Bambang Budijanto

Values and Participation

Development in Rural Indonesia

2009 / 978-1-870345-70-5 / x + 237pp

Socio-religious values and socio-economic development are inter-dependant, inter-related and are constantly changing in the context of macro political structures, economic policy, religious organizations and globalization; and micro influences such as local affinities, identity, politics, leadership and beliefs. The three Lopait communities in Central Java, Indonesia provide an excellent model of the rich and complex negotiations and interactions among all the above factors. The book argues that the comprehensive approach in understanding the socio-religious values of each local community is essential to accurately describing their respective identity which will help institutions and agencies, both governmental and non-governmental, to relate to these communities with dignity and respect.

Young-hoon Lee

The Holy Spirit Movement in Korea

Its Historical and Theological Development

2009 / 978-1-870345-67-5 / x + 174pp

This book traces the historical and theological development of the Holy Spirit Movement in Korea through six successive periods (from 1900 to the present time). These periods are characterized by repentance and revival (1900-20), persecution and suffering under Japanese occupation (1920-40), confusion and division (1940-60), explosive revival in which the Pentecostal movement played a major role in the rapid growth of Korean churches (1960-80), the movement reaching out to all denominations (1980-2000), and the new context demanding the Holy Spirit movement to open new horizons in its mission engagement (2000-). The volume also discusses the relationship between this movement and other religions such as shamanism, and looks forward to further engagement with issues of concern in wider society.

Alan R. Johnson

Leadership in a Slum

A Bangkok Case Study

2009 / 978-1-870345-71-2 xx + 238pp

This book looks at leadership in the social context of a slum in Bangkok from an angle different from traditional studies which measure well educated Thais on leadership scales derived in the West. Using both systematic data collection and participant observation, it develops a culturally preferred model as well as a set of models based in Thai concepts that reflect on-the-ground realities. This work challenges the dominance of the patron-client rubric for understanding all forms of Thai leadership and offers a view for understanding leadership rooted in local social systems, contrary to approaches that assume the universal applicability of leadership research findings across all cultural settings. It concludes by looking at the implications of the anthropological approach for those who are involved in leadership training in Thai settings and beyond.

Titre Ande

Leadership and Authority

Bula Matari and Life - Community Ecclesiology in Congo

2010 / 978-1-870345-72-9 xvii + 189pp

This book proposes that Christian theology in Africa can make significant developments if a critical understanding of the socio-political context in contemporary Africa is taken seriously. The Christian leadership in post-colonial Africa has cloned its understanding and use of authority on the Bula Matari model, which was issued from the brutality of colonialism and political absolutism in post-colonial Africa. This model has caused many problems in churches, including dysfunction, conflicts, divisions and a lack of prophetic ministry. Titre proposes a Life-Community ecclesiology for liberating authority, where leadership is a function, not a status, and 'apostolic succession' belongs to all the people of God.

Frank Kwesi Adams

Odwira and the Gospel

A Study of the Asante Odwira Festival and its Significance for Christianity in Ghana

2010 /978-1-870345-59-0

The study of the Odwira festival is the key to the understanding of Asante religious and political life in Ghana. The book explores the nature of the Odwira festival longitudinally - in pre-colonial, colonial and post-independence Ghana - and examines the Odwira ideology and its implications for understanding the Asante self-identity. The book also discusses how some elements of faith portrayed in the Odwira festival could provide a framework for Christianity to engage with Asante culture at a greater depth. Theological themes in Asante belief that have emerged from this study include the theology of sacrament, ecclesiology, eschatology, Christology and a complex concept of time. The author argues that Asante cultural identity lies at the heart of the process by which the Asante Christian faith is carried forward.

Bruce Carlton

Strategy Coordinator

Changing the Course of Southern Baptist Missions

2010 / 978-1-870345-78-1 xvii + 268pp

In 1976, the Southern Baptist Convention adopted its Bold New Thrusts in Foreign Missions with the overarching goal of sharing the gospel with every person in the world by the year 2000. The formation of Cooperative Services International (CSI) in 1985 and the assigning of the first non-residential missionary (NRM) in 1987 demonstrated the Foreign Mission Board's (now International Mission Board) commitment to take the gospel message to countries that restricted traditional missionary presence and to people groups identified as having little or no access to the gospel. Carlton traces the historical development along with an analysis of the key components of the paradigm and its significant impact on Southern Baptists' missiology.

Julie Ma & Wonsuk Ma
Mission in the Spirit:
Towards a Pentecostal/Charismatic Missiology
2010 / 978-1-870345-84-2 xx + 312pp

The book explores the unique contribution of Pentecostal/Charismatic mission from the beginning of the twentieth century. The first part considers the theological basis of Pentecostal/Charismatic mission thinking and practice. Special attention is paid to the Old Testament, which has been regularly overlooked by the modern Pentecostal/Charismatic movements. The second part discusses major mission topics with contributions and challenges unique to Pentecostal/Charismatic mission. The book concludes with a reflection on the future of this powerful missionary movement. As the authors served as Korean missionaries in Asia, often their missionary experiences in Asia are reflected in their discussions.

S. Hun Kim & Wonsuk Ma (eds.)
Korean Diaspora and Christian Mission
2011-978-1-870345-89-7

As a 'divine conspiracy' for Missio Dei, the global phenomenon of people on the move has shown itself to be invaluable. In 2004 two significant documents concerning Diaspora were introduced, one by the Filipino International Network and the other by the Lausanne Committee for World Evangelization. These have created awareness of the importance of people on the move for Christian mission. Since then, Korean Diaspora has conducted similar research among Korean missions, resulting in this book. It is unique as the first volume researching Korean missions in Diasporic contexts, appraising and evaluating these missions with practical illustrations, and drawing on a wide diversity of researchers.

GENERAL REGNUM TITLES

Vinay Samuel, Chris Sugden (eds.)
The Church in Response to Human Need
1987 / 1870345045 / xii+268pp

Philip Sampson, Vinay Samuel, Chris Sugden (eds.)
Faith and Modernity
Essays in modernity and post-modernity
1994 / 1870345177 / 352pp

Klaus Fiedler
The Story of Faith Missions
1994 / 0745926878 / 428pp

Douglas Peterson
Not by Might nor by Power
A Pentecostal Theology of Social Concern in Latin America
1996 / 1870345207 / xvi+260pp

David Gitari
In Season and Out of Season
Sermons to a Nation
1996 / 1870345118 / 155pp

David. W. Virtue
A Vision of Hope
The Story of Samuel Habib
1996 / 1870345169 / xiv+137pp

Everett A Wilson
Strategy of the Spirit
J.Philip Hogan and the Growth of the Assemblies of God Worldwide, 1960 - 1990
1997 /1870345231/214

Murray Dempster, Byron Klaus, Douglas Petersen (eds.)
The Globalization of Pentecostalism
A Religion Made to Travel
1999 / 1870345290 / xvii+406pp

Peter Johnson, Chris Sugden (eds.)
Markets, Fair Trade and the Kingdom of God
Essays to Celebrate Traidcraft's 21st Birthday
2001 / 1870345193 / xii+155pp

Robert Hillman, Coral Chamberlain, Linda Harding
Healing & Wholeness
Reflections on the Healing Ministry
2002 / 978-1- 870345-35- 4 / xvii+283pp

David Bussau, Russell Mask
Christian Microenterprise Development
An Introduction
2003 / 1870345282 / xiii+142pp

David Singh
Sainthood and Revelatory Discourse
An Examination of the Basis for the Authority of Bayan in Mahdawi Islam
2003 / 8172147285 / xxiv+485pp

For the up-to-date listing of the Regnum books see www.ocms.ac.uk/regnum

regnum

Regnum Books International

Regnum is an Imprint of The Oxford Centre for Mission Studies
St. Philip and St. James Church
Woodstock Road
Oxford, OX2 6HR
Web: www.ocms.ac.uk/regnum